Research in
Canadian Workers'
Compensation

Terry Thomason and Richard P. Chaykowski

EDITORS

Industrial Relations Centre
Queen's University at Kingston
1995

IRC Press, Industrial Relations Centre
Queen's University, Kingston, Ontario
© 1995, IRC Press
Printed and bound in Canada

Canadian Cataloguing in Publication Data

Main entry under title:

Research in Canadian workers' compensation

Includes bibliographical references and index.

ISBN 0-88886-364-0

1. Workers' compensation - Canada. I. Thomason, Terry.
II. Chaykowski, Richard P. (Richard Paul), 1958- . III. Queen's University
(Kingston, Ont.). Industrial Relations Centre.

HD7103.65.C3R4 1995   368.4'1'00971   C95-930978-0

Contents

Tables

Figures

Preface

Partly in response to the need to increase the information available to policymakers, the economic analysis of many aspects of Canadian workers' compensation systems has developed considerably in recent years. Yet, to our knowledge, prior to this volume there had been no comprehensive effort to bring together international researchers for the purpose of analysing a broad range of economic aspects of Canadian workers' compensation programs. The papers in this volume constitute a collection of institutional and applied empirical analyses of workers' compensation issues. Given the critical economic challenges confronting the provincial workers' compensation systems, we trust that these papers will contribute to our understanding of the substantive issues currently challenging policymakers and provide a basis for future analyses that will be required to faciliate the creation of policy into the next century.

With the exception of the introductory chapter, each of the papers in this volume was presented and discussed at a conference entitled 'Challenges to Workers' Compensation in Canada,' which we hosted at the School of Industrial Relations at Queen's University in April 1993. Our objective was to provide a forum in which preliminary versions of the research could be reviewed and discussed by researchers and policymakers from a variety of disciplinary perspectives. We are indebted to the conference participants for their important contributions to the development of the papers and, consequently, to this volume.

The conference was sponsored by the Institut de recherche en santé et en sécurité du travail du Québec, the Commission de la santé et de la sécurité du travail du Québec, the Ontario Workers' Compensation Institute, and the Workers' Compensation Board of Ontario. We gratefully acknowledge the significant financial support of these organizations, which was instrumental to making possible this conference. We also appreciate the substantial institutional support provided by the School of Industrial Relations at Queen's University. We are especially grateful to Barbara Gibson, Liann Joanette and Tracy Rolfe for their excellent assistance in the planning and management of the conference.

From the commencement of this project, we have worked jointly on all portions of this undertaking and this volume represents our combined efforts. Various stages of this project have greatly benefited from the helpful suggestions and support provided by John Frank, Richard Allingham, John F. Burton Jr., and Bryan Downie. We are also appreciative of the excellent support of our editor at the IRC Press, Carol Williams.

Richard P. Chaykowski   Terry Thomason

Contributors

Richard Allingham
Research and Evaluation Branch
Workers' Compensation Board
of Ontario

Marjorie Baldwin
Department of Economics
East Carolina University

John F. Burton Jr.
Institute of Management and
Labor Relations
Rutgers University

Richard J. Butler
Department of Economics
Brigham Young University

Richard Chaykowski
School of Industrial Relations
Queen's University

Jean-Michel Cousineau
Centre de recherche et développe-
ment en économique
Université de Montréal

Georges Dionne
Centre de recherche sur les
transports
Université de Montréal

Lynn Elinson
Medical and Occupational
Disease Policy Branch
Workers' Compensation Board
of Ontario

Anne-Marie Girard
Centre de recherche et
dévelopement en économique
Université de Montréal

Sandra Girard
Société canadienne
d'hypothèque et de logement

Morley Gunderson
Centre for Industrial Relations
University of Toronto

Douglas Hyatt
Department of Economics
University of Wisconsin

William G. Johnson
School of Health Administration
and Policy
Arizona State University

Boris Kralj
Research and Evaluation Branch
Workers' Compensation Board
of Ontario

Robert Lacroix
Département des sciences
économiques
Université de Montréal

Paul Lanoie
Institut d'économie appliquée
commerciales
École des hautes études
commerciales

David Law
Re-employment Hearings
Branch
Workers' Compensation Board
of Ontario

Silvana Pozzebon
École des hautes études
commerciales

Sandra Sinclair
Ontario Workers' Compensation
Institute

Pierre St-Michel
Department of Statistics and
Information Management
Commission de la santé et de la
sécurité du travail

Terry Thomason
Faculty of Management
McGill University

François Vaillancourt
Centre de recherche et
dévelopement en économique
Université de Montréal

Charles Vanasse
Centre de recherche sur les
transports
Université de Montréal

Canadian Workers' Compensation: Institutions and Economics

Richard P. Chaykowski and Terry Thomason

Workers' compensation is a social insurance program that provides cash benefits as well as medical and rehabilitative services to workers who have suffered a work-related injury or disease. Workers' compensation is one of the largest social programs in Canada, affecting the lives of at least a million Canadians each year. In 1991, Canadians experienced nearly 931,000 compensable injuries and received over $4.8 billion in workers' compensation benefits.

In recent years, Canadian workers' compensation programs have come under increasing scrutiny by stakeholders (i.e., employers and workers) and policymakers. Injured workers in some provinces have expressed considerable dissatisfaction with the assistance provided by provincial workers' compensation boards, one of which was characterized as a 'faceless, impersonal, even dehumanizing organization, which puts injured workers through a mail-order assembly line' (Weiler 1980, 92). At the same time, Canadian employers have become increasingly concerned about the escalating costs of workers' compensation, which have grown, in real terms, at an average annual rate of nearly 7 percent since 1960. Compensation benefits are currently equal to approximately 1.26 percent of the wages and compensation component of gross domestic product, compared to 0.60 percent in 1960. Some provincial governments, already contending with rising deficits in their general budgets, are disturbed by the significant underfunding of accident reserves and corresponding deficits in workers' compensation accounts.

Note: The order of authorship was determined alphabetically. Equal contributions were made by both authors. The authors thank John F. Burton, Jr. for helpful comments made on a previous draft. They also thank Eva Stamadianos for outstanding research assistance and the Association of Workers' Compensation Boards of Canada, Rigo Vettoretti of Health and Welfare Canada, and Noelle Sotack of the US Chamber of Commerce for providing data used herein.

Academic interest in workers' compensation has been nurtured by several provincial programs. In particular, Québec and Ontario have been engaged in research efforts. Recently, both provinces have created independent research agencies that sponsor and conduct research investigating various aspects of program funding, the delivery of benefits, and training and rehabilitation.[1] While the overall level of research activity devoted to issues in workers' compensation has increased in recent years, the growth in research on workers' compensation clearly lags that devoted to other governmental policies affecting the labour market.

This volume represents the first endeavour to assemble a range of primarily empirical economic analyses of Canadian workers' compensation issues. The collection includes both *economic* and *institutional* analyses of the effects of various features of workers' compensation programs and some of the emerging policy challenges. This chapter continues with a general overview of key historical developments in Canadian workers' compensation and of the current structure and operations of Canadian workers' compensation systems. A concise review of economic analyses of workers' compensation issues follows. The concluding section provides an overview of the chapters in the volume.

Historical Development of Workers' Compensation

Public Policy Prior to Compensation Programs

Canadian provinces first began to enact workers' compensation legislation around the turn of the twentieth century. Prior to that, liability for work accidents was determined according to the common law of negligence. Under this regime, employers were required to compensate injured workers only if the employer had failed to exercise 'due care' or the level of care that would have been exercised by a 'reasonable' person under similar circumstances. Employers who discharged these duties could not be held liable for injuries sustained as the result of a work-related accident, which, of course, precluded the injured worker from collecting compensation for most workplace accidents.

Assuming that an injured worker could demonstrate that the employer had failed to exercise reasonable care, the employer had a variety of defences available. Under the doctrine of contributory negligence, if it could be shown that an injured worker had failed to exercise

---

1 These agencies include the Institut de recherche en santé et en sécurité du travail in Québec and the Workers' Compensation Institute in Ontario. Both programs were engaged in substantial research efforts prior to the creation of these agencies.

reasonable care and thus had contributed to the occurrence of the accident, the worker assumed complete liability for the injury. The fellow-servant doctrine held that employers were not liable for accidents caused by co-workers. Finally, on the theory that the increased risk of accident in some occupations was reflected in the workers' wage, courts held that workers assumed liability for accidents caused by risks common to employment—a doctrine known as assumption of risk.

Although these common law rules originated in Great Britain during the pre-industrial era, they were developed and widely applied by courts in that country and in Canada and the United States with the beginning of industrialization.[2] Industrialization and the adoption of steam power by transportation and manufacturing industries led to a rapid escalation in the incidence of work accidents. Evidence from the US indicates that the judiciary there initially sought to protect these infant industries from increasingly costly litigation by devising rules that made it difficult for injured workers to collect damages (Friedman 1973).

As tort damages proved inadequate and as the death toll began to rise, public sentiment turned.[3] In 1880, Great Britain passed the *Employers' Liability Act*, which substantially eased the burden of proof for injured workers by eliminating the assumption of risk, fellow servant, and contributory negligence doctrines as employer defences. Provincial governments in Canada enacted similar legislation during this period. However, these statutes did not completely eliminate previous deficiencies in the law, which continued to require that the injured worker demonstrate employer negligence. The acts also limited employer's financial liability and placed time limitations on the workers' right to bring action (Dee, McCombie, and Newhouse 1986).

In 1881, Germany, under the leadership of Otto von Bismarck, became the first nation to introduce compulsory workers' compensation insurance. Germany's program was based on a system of collective liability whereby employers were categorized into industrial groups and each group was collectively liable for injuries to employees within the group. In 1897, Great Britain enacted legislation that made individual employers liable for compensation of industrial accidents. The British

2 For example, the fellow servant rule can be traced back to 1837 (*Priestly* v *Fowler* (1837), 3 M & M 1, 150 E.R. 1030), while the doctrine of contributory negligence has its origin in an 1809 case (*Butterfield* v *Forrester* (1809), 11 East 60, 103 E.R. 926).

3 However, Posner (1972) points out that, in the United States between 1875 and 1905, there was tremendous growth in work accident litigation and a corresponding increase in the proportion of plaintiffs who collected damages as the result of these actions. Friedman (1973) suggests that by the turn of the century there had been a judicial erosion of these common law doctrines, so that juries had begun to award substantial damages to some victims of industrial accidents. However, damages were awarded erratically and many victims received no compensation at all.

act permitted, but did not require, that the employer carry insurance with private carriers.

The Development of Workers' Compensation Programs

The first Canadian workers' compensation program was introduced in British Columbia in 1902 (effective 1903). Within the next ten years, Newfoundland (1908), Alberta (1908), Québec (1909), Manitoba (1910), Nova Scotia (1910), and Saskatchewan (1911) enacted similar legislation. With the sole exception of Manitoba, these early statutes were restricted to a few industries, primarily railways; factories; mines; quarries; engineering work; and the construction, repair and demolition of buildings.[4] This limited legislation provided for individual liability for work injuries, based on the British Act of 1897, but not for compulsory insurance.

The compensation of occupational injuries in Canada was to be fundamentally transformed when in 1913, an Ontario parliamentary commission headed by Sir William Ralph Meredith, the Chief Justice of Ontario, delivered its final report to the Ontario legislature (Meredith 1913). This report represented a radical departure from previous Canadian approaches to workers' compensation and soon led to legislation that established Ontario's workers' compensation program. Moreover, the model for workers' compensation advocated by Meredith was subsequently adopted by all Canadian jurisdictions, and continues to be the basic framework in all provinces (Association of Workers' Compensation Boards of Canada 1991, vii).[5]

In formulating his recommendations for legislation, Meredith drew upon features of both the German and British plans. But with respect to the critical issue of collective versus individual liability, Meredith opted for the German model. Meredith argued that by placing liability on the individual employer, the British system jeopardized the security of both small employers, who could be financially ruined by a catastrophic work accident, and their employees, who would have no assurance that compensation would be paid. Meredith (1913, 5) believed that this would be especially problematic in Canada:

[this] objection would be still more serious in a comparatively new country such as this, where many of the industries are small and conditions are much less stable than they are in the British Isles.

4 Manitoba limited application of the Act to establishments employing at least five workers.

5 Nova Scotia adopted a version of the Meredith plan in 1915. It was followed by British Columbia (1916), Manitoba (1916), Alberta (1918), New Brunswick (1918), Saskatchewan (1929), Québec (1931), Prince Edward Island (1949), and Newfoundland (1950).

Meredith (1913, 5) argued that a system of collective liability ensured that 'the injured workman and his dependents shall receive the compensation to which they are entitled' and that 'the employer would not be ruined by having to pay compensation.'

Meredith also embraced the 'no-fault' principle and a *quid pro quo* compromise between the existing rights of employers and employees under the common law of negligence. Meredith (1913, 15) noted under the draft proposal of the act:

> The workman will bear (1) the loss of all his wages for seven days if his disability does not last longer than that, (2) the pain and suffering consequent upon his injury, (3) his outlay for medical or surgical treatment, nursing and other necessities, (4) the loss of 45 percent of his wages while his disability lasts; and if his injury results in his being maimed or disfigured he must go through life bearing that burden also . . . .

This compensation is, of course, less than the damages the injured worker would receive through a tort action by which, if found negligent, the employer would be liable for the entire cost of the worker's loss (including psychic damages, such as pain and suffering and the loss of enjoyment of leisure activities). Under the Meredith plan,

> the workman is required, as the price of compensation he is to receive, to surrender his right to damages under the common law, if his injury happens under circumstances entitling him by the common law to recover. . . . (Meredith 1913, 15)

Meredith's proposal envisioned a strong, centralized system. The report recommended that the 'collection and administration of the accident fund' should be the responsibility of a government agency rather than private insurers and that this agency's decisions should be removed from the jurisdiction of provincial courts, with the exception of questions of law (Meredith 1913, 7).[6]

Compensation was to be paid 'as long as the disability caused by the accident lasts' (Meredith 1913, 13). Meredith explicitly rejected two features of compensation programs that are common in other countries, particularly the United States: the payment of lump sums and limitations on the duration of benefits for permanent partial disability. Meredith argued that both features would cause the disabled worker

---

6 Meredith even insisted that the monies paid by employers into the accident fund be called an *assessment* rather than a *premium*.

to become 'a burden on his relatives or friends or on the community' (Meredith 1913, 13).

Recent Legislative Developments in Ontario and Québec

Workers' compensation programs in Canada have undergone extensive revision since Meredith's 1913 report. Early reforms often focused on the expansion of coverage to include previously exempt employment, such as agricultural work, and the progressive liberalization of benefits. In recent years, reform proposals have advocated more fundamental change including: the creation of independent tribunals to which the worker (or employer) could appeal Board decisions, increased emphasis on the liability of individual employers through the creation of merit/demerit or experience-rating plans, and revision of the structure of compensation for permanent partial disability. These developments can be illustrated by the history of workers' compensation in Ontario and Québec since 1980.

Throughout the 1960s and 1970s injured workers in Ontario expressed considerable dissatisfaction with the provincial Workers' Compensation Board, which they considered to be a 'huge, autocratic bureaucracy which exercised its mandate in a paternalistic and defensive fashion' (McCombie 1984, 137). Increasing frustration and anger led to the formation of a number of injured worker interest groups, notably the Union of Injured Workers established in Toronto in May 1974. These groups organized a series of demonstrations to create pressure for reform of the existing program.

In this atmosphere, in 1980 Ontario commissioned a study of the workers' compensation program by Paul Weiler, former chairman of the Labour Relations Board of British Columbia. Eleven months later, Weiler delivered the first of three reports that, together, ultimately served as the basis for substantial revisions of Ontario's program. However, Weiler's recommendations were not without controversy.[7] Injured worker groups were able to derail proposed legislation based on the initial Weiler report and to have some of the language they found objectionable in early drafts of Bill 101 eliminated. The Bill was enacted in 1985 (McCombie 1984).

This legislation dramatically altered Ontario's program by liberalizing benefits and changing the administration of the system.[8] Bill 101

7 For example, some injured workers formed the 'Committee on the Weiler Inquiry,' which demanded that Weiler hold a public inquiry to provide interested parties with the opportunity to submit briefs and evidence. Rejection of the Committee's demand led to a series of demonstrations designed to influence the inquiry and resulting legislation.
8 Benefit liberalization included several major improvements: changing the basis of indemnity benefits from 75 percent of gross earnings to 90 percent of net, improving death benefits for surviving spouses and dependent children, and payment for the day of injury.

created the Workers' Compensation Appeals Tribunal (WCAT), an independent agency to serve as the final level of appeal from decisions of the Workers' Compensation Board. In addition, Bill 101 created three other agencies: the Industrial Disease Standards Panel, which conducts research and makes recommendations concerning the compensation of industrial diseases; and the Offices of the Worker and Employer Advisor, which provide information, advice, and representation to workers and employers, respectively.[9]

The creation of these agencies, and particularly the WCAT, has had profound implications for Ontario's workers' compensation program. No longer was authority and control of the program vested in a single agency, as Meredith envisioned in his original proposal. On the one hand the WCAT, which is detached from daily administration of the program, issued decisions that had significant cost implications, including decisions regarding the compensation of injured workers who are incapacitated due to chronic pain or chronic stress.[10] On the other hand, the transfer of authority from the WCB to the WCAT complicated the WCB's capacity to discharge its functions. The WCB has often been slow to react to WCAT decisions that reverse existing policy. Resulting delays have meant that the Board has continued to operate under policies declared invalid by the Tribunal, frequently for a considerable period.

In 1989, the Ontario government enacted Bill 162, which restructured the compensation of permanent partial disabilities by creating a dual-award system. This system provides an award for noneconomic loss based on the extent of the claimant's functional impairment and compensation based on the claimant's actual (or predicted) wage loss due to disability. One of the more widely heralded features of Bill 162 was its strong emphasis on worker rehabilitation, especially vocational rehabilitation. Bill 162 requires that the Board contact injured workers who have not returned to work to identify their need for rehabilitation. Within six months of injury, the Board must offer disabled workers vocational rehabilitation services. Futhermore, the Bill provided injured workers with incentives to encourage participation in rehabilitation programs by linking compensation benefits to the claimant's willingness to undergo rehabilitation. As well, employers were obligated to re-employ workers for a period of one year following the date of injury.

9 All of these changes evolved from recommendations contained in Weiler's first and second reports (Weiler 1980, 1983).
10 It is arguable that both conditions, which depend on subjective assessment of symptoms, are subject to significant 'moral hazard' problems, because claimants may extend the duration of disability benefits or submit false or exaggerated claims.

The transition to the new system has been complicated by personnel changes and conflicting advice offered agency panel members. The civil service bureaucracy has been reorganized several times in the last half dozen years, and both the chairman and the vice-chairman of the WCB resigned shortly after the New Democratic Party formed the provincial government in 1990. Occasionally, panels to the appeals tribunal, which are newly appointed for each case, issue contradictory decisions, creating confusion about policy implementation and future directions.

Workers' compensation legislation in Québec has also changed in the last decade. Amendments to the *Workers' Compensation Act* in 1977 liberalized benefits by making the employer responsible for the first five days of disability and by providing for automatic annual increases in benefits. In 1980, the Commission des accidents du travail (CAT), the agency then responsible for workers' compensation, was replaced by the more powerful Commission de la santé et de la sécurité du travail (CSST). The CSST is responsible for the administration of occupational safety and health regulations as well as the workers' compensation program. Inspection activities formerly conducted by the Ministries of Labour and Manpower, Environment and Energy and by the Office de la construction du Québec are now consolidated under the direction of the CSST.

In 1985, the National Assembly of Québec passed the *Act Respecting Industrial Accidents and Occupational Diseases* (*AIAOD*), which replaced the *Workers' Compensation Act*. This legislation introduced sweeping reforms, similar to those advocated by Weiler in his first report for Ontario. Like Bill 162, the *AIAOD* created a dual-award system for permanent partial disabilities and substantially enhanced the rehabilitation function, including recognition of the injured worker's right to reinstatement. Finally, the *AIAOD* revamped the appeals process in two ways. First, the Bureau de révision, an internal appeals unit with membership limited to CSST personnel, was replaced by a tripartite Bureau de révision paritaire. Second, an independent appeals tribunal, the Commission d'appel en matière de lésions professionnelles (CALP), was created to provide the final stage of appeal from decisions of the CSST.

Despite the objections of many within the labour movement, in June 1992 the National Assembly enacted Bill 35, which introduced several further amendments to workers' compensation legislation. These reforms were principally designed to reduce the influence of the claimant's treating physician, to facilitate both the CSST's and the employer's ability to challenge worker claims, to streamline the administration in order to reduce costs and delays in claim processing, and to reduce the costs of dispute resolution.

Successive legislative reforms in both Québec and Ontario have created a workers' compensation system that is substantially different from the one envisioned by Chief Justice Meredith 75 years ago. In particular, responsibility for workers' compensation has been decentralized. In both provinces, final authority for compensation decisions has been placed in the hands of an independent appeals tribunal. In Québec, decisionmaking authority has also been devolved to the treating physician and a tripartite internal appeals board. Ontario has created several additional agencies with responsibility for various aspects of the program—independent of the Workers' Compensation Board. In both provinces, these changes were adopted to mollify injured workers, who had become increasingly frustrated with inadequate procedural justice dispensed by a seemingly omnipotent government agency.

These substantive reforms, accompanied by ongoing benefit liberalization, have arguably resulted in a marked increase in Canadian workers' compensation costs. As examples, between 1980 and 1991, costs increased by over 265 percent in Québec and by over 295 percent in Ontario. In addition, the accident reserves of both provinces are substantially underfunded.[11] In 1992, Québec experienced a shortfall of $655 million, which increased its unfunded liability to over $3.5 billion, while Ontario posted a deficit of $681 million which raised its liability to over $11 billion.[12]

Two additional developments grew out of concern about the rising costs of compensation: (1) the restructuring of permanent partial disability compensation (which is a substantial component of indemnity costs), combined with an increased emphasis on vocational rehabilitation; and (2) an emphasis on accident prevention through experience-rating plans (Canadian Manufacturers' Association 1987).[13] These measures could be considered a means of reducing costs without affecting benefits; outright benefit reductions would be politically difficult, if not impossible. By combining wage-loss benefits with vocational rehabilitation, it is arguable that policymakers hoped to reduce costs as rehabilitated claimants returned to work more rapidly and their benefits ceased. The continued high levels of benefit costs suggest that these programs have not been completely successful.

11 These reserves pay the future costs of past injuries.
12 For 1992, Ontario's unfunded liability was over five times greater than 'current assessments' for that year.
13 Experience-rating represents a further derogation of the Meredith plan in that it is contrary to the notion of collective liability.

Institutional Features of Canadian Workers' Compensation Programs[14]

Workers' compensation programs perform two principal functions: first, they distribute compensation benefits to workers who have suffered an injury as the result of a work-related accident or illness; and second, they determine employer assessments used to finance these benefits. In this section, the principal characteristics of workers' compensation programs, including administration, benefits, financing, and benefit costs, are reviewed.

Administration of Injury Claims

In each province, the workers' compensation program is administered by a board or commission appointed by the government. The board is typically tripartite (with representatives of management, labour, and the public) and reports to the provincial government through a minister of the Crown (usually the minister of labour). The board is responsible for developing policies, within the framework of the legislation, for establishing and collecting employer assessments, determining benefit eligibility, and providing compensation. The day-to-day operation of these activities is directed by a president or chief executive officer, who is supported by a substantial civil service bureaucracy.

Claims may be initiated by the injured worker, the employer, or the treating physician. The decision of whether or not to compensate is usually made by an adjudicator within the board.[15] While in most provinces the worker has a right to select his or her treating physician, board physicians are responsible for rendering medical decisions concerning claimant eligibility for benefits and for determining the extent of disability. However, in Québec the treating physician's conclusions about the extent of disability and whether or not the injury is work-related are considered binding on the CSST.[16]

Should either the claimant or the employer object to the initial decision of a board adjudicator, all boards have an internal appeals mechanism by which the parties may challenge these decisions. The board

14 Much of the information presented in the following three subsections comes from two sources: Ison (1989) and the Association of Workers' Compensation Boards of Canada (1991).

15 In Québec, the employer is obliged to compensate an injured worker for the first 15 days of disability, based on a medical certificate issued by the claimant's treating physician.

16 Both the employer and the CSST have the right to challenge the treating physician's conclusions by requiring that the worker submit to a medical examination by a physician chosen by either the employer or the CSST. Disputes are submitted to the Bureau d'évaluation medicale, whose decisions are binding on the CSST. Of course, either party may appeal this decision to the CSST's internal appeal office (the Bureau de révision paritaire) and, ultimately, to an independent, external appeals tribunal (the Commission d'appel en matière de lésions professionnelles).

has exclusive jurisdiction with respect to the compensation of occupational injury or disease. Privative clauses limit the ability of the parties to appeal an adverse decision to the courts. In all but three provinces, board decisions may be appealed to an external review agency whose jurisdiction is limited to workers' compensation issues (e.g., the Workers' Compensation Appeals Tribunal in Ontario or the Commission d'appel en matière de lésions professionnelles in Québec).

Internal appeals are typically informal, without rules of procedure. While external appellate bodies follow procedural rules, these rules may be waived if the interests of the parties are not prejudiced. Legislation directs that board decisions be based on the 'merits and justice' of the case and that the board shall not be bound by previous decisions or rulings. Furthermore, most jurisdictions provide workers with an advocate, free of cost, to represent them in the appeals process. For example, in Ontario, advocacy services are provided by an independent agency (i.e., the Office of the Workers' Adviser) that reports directly to an assistant deputy minister of labour.

In most provinces, the boards hold other responsibilities in addition to the administration of the workers' compensation program. At one time, most boards were also responsible for administering occupational safety and health programs, although these duties have since devolved to separate administrative agencies in all jurisdictions except British Columbia and Québec. In some provinces, the board also administers programs that compensate crime victims. In Québec, the CSST manages the Protective Reassignment of Pregnant or Breast-feeding Workers Program, which provides compensation to female workers who are unable to work because they are pregnant or breast-feeding their infant children.

Compensation Benefits

Canadian workers' compensation programs offer three types of benefits to workers or the survivors of workers who have suffered an occupational injury or disease: medical aid; rehabilitative services; and various types of cash benefits, including temporary and permanent disability and survivor benefits.[17]

Medical Aid and Rehabilitative Services

Compensation programs pay for the cost of all medical aid necessary to restore the claimant's health to its pre-injury status,[18] although the

---

17 To be eligibile for compensation for an injury due to an industrial accident the worker must (1) be engaged in covered employment and (2) have suffered a personal injury that arises out of and in the course of employment.

18 This goes far beyond Meredith's original recommendations which required workers to bear the cost of the 'outlay for medical or surgical treatment, nursing and other necessaries' (Meredith 1913, 15).

boards have discretionary power to determine the scope and the nature of necessary aid.[19]

Workers' compensation programs also offer rehabilitative assistance to restore the claimant's earnings capacity to the pre-injury level. Rehabilitative services inlude both vocational and physical rehabilitation: vocational counselling, job placement, education, and training, as well as the adaptation of the worker's residence or vehicle to accommodate the worker's impairment. Some provinces provide 'social' rehabilitation services, including psychological and academic assistance designed to help the disabled worker adjust to personal or social problems resulting from the work accident.

In addition to specific services, compensation programs use a variety of incentives to encourage participation in rehabilitation programs. For example, Québec, Ontario, and New Brunswick obligate employers to reinstate employees who have suffered an occupational injury. Claimant benefits in several provinces are linked to participation in a rehabilitation program; for example, refusal to participate in a prescribed program may result in termination of benefits.

Cash Benefits

In terms of costs, the single most important benefit paid by workers' compensation is cash benefits, also termed indemnity benefits, which are paid to claimants who have suffered disability due to an occupational injury or disease, and to the dependent survivors of workers who have died as the result of a work-related accident or disease. Disability benefits may be categorized according to duration and extent of disability to produce a four-fold classification: temporary total, permanent total, temporary partial, and permanent partial.

Temporary benefits are paid up to the date of maximum medical improvement, the point at which further medical treatment is not expected to result in any improvement of the claimant's medical condition. At that point, the worker is usually no longer disabled and can return to work. If the claimant continues to experience the consequences of injury, he or she is eligible for permanent disability benefits. Total disability benefits, whether temporary or permanent, are paid to workers who have no wage-earning capacity, while partial benefits are paid to workers who retain some wage-earning capability.

Temporary Disability Benefits

With the exception of New Brunswick, temporary benefits begin on the first day after injury.[20] This contrasts with US programs that typi-

---

19 For example, the boards place limitations on treatment by some health-care providers, such as chiropractors.

20 There is a three-day waiting period in Nova Scotia. In some provinces the employer is required to pay for the day of injury.

cally require a three- to seven-day waiting period—similar to a deductible in an automobile or homeowner's insurance policy—before benefits begin. Temporary total disability benefits are paid weekly and, in most jurisdictions, are equal to either 75 percent of the claimant's gross pre-injury wage or to 90 percent of the claimant's pre-injury wage net of taxes. Temporary partial benefits are paid when the claimant has returned to work but is earning less than pre-injury wages. The weekly payment is equal to a proportion of the difference (either 75 percent of gross or 90 percent of net) between pre- and post-injury wages. Under both systems, benefit payments cannot be less than (or greater than) a specified minimum (or maximum).[21] The replacement rate (or coinsurance), minimum, and maximum for each Canadian jurisdiction are presented in Table 1.

Table 1

Workers' Compensation Benefit Characteristics, 1993

Province	Benefit formula	Benefit maximum	Benefit minimum	Maximum earnings covered	Cost of living adjustment
British Columbia	75% of gross	$727.81	$261.44	$50,000	Automatic semi-annual
Alberta	90% of net	525.83	217.48	42,000	Ad hoc
Saskatchewan	90% of net	551.2	317.77	48,000	Automatic annual
Manitoba	90% of net (80% after 24 mos)	541.09	171.28	47,000	Automatic annual
Ontario	90% of net	647.27	285.83	52,500	Automatic annual
Quebec	90% of net	568.26	213.91	46,500	Automatic annual
New Brunswick	80% of net (85% after 39 wks)	459.39	None	41,000	Automatic annual
Nova Scotia	75% of gross	519.23	147.11	36,000	Automatic annual
PEI	75% of gross	389.42	60	27,000	Ad hoc
Newfoundland	75% of net (80% after 39 wks)	466.54	200	45,500	Automatic annual
Northwest Territories	90% of net	640.31	301.44	47,500	Ad hoc
Yukon Territory	75% of gross	719.18	306.85	50,000	Automatic annual

Source: Association of Workers' Compensation Boards of Canada (1993c).

21 In most provinces, workers receive actual wages if benefits are less than the minimum.

Permanent Disability Benefits

Unlike programs in other jurisdictions, particularly the United States, Canadian programs have traditionally paid compensation benefits for the duration of the claimant's disability. Claimants who suffer a permanent disability typically receive benefits for the remainder of their life or their working life. The formula used to compute permanent total benefits is identical to that used for temporary total benefits.[22] Canadian jurisdictions use two approaches to the compensation of permanent partial disability.

In British Columbia, Alberta, Manitoba, Nova Scotia, Prince Edward Island, and the Northwest Territories, permanent partial benefits are based on a medical assessment of the extent of the claimant's 'clinical' or physical impairment.[23] Often this evaluation is made with reference to a rating schedule that lists disability ratings for a variety of impairments.[24] In some jurisdictions, these assessments are adjusted for age; for example, in British Columbia, the claimant's disability assessment is increased by 1 percent for each year over the age of 45, to a maximum of 20 percent. Weekly permanent partial benefits are then calculated by multiplying the disability rating by 75 (90) percent of the claimant's gross (net) pre-injury wage, subject to minimums and maximums. Benefits are paid over the remainder of the claimant's life. In several jurisdictions (Alberta, the Northwest Territories, Nova Scotia, and Prince Edward Island), workers are also eligible for supplementary benefits if the combination of post-injury earnings and the life pension is less than pre-injury earnings.

In other Canadian jurisdictions, claimants who suffer a permanent disability are eligible for a dual award that ostensibly compensates them for nonwork as well as work disability. Compensation for work disability is based on the claimant's wage loss due to an injury, while compensation for nonwork disability is based on the extent of the claimant's physical impairment. The claimant's labour market status is reviewed periodically to determine whether compensation is consistent with current lost earnings due to work disability.

For example, Ontario pays two benefits to most permanently disabled claimants: a Noneconomic Loss (NEL) and a Future Economic Loss (FEL) Award. NELs are based on the extent of the claimant's impairment, as assessed by a physician using disability ratings from the AMA *Guides to the Evaluation of Permanent Impairment*, Third Edition. FELs are

---

22 However, unlike temporary total benefits, permanently disabled workers do not receive compensation below the statutory minimum.

23 Medical assessments of the extent of the claimant's 'clinical' or physical impairment are conducted by a board physician.

24 For example, in Ontario prior to 1989, the amputation of the great toe was assigned a rating of 2.5 percent, while the loss of a kidney was assigned a rating of 15 percent.

determined within 18 months of the notice of accident and are based on the claimant's wage loss or loss of earning capacity. If the claimant is working, the FEL award is equal to 90 percent of the difference between the pre- and post-injury net average earnings, subject to minimums and maximums. If the claimant has not returned to work, benefits are equal to 90 percent of the difference between the pre-injury net average wage and the net average wage the claimant would have received if he or she completed a prescribed vocational rehabilitation program.

FELs are reviewed two years after the initial determination. If the claimant's earnings or earning capacity has changed since initial determination, the FEL is adjusted accordingly (e.g., if the claimant is earning wages that exceed pre-injury wages). Three years following this first review, the FEL is reviewed a second time and adjustments are made as required. Following this second review, the FEL becomes permanent until age 65.

Finally, in all jurisdictions except Alberta, Prince Edward Island, and the Northwest Territories, both partial and total permanent disability benefits are adjusted automatically to reflect changes in the cost of living. Table 1 indicates that these adjustments occur on an annual or semi-annual basis.

Survivor Benefits

Workers' compensation programs provide cash benefits to the dependent survivors of workers who have died as the result of an occupational injury. Provinces pay a lump-sum amount for funeral expenses and transportation of the body. In addition, all Canadian jurisdictions pay a pension to the surviving spouse. In most jurisdictions, the pension is equal to the amount the deceased worker would have received had he or she been 100 percent disabled, although in a few jurisdictions (Northwest Territories, the Yukon, and Prince Edward Island), the payment is a fixed monthly amount. In Québec, Newfoundland, and Nova Scotia, the spouse receives a lump sum based on the workers' income or (in Québec) on the age of the surviving spouse.[25] With the exception of Ontario and the Yukon, pension benefits cease upon remarriage, and in Alberta, New Brunswick, and Saskatchewan, these pensions depend on the employment status of the surviving spouse.

Most provinces augment spousal benefits according to the number of dependent minor children, while a few pay dependent benefits to children individually.[26] All provinces pay benefits to dependent minor

25 In Québec, in addition to a lump sum, the surviving spouse receives a pension for a maximum of three years that, depending on the age of the spouse, equals from 55 to 90 percent of the deceased worker's pre-injury wage.

26 In most provinces, benefits are extended past the age of majority, if and while the child pursues an education.

children (or their guardians) when the spouse is also deceased. Provinces also pay survivor benefits to other relatives such as the worker's parents, if they were dependent on the worker's earnings at the time of the accident. However, in most jurisdictions claims of the spouse or children take precedence. As with spousal benefits, payments to children or other dependents may be a lump sum, a fixed monthly amount, or a monthly pension equal to a proportion of the worker's earnings. Benefits for other dependents continue for as long as the deceased worker would reasonably have been expected to have supported them.

Financing

Canadian workers' compensation programs are financed through assessments on employers covered by provincial workers' compensation acts. Assessments are intended (but often fail) to cover all costs incurred by the program, including future liability for injuries, administrative costs, and the costs of special funds, such as second injury or disaster funds.[27] There are two categories of employers. Some organizations, including federal and provincial governments, crown agencies, railways, and airlines, are individually liable for compensation claims (i.e., they are self-insured). The remaining organizations are charged assessments based, at least in part, on the firm's payroll and the accident experience of all firms within the 'rate group.'

The assessment process for the latter category of firms begins with the classification of firms into rate groups based on industrial sector.[28] The number and nature of these rate categories varies substantially by province.[29] The assessment rate for each group, which is stated as a rate per $100 of payroll, is determined by the rate group's accident experience over the previous three to five years. Consequently, firms in more hazardous industries are required to pay greater assessments than firms in less hazardous industries. Table 2 presents data on provincial assessment rates for several representative industries. For example, in Nova Scotia in 1993, credit unions paid a rate equal to $0.39 per $100 of payroll whereas underground coal mines paid $20.86. Rates also vary considerably across provinces. As examples, rates for poultry packing

27 'Second injury' funds pay for the costs of injury that are attributable to the fact that a pre-existing condition has increased the severity of disability resulting from a second injury relative to what it would have been if there were no pre-existing condition. These funds are designed to encourage firms to employ workers with such conditions. Disaster funds pay for extraordinary losses due to catastrophic events (e.g., a single accident that results in the death or disability of a large number of workers).

28 Firms that are engaged in two or more industries pay separate rates for each portion of their business; thus the firm's employees are allocated to the sectors in which it conducts business.

29 For example, the Yukon uses 6 categories, while Alberta has 584 groups.

Table 2

Assessment Rates, by Industry and Province, 1993

Industry	British Columbia	Alberta	Sask.	Manitoba[1]	Ontario	Québec
Dairy farms	3.00	6.89	1.50	3.68	4.88	9.18
Underground coal mining	2.80	7.92	5.25	3.81	4.41	—
Poultry packing plants	2.04	9.63	4.65	6.19	4.13	6.84
Manmade fibres and yarns	1.79	—	1.40	2.06	2.53	2.64
Sawmill	3.46	6.11	3.50	7.89	8.21	—
Printing	0.74	0.99	0.30	1.08	1.80	2.36
Steel fabrication	3.99	5.33	6.25	4.88	6.07	4.61
Commercial construction	6.14	5.14	9.50	7.01	5.97	11.05
General trucking	4.03	6.76	4.00	6.44	5.91	8.23
Supermarkets	1.09	2.10	1.40	2.08	2.75	3.30
Credit unions	1.09	0.29	0.05	2.08	.50	0.57

Industry	New Brunswick	Nova Scotia	PEI	Newfoundland	Yukon Territory	NWT
Fruit and vegetable farms	2.65	3.18	4.12	2.59	2.00	1.70
Open pit coal mining	3.81	20.86	—	19.31	2.50	19.75
Poultry packing plants	5.48	3.34	3.94[2]	10.10	1.25	4.00
Manmade fibres and yarns	1.75	1.79	0.82	0.90	1.25	—
Sawmill	6.55	4.13	7.50	6.47	2.50	21.00
Printing	0.45	0.41	0.82	1.29	1.25	1.20
Manmade fibres and yarns	1.75	1.79	0.82	0.90	1.25	—
Commercial construction	4.25	5.14	6.18	6.15	2.50	10.25
General trucking	4.37	3.32	2.76	6.73	2.50	6.25
Supermarkets	0.70	1.00	0.92	2.07	1.25	1.20
Credit unions	0.31	0.39	0.35	0.45	0.75	0.55

Source: Association of Workers' Compensation Boards of Canada (1993b).
[1] Manitoba has a range of rates for each industrial classification, reflecting a built-in experience rating system. The single figure reported in this table is the midpoint of that range.
[2] Prince Edward Island has a range of rates for Poultry Packing Plants, reflecting the fact that it has more than one rate grouping for this classification. We report the midpoint of that range.

plants varied from $1.25 in the Yukon Territory to $2.04 in British Columbia and $10.10 in Newfoundland.

The individual firm's base assessment is determined by multiplying the assessment rate by the firm's 'assessable payroll.' Assessable payroll is limited by the maximum assessable earnings of each employee; that is, each employee's contribution to total payroll is capped at this maximum assessable figure. Again, this cap also varies by province.[30]

Most jurisdictions have also established firm-level, experience-rating programs, under which assessments are adjusted by the firm's accident experience, so that more hazardous firms in the rate group pay a

30 Applying these principles, a bank in Québec with an assessable payroll of $1,000,000 would pay $4,200, whereas a demolition firm with an identical payroll would be assessed $213,800.

lower rate than less hazardous firms. This adjustment may be either prospective or retrospective: a prospective plan adjusts the employer's premium for the current year based on previous experience, while a retrospective plan adjusts the previous year's assessment based on the firm's accident experience during that year.

The characteristics of provincial experience-rating programs vary widely. Some programs are restricted to certain industries. For example, Ontario's CAD-7 plan applies only to the construction industry. In addition, many programs limit participation to firms that pay over a minimum annual assessment. For example, participation in Alberta's Experience Rating Program is limited to employers remitting over $3,000 in premiums during the previous three years, while participation in Québec's Retrospective Plan is limited to firms with an annual premium of at least $420,500. Finally, the degree to which assessments are experience rated depends on employer size, so that assessments of larger employers are more dependent on the firm's own accident experience (and correspondingly less dependent on the group's accident experience) than are assessments of smaller employers.

The specific formulas used to determine the experience-rating adjustment are complex and vary significantly by province. Some approaches offer greater incentives for accident reduction than others. In addition, the extent to which employer assessments are affected by experience rating varies by province. For example, the Experience Rated Assessments Program of British Columbia limits surcharges and rebates to 33.3 percent of the base rate, while Manitoba's Experience Sensitive Rating Program limits rebates to 25 percent and surcharges to 40 percent of the base rate. Details from Alberta's Experience Rating Program appear in Exhibit A.

Experience: Claim Rates and Costs

Benefit costs for 1991, disaggregated by province and type of benefit, are presented in Table 3. These data indicate that, on a nationwide basis, combined temporary and permanent indemnity benefit costs represent over 70 percent of all benefit costs.[31] However, these data also display substantial interprovincial variation. Since accounting practices are not standardized across provinces, this variation may be due to differences in the way claim costs are categorized and reported, particu-

---

31 While the data in Table 3 do not permit us to distinguish between permanent disability and survivor pensions, data from the annual reports of the provincial boards indicate that survivor benefits represent a relatively small proportion of the total. For example, expenditure data from the *1992 Annual Report of the Workers' Compensation Board of British Columbia* indicate that survivor benefits are only slightly over 16 percent of the sum of long-term disability and survivor benefits (Workers' Compensation Board of British Columbia 1993).

larly for permanent and temporary indemnity benefits. Nevertheless, Table 3 indicates that in the Northwest Territories, medical expenditures account for less than 10 percent of total benefit costs, whereas in Ontario they account for more than one-third of total costs. The difference may be explained by the emphasis on vocational rehabilitation in Ontario.

Table 4 reports benefit costs and the number of recipients of Canadian workers' compensation programs between 1960 and 1991. These data indicate that benefit costs increased by nearly 4000 percent (or by over 600 percent in real terms) during this period. This represents an average annual rate of increase of approximately 12.5 percent (roughly 6.5 percent in constant dollars). At the same time, the claims rate has declined, especially during the last ten years. Consequently, the average cost per claim has increased substantially: the average real cost of compensation has more than quadrupled since 1960, rising from $1,222 in that year to $5,179 in 1991.

Most of the increase in the average real cost per claim has occurred since 1980. From 1960 to 1980, average real benefit costs rose by about 85 percent (approximately 3 percent per year). In contrast, since 1980, average costs increased by 130 percent (almost 9 percent a year)—a growth rate roughly three times greater than that during the previous 20 years.

Table 3

Benefit Costs, by Province and Type of Benefit, 1991

Province	Permanent disability or survivors $000s	% of total	Temporary disability $000s	% of total	Hospital and medical care $000s	% of total	Total $000s
British Columbia	176,084	34.97	207,922	41.29	119,582	23.75	503,588
Alberta	127,634	30.82	164,229	39.65	122,316	29.53	414,179
Saskatchewan	28,035	33.90	36,967	44.71	17,685	21.39	82,687
Manitoba	27,175	23.01	68,874	58.31	22,065	18.68	118,114
Ontario	665,000	31.89	679,000	32.57	741,000	35.54	2,085,000
Québec	338,060	25.49	755,209	56.94	232,995	17.57	1,326,264
New Brunswick	15,676	24.06	31,878	48.92	17,607	27.02	65,161
Nova Scotia	47,116	37.28	51,394	40.66	27,888	22.06	126,398
PEI	4,237	38.77	3,363	30.77	3,328	30.45	10,928
Newfoundland	4,527	6.88	33,471	50.83	27,845	42.29	65,843
NWT	9,848	78.17	1,862	14.78	888	7.05	12,598
Yukon	1,077	29.73	1,825	50.37	721	19.90	3,623
Canada	1,444,473	30.00	2,035,999	42.29	1,333,923	27.71	4,814,394

Source: Data were obtained through personal communication with Health and Welfare Canada.
Note: Data are preliminary and subject to revision.

The cost of various components of compensation also increased substantially over the 1960 to 1991 period, but with different patterns. Table 5 provides real aggregate benefit costs disaggregated by type of benefit, including indemnity benefit costs and hospital and medical-care costs, for this same period.

These data indicate that the growth in indemnity benefits over this period was approximately equal to the growth in costs for medical care and rehabilitation (around 13 percent per year or about 7 percent in constant dollars). However, indemnity benefits in constant dollars grew about 50 percent faster before 1980 than after that time—7.5 percent annually prior to 1980 compared to 5 percent annually after 1980. In contrast, medical benefits exhibited the opposite pattern: the growth rate for medical benefits after 1980 was twice as great as the rate before 1980 (5 percent per year prior to 1980 compared to 10 percent per year after 1980). Consequently, medical benefits as a proportion of total benefits declined somewhat steadily from 1964 until 1985, but increased markedly after that. This corresponds with the experience of compensation programs in the United States where medical benefits have increased considerably in recent years.[32]

32 Comparing Canadian and American programs, Pozzebon and Thomason (1993) found that medical benefits in the United States have increased more rapidly in recent years and account for a larger share of total benefits than medical benefits in Canada. They report that between 1984 and 1990 real medical benefits (in US dollars) grew at an average rate of 5.8 percent in Canada and 7.8 percent in the US; in 1990, medical benefits accounted for about 14 percent of total benefits in Canada, while they accounted for nearly 41 percent of total benefits in the United States.

Table 4

Benefit Recipients, Claim Rates, and Benefit Costs, 1960–1991

Year	Current benefit costs ($000s)	Real benefit costs ($000s)	Benefit recipients	Claim rates
1991	4,798,184	4,798,184	926,482	75.1
1990	4,510,145	4,763,015	1,027,397	81.7
1989	3,915,216	4,334,213	1,044,928	83.7
1988	3,634,692	4,223,740	1,065,699	87.0
1987	3,449,858	4,170,231	1,029,813	86.8
1986	3,167,050	3,996,817	1,065,663	92.4
1985	2,733,594	3,593,537	1,071,483	95.5
1984	2,480,098	3,387,320	1,031,965	94.4
1983	2,217,709	3,162,428	950,156	89.0
1982	1,966,340	2,964,780	1,011,757	95.3
1981	1,613,644	2,697,243	1,202,775	109.3
1980	1,349,128	2,533,630	1,211,823	113.2
1979	1,104,690	2,285,441	1,163,610	112.0
1978	997,604	2,252,194	1,073,840	107.5
1977	858,976	2,113,114	1,039,062	107.7
1976	775,166	2,059,494	1,044,505	110.2
1975	657,790	1,878,124	988,155	106.4
1974	521,398	1,649,134	1,046,557	114.7
1973	426,164	1,493,942	985,640	112.5
1972	367,683	1,389,269	880,454	105.5
1971	318,991	1,261,964	793,535	97.9
1970	307,711	1,252,682	793,670	100.2
1969	274,480	1,154,646	795,407	101.6
1968	237,706	1,045,244	765,358	100.8
1967	220,150	1,006,628	777,707	104.4
1966	211,117	1,001,615	779,085	107.6
1965	183,802	902,561	724,809	101.5
1964	163,824	823,689	665,258	100.7
1963	149,628	767,604	528,419	82.9
1962	139,975	729,952	564,788	90.7
1961	127,704	674,320	540,887	89.3
1960	123,967	660,111	540,201	90.6

Source: Benefit cost and claim data for 1960 through 1987 are from Health and Welfare Canada (1985 and 1989). Benefit cost and claim data for years after 1987 were obtained through personal communication with Health and Welfare Canada. Claim rates were computed by the authors using employment data from the Labour Force Survey. Costs reflect monies paid out in the current year for current and past claims and do not reflect increases to accident reserves. (Editors' note: These figures are different from those reported by Vaillancourt, below, which include increases to accident reserves.)

Note: Data for 1988–91 are preliminary and subject to revision. Real costs are in 1991 constant dollars and were computed using the Consumer Price Index. The claims rate is expresssed in claims per 1000 employees. Data exclude the Yukon and Northwest Territories due to a lack of available data in earlier years, and are therefore not comparable with totals for Canada in Table 3.

Table 5

Compensation Costs and Claims, by Type of Benefit, 1960–1991

Year	Real indemnity benefit costs ($000s)	Real hospital and benefit costs ($000s)	Hospital and medical care costs as % of total benefits
1991	3,465,873	1,332,311	27.77
1990	3,680,005	1,083,010	22.74
1989	3,352,437	981,776	22.65
1988	3,261,010	962,729	22.79
1987	3,273,545	896,686	21.50
1986	3,259,511	737,306	18.45
1985	2,971,554	621,983	17.31
1984	2,780,283	597,796	17.65
1983	2,561,934	593,284	18.76
1982	2,435,313	522,151	17.61
1981	2,155,809	530,328	19.66
1980	2,056,621	470,705	18.58
1979	1,841,930	437,515	19.14
1978	1,798,917	449,051	19.94
1977	1,682,300	426,925	20.20
1976	1,625,321	432,452	21.00
1975	1,484,752	391,948	20.87
1974	1,313,644	335,490	20.34
1973	1,154,117	339,825	22.75
1972	1,063,889	325,381	23.42
1971	947,010	314,954	24.96
1970	940,011	312,671	24.96
1969	867,924	286,722	24.83
1968	757,244	288,000	27.55
1967	727,484	279,144	27.73
1966	734,569	267,046	26.66
1965	643,767	258,793	28.67
1964	586,785	236,904	28.76
1963	554,521	213,083	27.76
1962	537,044	192,909	26.43
1961	492,381	181,939	26.98
1960	487,846	172,266	26.10

Source: Cost data for 1960 through 1987 are from Health and Welfare Canada (1985 and 1989) Cost data for years after 1987 were obtained through personal communication with Health and Welfare Canada.
Note: Data for 1988–91 are preliminary and subject to revision. Real costs are in 1991 constant dollars. Medical costs include the cost of rehabilitation. Costs reflect monies paid out in current year for current and past claims and do not reflect increases to accident reserves. Data exclude the Yukon and Northwest Territories due to a lack of available data in earlier years, and are therefore not comparable with total costs for Canada in Table 3.

The Economics of Accidents and Workers' Compensation[33]

The Costs of Workplace Accidents

Work accidents are an undesirable by-product of industrial activity. As such, there is a direct relationship between the level of goods and services produced and the incidence of work accidents; that is, work accidents are more frequent when production levels are high.[34]

Society is concerned with both outcomes of the production process: goods and services and accident costs. Accident costs include the cost of medical and rehabilitative services required to restore the injured worker to health, lost production due to work disability, and the psychic costs of illness and disability (including pain and suffering and the loss of enjoyment of leisure activities).

Both employers and workers affect the incidence and severity of work accidents. Employers can reduce accident rates by purchasing safety equipment, modifying machinery, training the workforce in safety procedures, and establishing and enforcing safety rules. Workers can reduce accident frequency by being more attentive and taking greater care on the job. Accident prevention activities entail costs, however, including direct, out-of-pocket expenditures on safety equipment as well as indirect costs, such as productivity losses incurred when processes are modified to accommodate safety concerns.

Parties who bear all or part of the cost of work injuries will be motivated to avoid accidents through investment in accident prevention. Specifically, the employer and worker will invest in prevention up to the point where the marginal cost of prevention equals the marginal reduction in accident costs.

Similarly, injured workers and employers can reduce the severity of work accidents by investing in medical or vocational rehabilitation following injury. The party financially responsible for the injured worker's lost earnings will be motivated to reduce the duration and extent of disability by investing in rehabilitation to the extent that benefits, in the form of increased post-injury earnings, exceed costs.

If the legal regime transfers all or part of the burden of accident costs from one party to another (e.g., the employer is liable for the injured worker's medical expenses and lost earnings), additional costs, termed transaction costs, are incurred. These costs include (1) administrative

33 This discussion is intended to be heuristic rather than rigorous and borrows from several sources including: Oi (1973), Shavell (1987), Krueger (1990a), Lanoie (1991), Diamond (1977), Rea (1981), and Bruce and Atkins (1993).

34 Work accidents are also a function of the technology employed by the firm, so that some industries are more hazardous than others.

costs associated with determining whether the employer should be held liable for damages and if so, the extent of those damages (e.g., the costs of obtaining and adducing evidence) and (2) the costs of administrative or judicial error, (i.e., costs incurred when employers are wrongly held liable for damages or, conversely, are wrongly acquited of responsibility).[35] Increased transaction costs reduce the incidence of both valid and invalid compensation claims and thereby affect accident and accident-prevention costs.

Public policy may be evaluated based on the extent to which it maximizes social welfare (or minimizes social costs).[36] This analysis has identified four costs associated with the problem of compensation for occupational accidents: accident costs, including both psychic costs and lost earnings; accident prevention costs; the costs of rehabilitative services; and, if someone other than the injured worker is responsible for accident costs, transaction costs.

Market Mechanisms, Workers' Compensation, and Efficiency

The efficiency of workers' compensation in the marketplace is examined in this section. First, the alternative—a world without workers' compensation (and tort litigation)—is considered.

The risk of work injury varies due to differences in technology across firms. In a world without compensation, workers are reluctant to work for hazardous firms, and such firms must offer wages greater than those paid by 'safe' firms in order to attract an adequate workforce. If workers are fully informed about the risk of injury, this premium (or compensating differential) will equal the expected cost of accidents. No rational person would work for less. Since hazardous firms must pay higher wages *ex ante*, they are motivated to reduce accidents up to the point where the marginal costs of prevention equal marginal benefits (i.e., the reduction in the wage rate). Workers may use the hazardous wage premium to purchase insurance against the risk of disability. If actuarially fair, insurance costs will equal the compensating differential.

---

35 In part, judicial errors impose costs by increasing the uncertainty of the outcome of the adjudication process—the process by which disputes over the assignment of liability for damages are resolved. The more uncertain the outcome, the more likely that a party will invest in resources designed to influence it. If, for example, the employer is certain that the adjudicator will award damages to the claimant, the employer will spare the expense of a hearing and will voluntarily pay damages to the injured worker. Hence, the costs associated with judicial error increase as uncertainty increases (i.e., as the probability of victory approches 0.5). Some empirical evidence supports this hypothesis. Roberts (1992) showed that there is a positive relationship between the incidence of workers' compensation disputes and uncertainty about recovery and future earnings ability.

36 Policy may also be examined on the basis of equity—the extent to which the policy fairly distributes social welfare or costs. This a more difficult standard to precisely define, and our discussion will be limited to the efficiency dimension.

In addition, injured workers (who are obliged to pay for accident costs) will undergo rehabilitation to the extent that benefits, in the form of increased earnings, exceed costs. Thus, workers will only undertake 'efficient' rehabilitation. Finally, since costs are not transferred from one party to another, no transaction costs are incurred. Therefore, assuming that workers are fully informed, a competitive labour market will result in an efficient allocation of accident-related costs.

Different results are obtained if workers are not fully informed. If they underestimate the probability of accident, the risk premium will be less than accident costs, and employers will underinvest in safety relative to the efficient level. If workers overestimate accident probability, the risk premium will be greater than accident costs, and insurers will overinvest in accident prevention.

Furthermore, information asymmetries may prevent the development of an insurance market. If workers possess information concerning the risk of injury that is unavailable to insurers, low-risk workers will not purchase insurance; the cost of insurance for low-risk workers will exceed the expected cost of accidents. Since only high-risk workers enter the market, accident costs will exceed premiums and insurers will be driven out.[37]

Finally, since rehabilitation costs are incurred prior to the payoff from rehabiliation (increased earnings), injured workers may forgo efficient rehabilitation if capital markets are imperfect and they are unable to secure financing. Similar problems arise if injured workers lack information about the opportunities for, and/or the effectiveness of, rehabilitation. If so, subsidization of rehabilitation programs may lead to greater social welfare.

Workers' compensation shifts some accident costs from the worker to the employer. As a result, the premium for hazardous work is reduced; the reduction is equal to the expected value of compensation benefits. If employers are perfectly experience rated, the level of occupational injuries is unaffected by the introduction of workers' compensation. As the *ex post* costs for employers (compensation benefits) increase, *ex ante* costs (the compensating differential) decline, so that employer accident costs remain unchanged. However, if the employer is not experience rated, *ex post* compensation costs do not increase, even though *ex ante* costs are reduced.

---

37 Similar market failures result when employers bear the cost of work injury and workers' compensation is not mandatory. For example, in such circumstances, employers may elect to risk bankruptcy rather than purchase insurance; if so, the employer will not consider the full cost of accidents when making safety investment decisions, leading to an underinvestment in accident prevention.

Workers' compensation benefits may be expected to have contradictory effects on claimant rehabilitation. First, indemnity benefits reduce the disabled-nondisabled earnings differential, so that workers have less incentive to pursue rehabilitation and return to work. On the other hand, medical and vocational rehabilitation benefits reduce the cost of these services and, consequently, increase consumption and hasten the claimant's return to work. Subsidization of rehabilitation programs may result in an inefficient overconsumption of rehabilitation services; claimants will undergo rehabilitation when total costs (including subsidized costs) are greater than the expected gain in earnings capacity.

In addition, workers' compensation programs incur transaction costs that are not incurred when injured workers automatically bear the burden of work accidents. Compensation programs must determine whether or not the injury is occupational and, if so, the extent to which the claimant suffers injury-related disability.[38] Compensation benefits will induce workers to report injuries that might otherwise have gone unreported (or, possibly, to initiate fraudulent claims).

Empirical Research

As indicated above, the existence of compensating differentials between hazardous and nonhazardous firms is a necessary condition for efficient allocation in the market context. Several studies have examined the wage-risk relationship by estimating a wage equation using industry-level, aggregate data. Those studies that use a risk measure based on occupational fatalities have typically found that wages increase with the risk of death; studies using other risk measures are less conclusive (see Moore and Viscusi 1989 for a review).[39]

While these data show that workers receive a premium for hazardous work, they do not indicate whether this premium is *fully* compensating. That is, these results do not establish whether or not the present discounted value of the premium is equal to the expected value of higher accident costs (see Ehrenberg 1988). While inconclusive, evidence indicates that workers may have inadequate information concerning job risks—that workers wrongly estimate the likelihood of low probability events such as work injuries (Dickens 1985).

38 To the extent that parties can influence the resolution of these issues, they will invest in resources, such as medical expertise or legal counsel, to obtain a favourable outcome. Of course, transaction costs incurred by workers' compensation programs are not nearly as substantial as those incurred by the system of tort litigation that it replaced. In addition to the issues presented by a compensation claim (e.g., the extent of damages), tort litigation requires determination of fault.

39 Several studies have also found a negative relationship between compensation benefits and the size of the compensating differential, as predicted by theory (Dorsey 1983; Arnould and Nichols 1983; and Moore and Viscusi 1989).

Substantial research evidence suggests that the incidence of both occupational accidents and workers' compensation claims is positively related to the level of benefits (Chelius 1973; 1974; 1977; 1982; Butler and Worrall 1983; Krueger 1990a). There are two hypotheses that potentially explain this relationship. Increased benefits may induce workers to report injuries that would otherwise have gone unreported (a 'reporting' effect). On the other hand, increased benefits may induce workers to take more risks, which leads to an increased incidence of occupational injuries (a 'true injury' effect).[40]

Butler and Worrall (1991) attempted to disentangle reporting from true-injury effects by estimating statewide indemnity and medical benefit costs as a function of benefit levels, arguing that medical costs, unlike indemnity costs, should be unaffected by increased claim reporting. They found that, while indemnity costs were positively related to benefit levels, there was a negative relationship between benefit levels and medical costs. They conclude that higher benefits induce employers to increase accident prevention efforts, thereby reducing the true injury rate (and medical costs). At the same time, higher benefits increased claim reporting (and indemnity costs).[41]

Furthermore, Smith (1990) analyzed compensation claim incidence by injury type and by the day of the week and time of day that the injury was first reported. His data suggest that some injuries that are reported as occupational actually occurred off the job. Smith hypothesized that workers are more likely to falsely report nonwork injuries on Mondays (or on Tuesdays after long weekends) compared to other days of the week, and at the beginning of the workday rather than at other times.[42] Examining injury frequency by day of the week and time of day, Smith (1990) estimated that 9 percent of Monday injuries were falsely reported.

Several studies also indicate that employer incentives are related to the degree to which compensation insurance is experience rated. Ruser (1991) showed that the relationship between benefits and injuries was smaller for larger firms. Since large firms are more fully experience rated than small firms, these results indicate that experience rating provides

40 It is important to note that reporting effects are partially driven by transaction costs. If there were no administrative costs, workers would not be reluctant to report claims. If there were no judicial errors, workers would not report fraudulent claims.

41 Since it is unlikely that death claims are subject to reporting effects, the relationship between benefits and occupational fatalities should reflect the true-injury effect. Moore and Viscusi (1989) found that occupational fatality—as opposed to injuries or compensation claims—are negatively related to compensation benefits, a result they attribute to enhanced prevention efforts by employers.

42 To test this hypothesis, Smith (1990) partitioned a sample of compensation claims into two types: type F injuries that can feasibly be misreported as having occurred at work, such as strains and sprains and type N, injuries that are difficult to report falsely as occupational, such as cuts and lacerations.

firms with incentives to reduce claims. Similar results were obtained by Worrall and Butler (1988) and Ruser (1985).

In addition, there is substantial evidence supporting the hypothesis that indemnity benefits delay the claimant's return to work or otherwise adversely affect rehabilitation. Several studies have shown that the duration of temporary total disability is positively related to the level of temporary benefits (Butler and Worrall 1985; Johnson and Ondrich 1990; Krueger 1990b; Dionne and St-Michel 1991). Specifically, these studies suggest that the benefit elasticity for disability duration is approximately twice as great as the elasticity for injury rates (a 10 percent increase in compensation benefits increases disability duration by 10 to 20 percent and the injury rate by 4 to 6 percent). Finally, Thomason (1993a; 1993b) and Worrall et al. (1993) have found that the probability of transition from temporary to permanent disability is positively related to the level of compensation benefits.

Finally, evidence indicates that compensation benefits induce employers to challenge worker claims, thus raising associated transaction costs. As noted by Ehrenberg (1988, 76),

> As long as workers' compensation benefits are at least partially experience rated, higher benefits will increase employers' incentives both to challenge claims and to encourage injured workers to speed their recovery and return to work.

Using a sample of Ontario firms, Hyatt and Kralj (1991) have shown, for example, that experience-rated employers are more likely to appeal adverse decisions of the Ontario Workers' Compensation Board than employers who are not experience rated. Similarly, in an examination of claims from New York, Thomason and Burton (1993) found that insurer adjustments (i.e., the termination or reduction of benefits) increased the probability that claimants will accept a lump-sum settlement, which were substantially less remunerative than the benefits the claimant would have received if she had not accepted the settlement. With this same sample, Thomason (1994) found that insurers were more likely to challenge the claims of workers who were vulnerable to financial pressures, including claimants who could not speak English.[43]

Benefit Liberalization and the Costs of Compensation

The basic economic analysis suggests that if workers are fully informed about the risks of accident, then a competitive market will result in an efficient level of work accidents. However, empirical evidence indicates that workers lack adequate information about job risks, suggesting that government-sponsored compulsory compensation insurance may be

---

43 On the other hand, Thomason (1994) found that, contrary to expectations, compensation benefits were negatively related to insurer challenges.

justified. On the other hand, unless firms are fully experience rated, workers' compensation will also result in inefficient levels of accident costs and accident prevention.

Taken together, these considerations suggest that it is not possible to determine, *a priori*, whether or not workers' compensation increases efficiency relative to a competitive market under imperfect information. To date, the *corpus* of empirical evidence is not yet substantial enough to unambiguously inform this public policy debate.

However, the theory and empirical research discussed above provide an explanation for the increased cost of Canadian compensation programs. As previously indicated, compensation costs increased substantially between 1960 and 1991. As noted, empirical research indicates that higher benefit levels are associated with higher reported accident rates and increased disability duration. The benefit liberalization that occurred during this period may have led to greater program utilization. If so, this relationship would be evidence of inefficiency to the extent that increased utilization is due to increased claim reporting or malingering.[44]

Data with respect to benefit generosity (from 1960 to 1991) are provided in Table 6.[45] During this period, the average real maximum benefit in Canada increased by 1.27 percent annually compared to an average annual increase of 5.07 percent in real per claim benefit costs. Both variables grew more rapidly prior to 1980 than during the period after 1980: the real average benefit maximum rose by 1.76 percent annually before 1980 and 0.46 percent afterward; similarly, real per claim benefit costs increased by 9 percent annually before 1980 and 3 percent per year between 1980 and 1991 (see Table 7).

These data suggest that the direct effect of higher indemnity benefits is partially, although not completely, responsible for the increase in compensation costs from 1960 to 1991, and especially for the increase from 1960 to 1980.[46] However, the research reviewed above suggests

44 Of course, it is arguable that prior to this liberalization, benefits were inadequate and that any increased program utilization is legitimate. For example, prior to liberalization, transaction costs prevented workers from reporting valid claims.

45 The generosity of indemnity benefits is primarily determined by four variables: the benefit maximum, the benefit minimum, the replacement rate, and the waiting period. Variation in the minimum has little impact on benefit generosity for two reasons: first, few claimants earn wages low enough to be affected by the minimum; and second, in most provinces minimum benefits are equal to the claimants pre-injury wage, if the wage is less than the statutory minimum. For example, assume that the replacement rate is equal to 75 percent of gross wages, that the minimum equals $50, and that the claimant earns $50 weekly. Thus, claimant benefits are equal to $37.50. If the minimum is raised to $100, then the benefit will increase to $50, so that a 100 percent increase in the benefit minimum, at most increases benefits by only 33 percent.

46 The decline in the waiting period could not account for increased per claim costs since a shorter waiting period affects claim frequency but not claim duration or severity. The replacement rate did not change during this period.

Table 6

Maximum Benefit, Waiting Period, and Replacement Rate, Nationwide Statistics, 1960–1991

Year	Real average maximum temporary benefits	Average waiting period (in days)	% of employment in provinces paying benefits equal to 90% of net earnings
1991	569.38	0.42	83.50
1990	519.08	0.41	83.86
1989	516.48	0.40	81.10
1988	514.28	0.40	81.45
1987	530.59	0.40	81.45
1986	537.08	0.80	42.14
1985	547.65	0.80	38.50
1984	541.55	1.06	38.57
1983	538.50	1.06	37.13
1982	500.61	1.06	37.13
1981	512.61	1.06	24.75
1980	475.23	1.06	25.16
1979	497.12	1.06	0.00
1978	499.68	1.06	0.00
1977	492.00	—	0.00
1976	462.88	1.06	0.00
1975	438.61	1.13	0.00
1974	417.40	1.14	0.00
1973	427.05	1.14	0.00
1972	370.19	1.14	0.00
1971	384.41	—	0.00
1970	390.23	1.34	0.00
1969	359.88	1.88	0.00
1968	373.79	2.67	0.00
1967	385.88	2.68	0.00
1966	380.00	2.67	0.00
1965	387.85	2.67	0.00
1964	364.90	2.67	0.00
1963	370.94	4.00	0.00
1962	364.13	4.00	0.00
1961	367.21	4.05	0.00
1960	290.97	4.05	0.00

Source: U.S. Chamber of Commerce (1960–1991).
Note: Average temporary benefit maximum and average waiting period are weighted averages, where weight is provincial employment. If the employer pays for the day of injury, the waiting period is considered equal to zero. If benefits are equal to 90 percent of net earnings, temporary benefit maximum is equal to that for a single worker with no children. Real maximum benefits are in 1991 constant dollars. Data exclude the Yukon and Northwest Territories due to unavailability of data in earlier years.

Table 7

Real Per Claim Benefit Costs and Medical-Aid Only Claim as a Proportion of Total Claims, 1960–1991

Year	Real benefit costs per claim	Medical-aid only claims as a % of total claims	Year	Real benefit costs per claim	Medical-aid only claims as a % of total claims
1991	5,179	43.36	1975	1,901	55.37
1990	4,636	42.45	1974	1,576	54.78
1989	4,148	41.24	1973	1,516	55.52
1988	3,963	42.54	1972	1,578	55.51
1987	4,050	40.62	1971	1,590	60.53
1986	3,751	43.62	1970	1,578	61.88
1985	3,354	46.80	1969	1,452	63.44
1984	3,282	49.21	1968	1,366	65.29
1983	3,328	48.48	1967	1,294	65.64
1982	2,930	48.82	1966	1,286	65.55
1981	2,243	51.49	1965	1,245	65.67
1980	2,091	53.27	1964	1,238	65.20
1979	1,964	53.96	1963	1,453	65.17
1978	2,097	54.96	1962	1,292	67.19
1977	2,034	56.23	1961	1,247	67.94
1976	1,972	54.70	1960	1,222	66.90

Source: Cost data for 1960 through 1987 are from Health and Welfare Canada (1985 and 1989). Cost data for years after 1987 were obtained through personal communication with Health and Welfare Canada.

Note: Data for 1988–91 are preliminary and subject to revision. Real costs are in 1991 constant dollars. Medical costs include the cost of rehabilitation. Costs reflect monies paid out in current year for current and past claims and do not reflect increases to accident reserves. Data exclude the Yukon and Northwest Territories due to the unavailability of data in earlier years, and are therefore not comparable with total costs for Canada in Table 3.

that increasing compensation benefits also affects program utilization. Specifically, higher benefits are associated with higher claims rates and, more importantly, with increased disability duration.[47] Evidence presented in Table 7 supports this hypothesis: medical-aid-only claims, as a proportion of total claims, declined from a high of nearly 68 percent in 1961 to roughly 53 percent in 1980. In other words, workers were increasingly more likely to file claims involving indemnity benefits over this period.

As indicated, the costs of workers' compensation have increased substantially over the last three decades. Some policymakers have begun to question the continued viability of the public provision of workers' compensation in the face of these escalating costs. Our review of the literature suggests that economic analysis increases our understanding of this and other problems facing workers' compensation pro-

47 As noted, the effect of benefits on duration is twice as great as its effect on claim frequency.

grams in Canada and can help inform and guide future policy making. We believe that the papers contained in this book, and summarized in the following section, represent a substantial contribution to this understanding.

Economic Analyses of Canadian Workers' Compensation

This section provides a summary of each chapter in this volume, highlights the main focus of the research and reviews the principal results or conclusions. Several chapters examine important institutional aspects of workers' compensation, including policies respecting the compensation of occupational disease, the recent fiscal history of Canadian workers' compensation programs, and the development of the duty to re-employ injured workers. These studies are complemented by research that provides substantial new evidence concerning a number of important issues affecting Canadian workers' compensation programs, including processes determining the incidence and severity of work injuries, the efficacy of government safety regulation, and the effect of rehabilitation programs on the likelihood of re-employment. Taken together, the chapters represent a unique blend of institutional and empirical analyses that examine a broad range of workers' compensation issues.

One objective of workers' compensation is to promote workplace safety and reduce the incidence and severity of occupational accidents. Governments have also attempted to address health and safety concerns through the imposition of standards designed to regulate the behaviour of the firm. These regulations are sometimes imposed on worker conduct (e.g., requiring the worker to wear protective equipment, such as hard hats or respirators), but more frequently they are imposed on the firm (e.g., requiring that hand rails be placed on walkways above a certain height or stipulating the load that ladders must support).

Jean-Michel Cousineau, *Sandra Girard*, and *Paul Lanoie* focus on whether the extent of government regulation (e.g., inspections, fines, prosecutions, requirements for safety committees, or prevention programs) has an impact on changes in accident rates for several specific categories of worker injuries (e.g., 'falls or slips') as well as on changes in the overall rate of injuries. Cousineau, Girard, and Lanoie use disaggregated industry-level injury, safety enforcement, and establishment data for 23 industries in Québec over the period from 1982 to 1984. With the exception of inspections, regulatory policies in Québec were generally found to be negatively associated with changes in the injury rates of specific categories of accidents. That is, increased government regulation does seem to reduce work injuries. In addition, increases in both average hours worked and average firm size are found to be positively and negatively associated, respectively, with changes in accident rates. Cousineau, Girard, and Lanoie note that these findings are generally consistent with results from the United States.

One important result for the design of workers' compensation programs emerging from the American literature is the positive relationship between benefit levels and the likelihood that workers will report a compensable injury. *Terry Thomason* and *Silvana Pozzebon* analyze individual-level data from the Labour Market Activity Survey (supplement to Statistics Canada's Labour Force Survey) for the years 1986–87 and 1988–89 in order to examine this issue for Canada. This study is among the first to examine the probability of injury using individual-level micro-data and is the first to analyze accident rates using data from all ten provinces.

Thomason and Pozzebon find that, after controlling for a range of factors that affect claims incidence, the likelihood that a worker will receive workers' compensation benefits is positively associated with benefit levels in the program. However, they also find that claims incidence is associated with workers' occupational and demographic characteristics, such as job tenure and weekly hours of work. Their results, which are consistent with those from American studies, constitute the first evidence for these relationships for Canada.

William Johnson, Richard Butler, and *Marjorie Baldwin* examine the determinants of the duration of the first spells of work absences of injured workers, including individual personal characteristics (e.g., age, education, marital status, union status), job attributes (industry, region), as well as the benefit/wage ratio. Their analysis thus employs individual-level micro-data, including information derived from a comprehensive survey of all permanently impaired workers compiled by the Ontario Workers' Compensation Board in 1989–90, combined with administrative data from the Ontario Workers' Compensation Board.

Individual characteristics examined in this study have typically been found to have a significant impact on absence duration in American studies, and the results obtained in this study are generally consistent with previous findings. However, in striking contrast to US research, Johnson, Butler, and Baldwin find that union status is associated with a shorter duration of first spells of post-injury work absence, suggesting that Canadian unions facilitate claimants' return to work. Another important finding is evidence of gender differences in the effects of worker characteristics (such as marital status) on the duration of work absences, which may reflect underlying differences in household responsibilities. This result raises a number of important policy issues, particularly concerning the design of rehabilitation strategies for injured workers.

As the authors explain, their analysis of the first spells of work absence is an important but, nonetheless, limited step toward a more complete examination of the effect of accidents on employment outcomes, since the majority of injured workers experience additional work absences subsequent to the first spell. The next stage in this line of research is to examine the complete history of work absences of injured workers.

Since injured workers possess information concerning their health status unknown to the workers' compensation board (insurer), the possibilty of a type of 'moral hazard' arises, whereby the injured worker has an incentive to extend the duration of work disability. *Georges Dionne, Pierre St-Michel*, and *Charles Vanasse* examine this moral hazard using individual-level data for 1987 for accident claims from the Commission de la Santé et de la Sécurité du Travail du Québec. Specifically, they estimate injury duration as a function of insurance coverage for different injury types.

Dionne, St-Michel, and Vanasse supplement compensation claims data with information from a survey of injured workers to construct a database that includes such information as the duration of work absence, personal attributes (e.g., age, gender), job characteristics (e.g., industry, union status), and earnings. They hypothesize that injuries that are relatively easy to diagnose (such as contusions, amputations, fractures, and friction burns) are less subject to moral hazard than injuries, such as lower back pain or sprains, that are difficult to diagnose. Consequently, they expect that the relationship between insurance coverage—the extent to which compensation benefits replace lost work income—and claim duration will be greater for easily diagnosed injuries.

Their results provide support for this hypothesis. Their research has several important policy implications. First, they conclude that partial insurance coverage (in the form of a replacement rate or coinsurance less than 100 percent) is not sufficient to deter this type of moral hazard and that compensation boards should selectively monitor or audit workers' post-injury recovery. In addition, their empirical analysis demonstrates and illustrates a procedure by which compensation boards can identify those injuries that most require auditing.

The study by *Boris Kralj* examines whether linking an individual employer's compensation assessment to the firm's own claim experience has an impact on the duration of injury claims. Since claim costs are significantly affected by claim duration and since claim costs affect employer assessments under a system of experience rating, experience-rated employers may be expected to have an incentive to reduce claim duration, all else being equal.

Kralj analyzes micro-data for individuals in the Ontario construction industry who have experienced a total temporary disability. The data include information on personal characteristics, compensation benefits, the type of injury, as well as characteristics of the employer. The data are derived from administrative files of the Ontario Workers' Compensation Board and consist of two cross-sections: the first, from 1983, was taken at a point prior to the introduction of experience rating in the construction industry in 1984 and the second, from 1988, was taken after the program had been in place for four years. Kralj is therefore able to examine the likely impact of introducing experience rating on claim duration.

Interestingly, the main finding is that the introduction of experience rating is actually associated with greater claims duration—a result that is inconsistent with expectations. However, Kralj's findings are in accord with previous research using Québec data but contrary to American studies. But Kralj also obtains some evidence that the expected effect of experience rating on claim duration may occur for more severe injuries. This research for Ontario is an important addition to an earlier analysis of Québec data by Lanoie (1992), and together these studies point to a need for more research in this area.

The level of compensation awarded to workers who have experienced permanent losses resulting from injuries or diseases remains a fundamental challenge for workers' compensation policymakers. *Sandra Sinclair* and *John F. Burton, Jr.* assess the results of a research project sponsored by the Ontario Workers' Compensation Board that attempts to examine this issue for noneconomic loss. As Sinclair and Burton explain, a permanent worker impairment can result in both work disability and noneconomic loss associated with the general disutility of a permanent impairment; while both types of loss are now compensated in Ontario following the passage of Bill 162, there is no standard against which to judge the extent of noneconomic loss.

Ontario currently uses what is widely accepted as the best available guide to valuing losses, the *Guide to the Evaluation of Permanent Impairment* published by the American Medical Association. This guide essentially provides a chart of clinical *ratings* or *values* for different impairments. Sinclair and Burton examine results from a unique survey sponsored by the Ontario Workers' Compensation Board, which collected data from separate samples of injured workers and the general population in order to obtain individual ratings of 'loss' resulting from various degrees of impairment. Overall, Sinclair and Burton find that survey ratings obtained from both samples are (statistically significantly) different—they are higher—than the values obtained from the AMA *Guide* currently used by the Ontario Board. These results have been noted with interest by both policymakers and stakeholders.

Sinclair and Burton note the need for further comparative analysis of disability ratings systems (e.g., by body-system groupings). They also note that, despite the interest of policymakers and stakeholders, there are important outstanding issues, particularly the potential cost implications of adopting alternative ratings. Given the use of noneconomic loss benefits in several provinces, the results obtained by Sinclair and Burton, debunking the leading method of determining the degrees of noneconomic loss, provide a substantial foundation for further research in this area.

One of the unique features of the 1989 reforms of Ontario's workers' compensation legislation enacted under Bill 162 is the requirement imposed on employers both to re-employ injured workers and to 'accommodate' their return to the workplace. *Morley Gunderson, Douglas Hyatt*, and *David Law* examine the underlying rationale, the essence, the general context, and the cost implications of re-employment and accommodation requirements.

After reviewing the rationale for these reforms, Gunderson, Hyatt, and Law relate these two requirements to the broader legal and legislative development of accommodation requirements. In particular, they explain that the requirement to re-employ workers is currently provided by the workers' compensation legislation of two provinces, Ontario and Québec, but is absent from most American jurisdictions. Broader requirements to 'accommodate' are also provided by the human rights legislation of provincial jurisdictions and have emerged through recent developments in the Canadian courts; in the United States, the 1992 *Americans With Disabilities Act* includes accommodation requirements for injured workers. Requirements to accommodate injured workers are therefore in a formative stage. Gunderson, Hyatt, and Law also examine the specific re-employment and accommodation requirements found in the Ontario workers' compensation legislation and the relationship between legislative provisions and guidelines used by the Ontario Human Rights Commission to assess employer accommodation efforts. These guidelines have been adopted by the Ontario Workers' Compensation Board.

Two related issues are of considerable interest to stakeholders of the workers' compensation system: the potential costs imposed on employers by accommodation provisions and the extent to which these costs are shifted to injured workers. Gunderson, Hyatt, and Law conclude their review with a discussion of research using Ontario data, which suggests that partial cost-shifting occurs when injured workers are re-employed by firms other than the worker's employer at the time of the work accident. However, these data also indicate that 'accident employers' are unable to shift costs, presumably due to statutory accommodation requirements.

The ability of injured workers to return to work and regain pre-injury earnings capacity has significant social (i.e., both private and public) and economic implications. The historical emphasis on vocational rehabilitation and the recent enhancement of vocational rehabilitation programs under Ontario's Bill 162 highlight the importance of these programs as a means of facilitating the return of injured workers to the workforce. *Richard Allingham* and *Douglas Hyatt* empirically explore the relationship between vocational rehabilitation and the likelihood that injured workers will subsequently return to work.

Allingham and Hyatt use micro-data on injured workers from the administrative files of the Ontario Workers' Compensation Board and from the 1989–90 *Survey of Ontario Workers with Permanent Impairments*. These data include detailed information on variables expected to affect the disabled worker's return to work, such as the worker's rehabilitation status, the extent of 'residual disability,' personal characteristics (e.g., education), and injury characteristics (e.g., nature of the injury). The results suggest that participation in a vocational rehabilitation program has a positive impact on the likelihood that an injured worker will return to work.

There are relatively few studies of the impact of rehabilitation programs on re-employment probability, and this chapter provides the first such analysis using Canadian data. The results serve to underscore the importance of vocational rehabilitation and, as the authors note, provide a first step toward a broader understanding of the effects of rehabilitation programs on the labour market experience of injured workers, including such dimensions as their earnings and employment turnover patterns.

The empirical analysis of the determinants of accidents and wages in Québec by *Jean-Michel Cousineau, Robert Lacroix,* and *Anne-Marie Girard* builds on a substantial literature in the United States and Canada. Their research is unique in that they use occupation-level data, whereas previous studies examined industry-level data. Occupational data permits Cousineau, Lacroix, and Girard to control for potential heterogeneity of risk across occupations and to capture job-level work conditions more directly.

Their data set combines information from three sources: administrative data from the Commission de la santé et de la sécurité du travail, which supports the creation of a measure of the occupational accident rate; the 1981 Census of Canada, which yields various sociodemographic variables; and the *Canadian Classification and Dictionary of Occupations* which provides job attributes, such as working conditions and education and training requirements.

Cousineau, Lacroix, and Girard obtain several significant results using an instrumental variable analysis that controls for the endogeneity of wages. As expected, the accident rate varies inversely with wages. Job conditions (e.g., heat, humidity, noise, and required strength) also have a significant impact on the accident rate. Interestingly, accident probability is negatively related to work experience and the level of education and/or training required by the occupation. The authors attribute these results to the negative relationship between accident costs and the injury rate, since more experienced and highly skilled workers are more difficult to replace than less experienced and less skilled workers.

The authors note that the relationship between accident rates and labour costs (as proxied by experience and required training) implies that policy measures that enhance labour market information could reduce the accident rate, as could an employer tax on injuries.

Perhaps due to potentially substantial cost implications, one of the more controversial areas of workers' compensation is the compensation of disabilities attributable to occupational diseases. *Lynn Elinson* provides a comprehensive review of the historical development of the compensation of occupational disease in Ontario and the current management of these diseases under the Ontario *Workers' Compensation Act.*

Defining occupational disease is a complex problem. Elinson's critical assessment of this difficult issue is complemented by a discussion of contemporary Ontario policymaking and the functioning of claims practice regarding occupational diseases. Particularly challenging is the adjudication of disease claims. Elinson concludes her discussion by identifying future directions for compensation policy in this area.

François Vaillancourt provides an extensive overview of the changes in the financial position of workers' compensation boards in Québec, Ontario, and British Columbia over the period from 1982 through 1991. Vaillancourt begins by characterizing trends in revenues and costs in the three provinces. He then documents the development of unfunded liabilities in Ontario and Québec over the past decade. Vaillancourt proceeds to examine the structure of the growth in costs: measured in real terms, both total expenses and current claims costs have increased (whether measured as aggregate costs or measured on a per-accident basis). Vaillancourt highlights the significant differences in the financial trends in British Columbia, Ontario, and Québec. Vaillancourt provides a detailed description of the trends in workers' compensation costs that have given rise to the substantial unfunded liabilities that now confront policymakers in Ontario and Québec. His examination of financial developments in workers' compensation provides a motivation for further analytical investigation of the reasons for the differing trends in the financial positions of the provinces.

Most studies in this volume focus on the experience of workers' compensation programs in Ontario and Québec, the two largest jurisdictions in Canada. However, the characteristics of compensation programs vary significantly across Canadian jurisdictions. In addition, despite the considerable contributions made by the research presented here, many important questions remain unanswered. Most workers' compensation research has examined data from the United States, although there are considerable differences between Canadian and American programs. Workers' compensation is a costly program critical to the well-being of Canadian workers and employers alike. Unfortunately, relatively little is known about how Canadians respond to different policies and programs. Extending research on workers' compensation to other issues and jurisdictions should be a major priority of the provinces in the years to come.

References

Arnould, Richard and Len Nichols. 1983. Wage-risk premiums and workers' compensation: A refinement of estimates of compensating wage differentials. *Journal of Political Economy* 91:332–40.

Association of Workers' Compensation Boards of Canada. 1991. *Comparison of workers' compensation legislation in Canada*. Edmonton: The Association.

———. 1993a. *Workers' compensation experience rating programs in Canada*. Edmonton: The Association.

———. 1993b. *Workers' compensation industry classifications and assessment rates in Canada*. Edmonton: The Association.

———. 1993c. *Benefit comparisons as of January 1, 1993*. Edmonton: The Association.

Bruce, Christopher J. and Frank J. Atkins. 1993. Efficiency effects of premium-setting regimes under workers' compensation: Canada and the United States. *Journal of Labor Economics* 11:S38–S69.

Butler, Richard J. and John D. Worrall. 1983. Workers' compensation: Benefit and injury claim rates in the seventies. *Review of Economics and Statistics* 65:580–99.

———. 1985. Work injury compensation and the duration of nonwork spells. *Economic Journal* 95:714–24.

———. 1991. Claims reporting and risk bearing moral hazard in workers' compensation. *Journal of Risk and Insurance* 58:191–204.

Canadian Manufacturers' Association. 1987. *Workers' compensation in Canada: Facing new realities.* Ottawa: The Association.

Chelius, James R. 1973. An empirical analysis of safety regulation. In *Supplemental studies for the National Commission on State Workmen's Compensation Laws*, edited by M. Berkowitz, vol.3, pp.53–66. Washington, DC: US Government Printing Office.

———. 1974. The control of industrial accidents: Economic theory and empirical evidence. *Law and Contemporary Problems* 38:700–729.

———. 1977. *Workplace safety and health: The role of workers' compensation.* Washington, DC: American Enterprise Institute.

———. 1982. The influence of workers' compensation on safety incentives. *Industrial and Labor Relations Review* 35:235–42.

Dee, Garth, Nick McCombie, and Gary Newhouse. 1987. *Workers' compensation in Ontario.* Toronto: Butterworths.

Diamond, Peter. 1977. Insurance theoretic aspects of workers' compensation. In *Natural resources, uncertainty, and general equilibrium systems*, edited by A.S. Blinder and P. Friedman. New York: Academic Press.

Dickens, William T. 1985. Occupational safety and health and 'irrational' behavior: A preliminary analysis. In *Workers' compensation benefits: Adequacy, equity, and efficiency*, edited by J.D. Worrall and D. Appel, pp.19–40. Ithaca, NY: ILR Press.

Dionne, Georges and Pierre St-Michel. 1991. Workers' compensation and moral hazard. *Review of Economics and Statistics* 73:236–44.

Dorsey, Stuart. 1983. Employment risks and fringe benefits: Further tests for compensating differentials. In *Safety and the workforce: Incentives and disincentives in workers' compensation*, edited by J.D. Worrall, pp.87–102. Ithaca, NY: ILR Press.

Ehrenberg, Ronald G. 1988. Workers' compensation, wages, and the risk of injury. In *New perspectives in workers' compensation*, edited by J.F. Burton, pp.71–96. Ithaca, NY: ILR Press.

Friedman, Lawrence M. 1973. *A history of American law.* New York: Touchstone.

Health and Welfare Canada. 1985. *Social security statistics: Canada and provinces, 1958–59 to 1982–83.* Ottawa: Supply and Services Canada.

———. 1989. *Social security statistics: Canada and provinces, 1963–64 to 1987–88.* Ottawa: Supply and Services Canada.

Hyatt, Douglas E. and Boris Kralj. 1991. The impact of workers' compensation experience rating on employer appeals activity. University of Toronto, Toronto. Mimeographed.

Ison, Terence G. 1989. *Workers' compensation in Canada.* 2d ed. Toronto: Butterworths.

Johnson, William G. and Jan Ondrich. 1990. The duration of post-injury absences from work. *Review of Economics and Statistics* 72:578–86.

Krueger, Alan B. 1990a. Incentive effects of workers' compensation. *Journal of Public Economics* 41:73–99.

———. 1990b. Workers' compensation insurance and the duration of workplace injuries. Working paper, National Bureau of Economic Research, Boston.

Lanoie, Paul. 1991. Occupational safety and health: a problem of double or single moral hazard. *Journal of Risk and Insurance* 58:80–100.

——. 1992. The impact of occupational safety and health regulation on the risk of workplace accidents: Québec, 1983–87. *Journal of Human Resources* 27:643–60.

McCombie, Nick. 1984. Justice for injured workers: A community responds to government reform. *Canadian Community Law Journal* 7:136–73.

Meredith, Sir William Ralph. 1913. *Final report on laws relating to the liability of employers to make compensation to their employees for injuries received in the course of their employment which are in force in other countries.* Toronto: L.K. Cameron.

Moore, Michael J. and W. Kip Viscusi. 1989. *Compensation mechanisms for job risks: Wages, workers' compensation, and product liability.* Princeton, NJ: Princeton University Press.

Oi, Walter Y. 1974. On the economics of industrial safety. *Law and Contemporary Problems* 38:669–99.

Posner, Richard. 1972. A theory of negligence. *Journal of Legal Studies* 1:28–96.

Pozzebon, Silvana and Terry Thomason. 1993. Medical benefit costs in Canadian workers' compensation programs: A comparative perspective. *Benefits Quarterly* 9, 4:32–41.

Rea, Samuel A., Jr. 1981. Workmen's compensation and occupational safety under imperfect information. *American Economic Review* 71:80–93.

Roberts, Karen. 1992. Predicting disputes in workers' compensation. *Journal of Risk and Insurance* 69:252–61.

Ruser, John W. 1985. Workers' compensation insurance, experience rating, and occupational injuries. *Rand Journal of Economics* 16:487–503.

——. 1991. Workers' compensation and occupational injuries and illnesses. *Journal of Labor Economics* 9:325–50.

Shavell, Steven. 1987. *Economic analysis of accident law.* Cambridge, MA: Harvard University Press.

Smith, Robert S. 1990. Mostly on Mondays: Is workers' compensation covering off-the-job injuries? In *Benefits, costs, and cycles in workers' compensation,* edited by P.S. Borba and D. Appel, pp.115–28. Boston: Kluwer.

Thomason, Terry. 1993a. The transition from temporary to permanent disability: Evidence from New York state. In *Workers' compensation insurance: Claim costs, prices, and regulation,* edited by D. Durbin and P.S. Borba, pp.69–97. Boston: Kluwer.

——. 1993b. Permanent partial disability in workers' compensation: Probability and costs. *Journal of Risk and Insurance* 60:570–90.

——. 1994. Correlates of workers' compensation claims adjustment. *Journal of Risk and Insurance* 61:59–77.

Thomason, Terry and John F. Burton. 1993. Economic effects of workers' compensation in the United States: Private insurance and the administration of compensation claims. *Journal of Labor Economics* 11:S1–S37.

U.S. Chamber of Commerce. 1960–1991. *Analysis of workers' compensation laws of the United States.* Washington, DC: The Chamber.

Weiler, Paul C. 1980. *Reshaping workers' compensation for Ontario.* Toronto: Ontario Ministry of Labour.

——. 1983. *Protecting the worker from disability: Challenges for the eighties.* Toronto: Ontario Ministry of Labour.

Workers' Compensation Board of British Columbia. 1993. *Workers' Compensation Board of British Columbia annual report 1992, part 1—corporate and financial information.* Victoria: The Board.

Worrall, J.D. and R.J. Butler. 1988. Experience rating matters. In *Workers' Compensation insurance pricing*, edited by D. Appel and P.S. Borba, pp.81–94. Boston: Kluwer.

Worrall, J.D., D. Durbin, D. Appel, and R.J. Butler. 1993. The transition from temporary total to permanent partial disability: A longitudinal analysis. In *Workers' compensation insurance: Claim costs, prices, and regulation*, edited by D. Durbin and P.S. Borba, pp.51–68. Boston: Kluwer.

Safety Regulation and Specific Injury Types in Québec

Jean-Michel Cousineau, Sandra Girard and Paul Lanoie

Government intervention in occupational safety and health (OSH) has been increasing in North America during the last two decades. In the United States, safety regulation is the responsibility of the Occupational Safety and Health Administration (OSHA), created in 1970 to promote safety in the workplace. The OSHA set numerous new safety standards and implemented measures such as inspections of firms, fines and prosecutions to enforce them. Some of these standards address worker conduct (for example, one prohibits speeding while driving a forklift truck); however, most are imposed on firms and stipulate either equipment specifications, such as the width of railings, or equipment performance, for example, the weight that ladder rungs must be able to support. Canadian provinces followed a similar strategy in the 1970s, but they also adopted several safety-enhancing measures not present in the United States. These measures include the right to refuse hazardous tasks, the creation of joint worksite safety committees, mandatory prevention programs, and the right to protective reassignment.[1] The last two measures have been adopted only in the province of Québec where the agency responsible for occupational safety and health (Commis-

Note: The authors gratefully acknowledge the financial support of the Fonds pour la formation de chercheurs et l'aide de la recherche.

1 The right to refuse hazardous tasks allows a worker to refuse to carry out tasks he or she believes to be 'abnormally' dangerous. The joint worksite safety committees usually assume the responsibility of obtaining and disseminating information on occupational safety and health, identifying the sources of hazard to workers, and recommending to the employer means of eliminating hazards. Equal representation of management and workers on a committee is compulsory. A prevention program must meet the approval of the occupational health and safety agency and must address the training and supervision of workers, inspections, accident investigations, personal protective equipment, as well as the maintenance and disclosure of records. In Québec, prevention programs, and the safety committees which implement the programs, are imposed only on firms with more than 20 employees. Protective reassignment gives workers who can provide a medical certificate attesting to the potential danger of their job the right to be transferred to another job within the same firm. To date, this right has only been used by pregnant women.

sion de la santé et de la sécurité du travail or CSST) has placed particular emphasis on accident prevention since its creation in 1980. The Canadian approach seems to express more confidence in workers' ability to participate in solving occupational safety problems.

American econometric studies using aggregate data at the industry level have found that OSHA regulation has had little or no impact on workplace safety (see Curington 1988 or Viscusi 1986 for a review). In Canada, studies by Lanoie (1992a, 1992b) on the impact of CSST regulation have produced similar results. However, more encouraging results have been observed in the United States by those focusing on specific injury types that engineers believe may be prevented more easily than others through safety regulation (Mendeloff 1979; Curington 1986). Incidentally, Mendeloff reports a review of the violations of safety standards cited in Wisconsin and California accident investigations showing that over one-half involved machines with hazards relating to 'caught in or between' (CIOB) injuries, 'struck by or striking against' (SBOSA) injuries and 'falls or slips' (FOS) injuries. No existing analysis, however, has considered the performance of any Canadian occupational safety and health board in reducing accidents that result in these types of injury. This analysis examines the effectiveness of policies adopted by the Québec CSST in reducing the frequency of these specific types of injury.

In contrast to previous studies of the impact of safety regulation on specific injury types, this study considered direct measures of the intensity of regulation adopted by the CSST to estimate this equation, instead of relying on less precise estimation procedures. For example, Curington (1986) ascertained, through dummy variables shift effects, whether or not there was a downward trend in accidents in New York State after the creation of OSHA in 1970, while Mendeloff (1979) assessed, for California, whether or not there was a significant difference between the observed injury rate with OSHA and predictions of the rate that would have been observed without it. As well, following Cooke and Gautschi (1981), the determinants of *changes* in injury rates were examined to avoid drawing spurious inferences caused by simultaneity biases. Such biases could occur because more accidents in a given industry may lead to more intensive intervention by the CSST. In Québec, safety committees and prevention programs are compulsory only in three targeted groups of high-risk industries, providing evidence that the intervention of the CSST is more likely to be related to the absolute level of risk than to the change in risk. This issue has been neglected in previous research.

The next section presents the specification of the injury rate equation and the data. The following section discusses the empirical results, and concluding remarks are presented in the final section.

Specification of the Injury Rate Equation and Data

The impact of government intervention in OSH on the risk of accident can be analyzed using a theoretical model where the risk is influenced by firms and workers.[2] In particular, this means that, in their maximizing decisions, firms and workers have to choose a level of risk-preventing activity. The firm may, for example, invest in safer technology or the workers may decide whether or not to wear safety goggles.

It is intuitive that the strengthening government prevention policies, by increasing the penalty for non-compliance with safety standards, for example, should lead to a reduction in the risk of accident. Higher expected costs of accidents for employers should induce them to devote more resources to safety. This would not be true, however, if firms already complied with safety standards, or if the effect of a better environment were offset by workers' becoming less careful because they believe they work under safer conditions (see Lanoie 1991, for a formal argument).

From this brief discussion, it is possible to define an injury rate equation of the following form:

$$
\begin{aligned}
\Delta INJURY_{it} = \beta_0 &+ \beta_1 \bullet \Delta INSPECTION_{it} + \beta_2 \bullet \Delta INFRACTION_{it} + \\
&\beta_3 \bullet \Delta PROSECUTION_{i,t-1} + \beta_4 \bullet \Delta REFUSAL_{it} + \\
&\beta_5 \bullet \Delta PROGRAM_{it} + \beta_6 \bullet \Delta COMMITTEE_{it} + \\
&\beta_7 \Delta\%HOURS + \beta_8 \bullet \Delta\%SIZE + e_{it} \,,
\end{aligned}
\tag{1}
$$

where e_{it} is an error term.

Table 1 provides the exact definition of all the variables used in the analysis, their mean, standard deviation, and statistical source. The change in the injury rate ($INJURY_{it}$ - $INJURY_{i,t-1}$), and not its absolute level, was of interest.[3] $INJURY_{it}$ is the rate of injuries per worker in industry i at time t. Four different injury rates are used as the dependent variable: the global injury rate and, as in previous studies[4] of specific injury

---

2 Viscusi (1979), Rea (1981), Lanoie (1991, 1992a) and Krueger (1990) present different versions of such a model. Curington (1986) and Carmichael (1986) present models where the risk of accident is only affected by a firm's behaviour.

3 For the dependent variable and the SEM variables, the change in percentage is not used. In effect, because certain industries are relatively small (e.g., the leather industry) and because the occurrence of accidents and of certain CSST interventions (e.g., prosecutions, refusals) are being more or less random, the use of variables expressed as a percentage change would generate outlier observations that could bias the results. For instance, suppose that, in a small industry, the number of prosecutions goes from one to four from one year to the next, this 300 percent increase would probably exaggerate the importance of the phenomenon. Furthermore, in certain cases, the calculation of a percentage change was not possible because the denominator was zero.

4 Mendeloff (1979) studies the rate of injuries from these causes and from 'strain or overexertion'; Curington (1986) does not examine the rate of FOS injuries.

Table 1

Definition, Mean, Standard Deviation and Source of All Variables[1]

Variable	Definition	Mean	Standard deviation	Statistical source
Dependent Variables				
$\Delta INJURY_{it}$	Global injury rate: Δ (nb. of injuries with at least one workday lost/nb. of full-time (f.t.) employees)	0.774 E-2	0.443 E-1	CSST databank STAT 35
	Rate of 'struck by or striking against' injuries: Δ (nb. of injuries of this type with at least one workday lost/nb. of f.t. employees)	0.409 E-2	0.152 E-1	Idem
	Rate of 'caught in or between' injuries: same definition	-0.147 E-3	0.549 E-2	Idem
	Rate of 'falls or slips' injuries: same definition	0.721 E-3	0.576 E-2	Idem
Independent Variables				
Safety-enforcing Measures				
$\Delta INSPECTION_{it}$	Δ (Total nb. of inspections[2]/1000 f.t. employees)	0.474 E-3	0.651 E-2	CSST Annual Reports
$\Delta INFRACTION_{it}$	Δ (Nb. of fines imposed/1000 f.t. employees)	-0.115 E-3	0.784 E-3	CSST (1988)
$\Delta PROSECUTION_{i,t-1}$	Δ (Nb. of prosecutions launched/1000 f.t. employees)	0.348 E-4	0.616 E-3	Idem
$\Delta REFUSAL_{it}$	Δ (Nb. of interventions from CSST officials for refusals /1000 f.t. employees)	0.399 E-4	0.210 E-4	CSST Annual Reports
$\Delta PROGRAM_{it}$	Δ Percentage of firms that have adopted a prevention program	0.193	0.353	Idem
$\Delta COMMITTEE_{it}$	Δ Percentage of firms that have created a safety committee	0.365 E-1	0.098 E-1	Idem
Control variables				
$\Delta\%HOURS_{it}$	$\Delta\%$ (Average number of hours worked per worker per week)	0.953	2.352	Statistics Canada 72-002
$\Delta\%SIZE_{it}$	$\Delta\%$ (Nb. of f.t. employees/Nb. of establishments)	0.468	21.973	CSST Annual Reports

Source: CSST 1983, 1988; Statistics Canada.

[1] Data are at the industry level on a yearly basis (1982–1984) N=46. The industries are: building and public works; chemical industry; forestry and sawmills; manufacturing of metal products; wood industry; rubber and plastic products industry; manufacturing of nonmetal mineral products; public administration; food and beverage industry; furniture and furnishing industry; paper industry and related activities; transportation and storage; trade; leather industry; manufacturing of machinery; textile industry; other business and personal services; printing, publishing and related activities; manufacturing of oil and coal products; manufacturing of electrical products; hosiery and apparel; finance insurance and real estate.

[2] These inspections include regular inspections, inspections following workers' complaints, and inspections following an important accident.

types, the rate of CIOB injuries, the rate of SBOSA injuries and the rate of FOS injuries. These injuries represent 53 percent of all injuries.

Concerning the independent variables, the intensity with which prevention policies are implemented is approximated by the rate of safety-enforcing measures (SEMs). In Québec, there are six types of SEMs that can be documented: inspections ($\Delta INSPECTION_{it}$); fines imposed for infractions or non-compliance with safety standards ($\Delta INFRAC-TION_{it}$); prosecutions in case of persistent violations of safety standards ($\Delta PROSECUTION_{it}$); applications of the right of refusal ($\Delta REFUSAL_{it}$); requirement for a prevention program ($\Delta PROGRAM_{it}$); and requirement for a safety committee ($\Delta COMMITTEE_{it}$). The first four variables are expressed as a rate per 1,000 workers, while the last two are expressed as the percentage of firms in the industry that have a program or a committee. One should also note that the change in the prosecution rate is taken at the period t - 1 since the available data set records prosecutions whose outcome is typically not known within the same year they are initiated due to legal delays. Furthermore, the prevention program and safety committees' policies are implemented in the same categories of firms and the simple correlation between these two variables is fairly high (around .80). Therefore, results are presented with either variable, but not both, in the specification. As was argued in the beginning of this section, the predicted signs of the coefficients associated with safety-enforcing measures are ambiguous. However, SEMs are clearly intended by OSH authorities to reduce the risk of workplace accidents and, in conformity with this objective, the coefficients associated with these policies are expected to be negative.

Two control variables that are often encountered in the literature were included in the specification. The percentage change in the average number of hours worked per worker per week ($\Delta\%HOURS_{it}$)[5] was included to capture business cycle effects and was expected to take a positive sign (see Viscusi 1979). Indeed, during a cycle upswing, the price of foregone output increases and, therefore, the cost of devoting inputs to accident prevention rather than production of output rises, thereby inducing firms to reduce their safety expenditures which, in turn, increases the risk of accident. Moreover, if the workpace is accelerated during a cycle upswing, the chance of an accident increases. The percentage change in the average firm size in a given industry ($\Delta\%SIZE_{it}$) was also included and was expected to take a negative sign because large firms are likely to benefit from economies of scale in providing safety (see Chelius 1974). Furthermore, workers' compensation premiums paid by larger firms are more likely to be experience rated,

---

5 We have also used the percentage change in employment as a variable capturing business cycle effects. The results were not qualitatively different from those presented here. See Girard (1991) for a complete set of results.

that is, to reflect their own risk experience, possibly giving them a stronger motive, to invest more resources in safety in order to reduce their insurance costs.

For the estimation, pooled time-series and cross-section data were used. Annual data cover 1982 to 1984 inclusively.[6] The data for 23 industries,[7] are at the two- or three-digit industry level and cover most sectors of economic activity (see Table 1). The data regarding injury rates can be found in the databank STAT 35, obtained from the CSST.[8] Data related to CSST prevention policies and data on the average size of firms are published in the CSST Annual Reports, while data on the average number of hours worked per week are published by Statistics Canada.

Empirical Results

Table 2 reports our results related to four different injury rates: the global injury rate, the rate of SBOSA injuries, the rate of CIOB injuries, and the rate of FOS injuries. For each rate, two specifications of equation (1) are presented: one including the prevention program variable and the other including the safety committee variable. The equations were estimated using ordinary least-squares adjusted by White's (1980) heteroskedastic-consistent covariance matrix to correct the estimates for unknown forms of heteroskedasticity. In general, the explanatory power (2) of the regressions is relatively high considering this kind of model.

Among the safety-enforcing measures, the coefficient of the rate of infractions ($\Delta INFRACTION_{it}$) is, as expected, negative and significant in all specifications, but the absolute value of its elasticity in equations related to the specific injury rates is larger than or equal to the absolute value of its elasticity in the global injury rate equation.[9] The elasticities are -.345 in the global injury rate equation, and -.344, -5.084 and -.562 respectively in the SBOSA, CIOB and FOS injury rate equations. Furthermore, the coefficient for the rate of prosecutions ($\Delta PROSECUTION_{it}$) is negative and significant in the CIOB injuries equation, but not significant in the equation predicting the global injury rate. Similarly, the

6 The estimation period is relatively short because the databank used covers the period from the beginning of 1981 to the middle of 1985, when there was a change in the compensation legislation, and because the prosecution variable is lagged one period. The data for the year 1985 cannot be used. Furthermore, we cannot have access to a databank in which injuries are stratified by injury types for the period following 1985.

7 Usually, industry dummies are included in the studies of safety regulation to capture industry specific effects, but, since we are interested in the change in injury rates, we only consider independent variables that have changed over the period.

8 This extensive data set is also used by Cousineau, Lacroix and Girard (1992) in their study of compensating differentials for risky jobs.

9 These results are not directly comparable with those of Lanoie (1992a, 1992b) since the estimation periods are not the same.

Table 2

The Injury Rate Equations (N=46), OLS Estimates, Coefficients (t-statistics)

	Δ Global		Δ 'Struck by or striking against'	
Constant	-0.47 E-4	-0.11 E-2	0.78 E-3	0.19 E-3
	(-0.01)	(-0.27)	(0.64)	(0.18)
$\Delta INSPECTION_{it}$	3.869**	3.951**	1.589**	1.510**
	(2.42)	(2.22)	(4.36)	(3.67)
$\Delta INFRACTION_{it}$	-23.807**	-23.286**	-12.036**	-12.262**
	(-3.15)	(-3.11)	(-4.62)	(-3.90)
$\Delta PROSECUTION_{i,t-1}$	-11.849	-11.169	-5.967	-6.127
	(-1.07)	(-0.97)	(-1.60)	(-1.53)
$\Delta REFUSAL_{it}$	22.989	23.586	14.261**	13.401**
	(1.05)	(1.11)	(2.56)	(2.36)
$\Delta PROGRAM_{it}$	-0.93 E-2		-0.19 E-2	
	(-1.09)		(0.60)	
$\Delta COMMITTEE_{it}$		-0.023		0.61 E-2
		(-0.50)		(0.32)
$\Delta \%HOURS_{it}$	0.58 E-2**	0.53 E-2**	0.14 E-2**	0.14 E-2**
	(2.15)	(2.23)	(2.23)	(2.38)
$\Delta \%SIZE_{it}$	-0.90 E-3**	-0.89 E-3**	-0.22 E-3**	-0.24 E-3**
	(-3.801)	(-3.99)	(-3.93)	(-3.99)
R^2	.622	.618	.689	.688
F	10.821	10.654	12.312	11.806

	Δ 'Caught in or between'		Δ 'Falls or slips'	
Constant	-0.49 E-3	-0.55 E-3	0.14 E-3	-0.99 E-4
	(-1.08)	(-1.29)	(0.19)	(-0.15)
$\Delta INSPECTION_{it}$	0.529**	0.667**	0.760**	0.775**
	(3.67)	(3.54)	(4.09)	(3.65)
$\Delta INFRACTION_{it}$	-7.080**	-6.504**	-3.91**	-3.530**
	(-4.27)	(-4.86)	(-3.95)	(-3.55)
$\Delta PROSECUTION_{i,t-1}$	-5.251**	-4.647**	-0.445	-0.309
	(-2.86)	(-2.71)	(-0.32)	(-0.21)
$\Delta REFUSAL_{it}$	-4.091	-2.784	-3.795	-3.696
	(-1.41)	(-1.12)	(-1.28)	(-1.33)
$\Delta PROGRAM_{it}$	-0.39 E-2**		-0.19 E-2*	
	(-2.18)		(-1.92)	
$\Delta COMMITTEE_{it}$		-0.022**		-0.46 E-2
		(-3.18)		(-0.79)
$\Delta \%HOURS_{it}$	0.42 E-3**	0.45 E-3**	0.42 E-3	0.44 E-3
	(1.98)	(2.04)	(1.14)	(1.23)
$\Delta \%SIZE_{it}$	-0.76 E-4**	-0.57 E-4**	-0.98 E-4**	-0.97 E-4**
	(-2.51)	(-2.11)	(-3.28)	(-3.33)
R^2	.599	.629	.624	.613
F	4.424	5.463	7.715	6.889

**Significant at 5 percent level (two-tailed test).
*Significant at 10 percent level (two-tailed test).

coefficient of the prevention programs variable ($\Delta PROGRAM_{it}$) is negative and significant in the equations predicting FOS and the CIOB injury rates but not elsewhere. In that last equation, the safety committee variable has also a negative and significant coefficient. Overall, our results are consistent with those in the American literature showing that regulation has a greater impact on specific injury rates than on global injury rate.

Unexpectedly, the coefficient for the inspection rate variable ($\Delta INSPECTION_{it}$) is positive and significant in all specifications. One plausible reason for this is the existence of a simultaneity bias in spite of the use of the change in the injury rates and the change in the SEMs as dependent and independent variables respectively. This would imply that greater changes in the injury rates lead to greater changes in the inspection rate. The hypothesis of exogeneity could not be rejected following testing for the non-exogeneity of the rate of inspections, using the Hausman (1978) test.[10] Another explanation for the positive sign is that, in 1983, the CSST adopted a policy to expand its inspection effort (see CSST 1983) while, at the same time, injury rates increased due to the economic recovery. This phenomenon may not have been detected by the Hausman test since a causal relation between the two events does not necessarily exist. However, the *HOURS* variable may have captured a significant portion of the recovery effect.[11]

The coefficient of the refusal rate variable ($\Delta REFUSAL_{it}$) is negative, but not significant in most specifications, except in the equation related to the 'struck by or striking against' injuries in which it is unexpectedly positive and significant. A Hausman exogeneity test was performed that did not reject the exogeneity of the refusal rate variable. One plausible explanation for the positive sign could be that the right of refusal was introduced in 1981 but, because it was new and not well-known, it was not often used before 1983 (see, CSST 1983). Also, at the same time, injury rates were increasing due to the economic recovery. Another possible reason could be that the refusal rate is a variable that

10 Two different instruments were used: the number of workers in the industry and the number of establishments. These variables were shown to have a relatively high correlation with the inspection rate, but not with the injury rates. Complete results are available in Girard (1991).

11 A final, and more 'pessimistic,' explanation for the positive sign is that firms have a fixed budget to devote to safety. (In his theoretical model, Curington (1986) also assumes that firms have a fixed safety budget.) Therefore, expenditures on fines resulting from inspections, or on prevention programs reduce the budget for other safety features, which may lead to a higher injury rate. Similarly, it is possible that safety items required by inspectors are less efficient than those the firm would otherwise choose and, assuming a fixed budget, this would also lead to more injuries. Unfortunately, the available data does not allow a test of this hypothesis.

captures a union militancy effect since refusals occur mainly in unionized firms.[12] Note that Lanoie (1992b) shows that the unionization rate in a given industry is positively related to the frequency of all accidents.

Finally, coefficients for the two control variables ($\Delta\%HOURS_{it}$ and $\Delta\%SIZE_{it}$) have the expected sign in all specifications, and almost all are significant. This suggests that changes in the average number of hours worked per worker per week are positively associated with changes in injury rates, whereas changes in the average size of firms are negatively associated with changes in injury rates. These results are common in the rest of the literature. Interestingly, given the values of elasticity at the point of means, the CIOB injuries variable is more sensitive to all of the independent variables. This suggests that the prevention of such injuries may be easier whether one uses regulation, financial incentives (since the *SIZE* variable may capture the degree of experience rating) and/or reduces the work pace and fatigue due to overtime work.

Conclusion

How effective are policies adopted by the Québec CSST in reducing the global injury rate and the rates of specific types of injury that engineers believe may be more easily prevented than others through safety regulation, i.e., the CIOB, SBOSA and FOS injuries? The results of this analysis showed that the rate of fines imposed after an infraction had an impact on all injury rates, but that the impact was the same, or greater, on specific injury rates as on the global rate. This suggests that monetary incentives seem to work well in improving workplace safety. Furthermore, prosecutions were shown to have a negative effect on CIOB injuries, while prevention programs, to our knowledge, unique in North America, also had a desirable influence on this category of injuries and on the FOS injuries. The results thus suggest that an approach relying on workers' ability to solve safety problems is an adequate complement to more traditional safety-enforcing measures in reducing accident rates.

Overall, the findings confirm those of the American literature showing that the impact of safety regulation is larger on specific injury types than on the global injury rate. These specific injuries represent only half of all injuries, and policymakers may have to rely on other policy instruments, such as financial incentives for employees, to substantially improve safety in the workplace.

12 This point was raised in a conversation with an official of the Québec Institut de recherche en santé et sécurité du travail.

References

Carmichael L. 1986. Reputations for safety: Market performance and policy remedies. *Journal of Labor Economics* 4:458–72.

Chelius, James R. 1974. The control of industrial accidents: Economic theory and empirical evidence. *Law and Contemporary Problems* 38:700–729.

CSST (Commission de la santé et de la sécurité du travail).1983 *Annual report.* Montreal: Government of Québec.

———. 1988. Statistiques sur les avis d'infraction et les poursuites. Unpublished report.

Cooke, W.N. and F.H. Gautschi III. 1981. OSHA, plant safety programs and injury reduction. *Industrial Relations* 20:245–57.

Cousineau, J.M., R. Lacroix, and A.-M. Girard. 1992. Occupational hazard and wage compensating differentials. *Review of Economics and Statistics* 74:166–69.

Curington, W.P. 1986. Safety and workplace injuries. *Southern Economic Journal* 53:51–72.

———. 1988. Federal vs state regulation: The early years of OSHA. *Social Science Quarterly* 69:341–60.

Girard, S. 1991. L'impact de la reglementation en santé et sécurité au travail sur les accidents du travail au Québec. MA thesis, Department of Economics, University of Montreal.

Hausman, J.A. 1978. Specification tests in econometrics. *Econometrica* 46:1251–71.

Krueger, Alan B. 1990. Incentive effects of workers' compensation insurance. *Journal of Public Economics* 41:73–99.

Lanoie, Paul. 1991. Occupational safety and health: A problem of double or single moral hazard. *Journal of Risk and Insurance* 58:80–100.

———. 1992a. Safety regulation and the risk of workplace accidents in Québec. *Southern Economic Journal* 59:950–65.

———. 1992b. The impact of occupational safety and health regulation on risk of workplace accidents: Québec, 1983–1987. *Journal of Human Resources* 27:643–60.

Mendeloff, J. 1979. *Regulating safety: An economic and political analysis of occupational safety policy.* Cambridge, MA: MIT Press.

Rea, Samuel A., Jr. 1981. Workmen's compensation and occupational safety under imperfect information. *American Economic Review* 71:80–93.

Statistics Canada. *Employment, earnings and hours.* Ottawa: Supply and Services Canada, monthly.

Viscusi, W. Kip. 1979. The impact of occupational safety and health regulation. *Bell Journal of Economics* 10:117–40.

———. 1986. The impact of occupational safety and health regulation, 1973–1983. *Rand Journal of Economics* 17:567–80.

White, H. 1980. A heteroskedasticity-consistent covariance matrix estimator and a direct test for heteroskedasticy. *Econometrica* 48:817–38.

The Effect of Workers' Compensation Benefits on Claim Incidence in Canada: An Analysis of Micro-Level Data

Terry Thomason and Silvana Pozzebon

Workers' compensation is one of the largest social insurance programs in Canada. Over one million Canadians reported experiencing an industrial accident in 1989; more than 650 thousand of these accidents resulted in a disabling injury where the worker lost at least one day of work. In that same year, provincial programs paid nearly $4 billion in compensation benefits, accounting for 1.48 percent of the total national payroll.

Figure 1 presents a graph of the incidence of accepted lost-time compensation claims per thousand workers in Canada and the Maritime provinces for the years 1982 to 1990.[1] The number of claims in Canada rose from about 45 lost-time claims per 1000 workers at the beginning of the decade to a high of approximately 51 claims per 1000 workers in 1986. Claims incidence fell over the next three years, although the rate at the end of the decade was higher than it was at the beginning. A trend analysis of these data indicates that claim frequency increased by approximately one-half of a claim per year during this period.

However, the national data mask substantial interprovincial variation in claims incidence and trends. Figure 1 shows that, with the exception of Newfoundland, there were fewer lost-times claims from 1982 to 1990 in the Maritime provinces than in Canada as a whole. The data also indicate that compensation claim rates rose faster than the national average in three of the four Atlantic provinces. In particular, a trend analysis reveals that the rate of lost-times claims per thousand workers increased by about two claims each year in Prince Edward Island.

Note: The authors thank Rick Chaykowski and the other participants of the 'Challenges to Workers' Compensation in Canada' Conference for their helpful comments on a previous draft. They are also grateful to Michele Greiche for superlative research assistance.

1 Figures 1 through 4 are based on data reported in Table A.1. That table also reports the slope of trend regressions predicting claim rates for Canada as well as each region and province.

Figure 1
Claim Rates, Maritime Provinces, 1982–1990

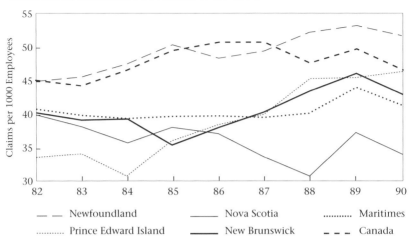

Claim frequency patterns for the Prairie provinces present a some-what different picture (see Figure 2). Similar to the Maritimes, the incidence of lost-time claims for the Prairies was lower than the national average. But compensation claim rates for the Prairie provinces increased less rapidly than in Canada overall. Finally, Figure 3 shows that while the claims rate for Québec had dropped slightly by 1990, during the 1982–1990 period lost-time compensation claims were substantially higher in Québec than in any other province. By the end of the decade, workers in Québec were twice as likely to suffer a compensable disabling work injury as workers in the Prairie provinces.

Studies using American data suggest that characteristics of workers' compensation programs influence the frequency of occupational injuries and compensation claims.[2] In particular, these studies indicate that injury and claim rates are positively related to compensation benefits. Although a comparison suggests that Canadian programs are more generous than their American counterparts (Thomason 1992), there are few studies examining the effects of economic incentives on claim frequency in the Canadian context. The research reported in this chapter attempts to remedy this deficiency by using a national sample of individual Canadian workers to estimate the probability that a worker will collect workers' compensation benefits at some time during 1987 or 1989.

2 For a review of this literature, see Thomason and Burton (1993).

Figure 2
Claim Rates, Prairie Provinces, 1982–1990

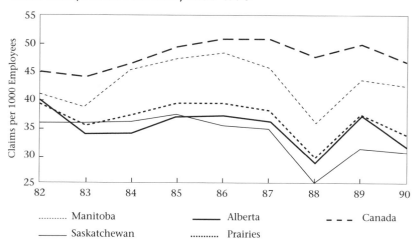

Manitoba   Alberta   – – – Canada
Saskatchewan   ·········· Prairies

Figure 3
Claim Rates, Québec, Ontario and British Columbia, 1982–1990

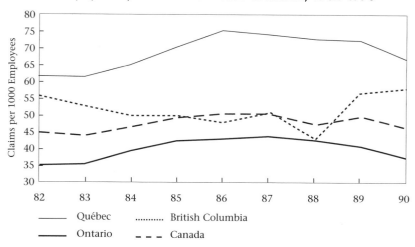

Québec   ·········· British Columbia
Ontario   – – – Canada

In the next section, economic theory explaining the incidence of workers' compensation claims is discussed, and pertinent empirical literature reviewed. The relevant features of Canadian workers' compensation programs are then described. In the fourth section, the data set analyzed in the study and the statistical method employed are described. Results and the conclusion follow.

Economic Analysis of Work Accidents

Theoretical analyses of the impact of a change in workers' compensation benefit levels on accident rates typically begin with the assumption of a perfectly competitive world. According to the model, workers at the margin are mobile and possess complete and accurate information concerning both the risks of employment and the costs of accidents.[3] These analyses also assume that employer liability insurance is fully experience rated; employers are legally obligated to pay for the full cost of accidents attributed to their firms. In this world, accident rates are unaffected by changes in benefit levels. Because workers are aware of the expected costs of accidents and are free to choose between hazardous and nonhazardous employment, employers in hazardous industries must necessarily pay a wage greater than that paid by employers in nonhazardous industries. This wage premium is equal to the expected cost of injuries borne by workers employed in those industries.[4] If the wage differential between safe and dangerous employment is less than the expected costs of injury, workers will choose to work in non-hazardous jobs. Employers in hazardous industries will thus be obliged to pay wages in excess of those paid by other employers in order to attract labour. In other words, fully experience-rated employers bear the full cost of accidents, either in the form of *ex ante* wage premiums or in the form of *ex post* compensation benefits.

Workers' compensation benefits reduce the portion of *ex post* accident costs borne by employees. Lower *ex post* costs for workers result in corresponding reductions in the wage differential between hazardous and nonhazardous employment. Since experience-rated employers bear the full cost of accidents, their incentive to prevent accidents is unaffected by a change in benefit levels. Higher benefits are offset by lower *ex ante* wages. However, when employers bear the full cost of accidents, workers will lack the motivation to avoid accidents, assuming that accident prevention measures involve some disutility for the worker.[5]

If the assumption of fully experience-rated firms is relaxed, different results are obtained. Firms that are not fully experienced rated do not bear the complete cost of *ex post* compensation. For these firms, insurance costs are determined, in part, by the accident experience of

---

3 More formal analyses of the economics of occupational accidents may be found in a number of sources including Diamond (1977), Krueger (1990), Lanoie (1991), Oi (1974), and Rea (1981).

4 Workers are assumed to be risk neutral.

5 This describes the equilibrium condition where, by definition, all cost minimizing technology has been employed. Prior to achieving equilibrium, workers could employ cost-effective, safety-prevention measures and split the resulting savings with the firm.

all firms within the rating class to which the firm belongs.[6] Since the individual firm has only a marginal impact on the total incidence of accidents for the class, each firm has only a marginal effect on the cost of insurance. The *ex post* costs of an accident are, in effect, shared among all firms within the class.

Yet, firms that are partially experience rated continue to bear the full costs of accident prevention while reaping only some of the advantages. More generous compensation benefits will decrease the *ex ante* wage differential by an amount equivalent to the size of the benefit increase, while only marginally increasing *ex post* compensation costs for the individual employer. Accidents can be expected to increase following a rise in benefit levels for partially experience-rated firms, since employer gains from accident prevention, in the form of a reduction in the compensating wage differential, decrease.

The majority of Canadian firms are not fully experience rated. The work-injury rate should therefore be positively related to compensation benefits. The theoretical relationship between benefits and accident rates has been confirmed in a number of empirical studies using American data. Chelius (1973, 1974, 1977, 1982, 1983), Ruser (1985, 1991), and Bartel and Thomas (1985) found that occupational injury rates are positively related to compensation benefits, while Butler and Worrall (1983), Butler (1983), and Chelius and Kavanaugh (1988) found that the workers' compensation claims frequency is also directly related to benefit levels. All of these studies examined rate data, that is, the number of injuries or compensation claims divided by employment or person-hours worked, aggregated by industry, by state, or by state and industry. An exception is Krueger (1990) who used a microsample containing information on individual workers to predict the probability that a worker will collect workers' compensation benefits over the course of a year. Krueger found that this probability is positively related to the level of benefits, corroborating prior research based on aggregate data.

There are few similar studies using Canadian data. Lanoie (1992a) and Fortin and Lanoie (1992) analyzed pooled cross-section, time-series data, aggregated by industry, from Québec for the period 1974 to 1987. The dependent variable in both studies was the number of claims involving at least one lost workday divided by the number of full-time employees in the industry. Contrary to previous American research, these studies detected a negative relationship between the replacement

6 Rating classes are industry and occupational categories used to establish insurance premiums called 'manual rates.' Manual rates are determined by the accident experience, that is, the number and severity of compensable injuries experienced by all firms in the rating class.

rate and the incidence of lost-time compensation claims in a variety of specifications.[7]

On the other hand, Lanoie's (1992b) analysis of Québec injury rates from 1983–1987 concluded that the frequency of lost-time injuries is positively and significantly related to the replacement rate. Similarly, Bruce and Atkins (1993) used time-series data from the forestry and construction sectors of Ontario to estimate occupational fatality rates. They estimated positive, although statistically insignificant, coefficients for the replacement ratio for both sectors. Overall, the empirical evidence based on both Canadian and American data, supports the theoretical premise that increased workers' compensation benefits are associated with a rise in job-related accidents.

Workers' Compensation Benefits in Canada

Canadian workers' compensation programs pay a variety of benefits to workers who have suffered an injury as the result of an occupational accident. These include compensation for all medical expenses related to the worker's injury, the costs of approved vocational rehabilitation programs, and indemnity benefits. The latter compensate workers for income lost due to a disability resulting from work injury. Indemnity compensation is based on the worker's pre-injury wage if the worker is totally disabled or the difference between the worker's pre- and post-injury wages if the worker is partially disabled.

As the information presented in Table 1 indicates, benefits are equal to 75 percent of gross wages (wage income before taxes or other deductions) in Prince Edward Island, Nova Scotia, Manitoba, and British Columbia. For the remaining provinces benefits are equal to 90 percent of net-wage income after deductions for taxes, contributions to the Canada or Québec Pension Plan, and Unemployment Insurance. In all provinces, indemnity benefits are subject to maximum and minimum amounts, which vary from one jurisdiction to another. Benefit maximums and minimums for 1987 are shown in Table 1. In those provinces that compute benefits on the basis of net wages, maximum benefits are based on the maximum insurable earnings in the province, which differ according to the number of dependents. Maximum benefit amounts for net-wage provinces reported in Table 1 assume that the worker has two dependents.

---

7 In one semi-reduced specification estimated by Fortin and Lanoie (1992), the relationship between the replacement rate and claim frequency was positive although statistically insignificant.

Table 1

Characteristics of Canadian Workers' Compensation Programs, 1987

Province	Replacement rate	Maximum[1] weekly benefit	Maximum covered earnings	Minimum[2] weekly benefit
Newfoundland	90% of net	$533.64	$45,500	$200.00
Prince Edward Island	75% of gross	$288.47	$28,000	$60.00[3]
Nova Scotia	75% of gross	$403.85	$20,000	$120.00
New Brunswick	90% of net	$424.75	$31,900	None[4]
Québec	90% of net	$443.78	$35,500	$174.00[5]
Ontario	90% of net	$444.44	$33,600	$225.11
Manitoba	75% of gross	$461.54	$32,000	$159.94
Saskatchewan	90% of net	$586.53	$48,000	$201.98[6]
Alberta	90% of net	$506.63	$40,000	$168.00
British Columbia	75% of gross	$591.17	$41,100	$205.86

Source: Association of Workers' Compensation Boards of Canada (1987).
[1] Maximum benefit for provinces that pay 90 percent of net earnings assumes that the worker has two dependents.
[2] Benefits are equal to actual earnings if earnings are less than the stated minimum.
[3] The Board may fix earnings at $15 per week if actual earnings are less than $15.
[4] Minimum set at 50 percent of industrial aggregate earnings for the province after two years have elapsed from the date of injury.
[5] Minimum equal to minimum salary or the minimum wage for a normal work week as established under the Act respecting labour standards.
[6] Absolute minimum of $201.98 after two years.

Data and Methodology

The data analyzed in this paper are from the 1986–87 and 1988–89 longitudinal panels of the Labour Market Activity Survey. The Labour Market Activity Survey (LMAS) was conducted in 1987, 1988, 1989, and 1990, to supplement the Labour Force Survey (LFS). The LFS includes a stratified sample of 45 thousand households and 60 thousand individuals. Both surveys were administered by Statistics Canada, a government agency which provides monthly unemployment and labour force participation statistics, as well as other data. The LMAS collected information about the work history of all household members, including their wage, normal hours of work, and other job characteristics. Demographic information and information concerning participation in various social insurance programs were also collected. Households in the 1986 and 1988 LMAS surveys were resurveyed in 1987 and 1989, respectively. Data from these later years were matched with those from the earlier surveys to create the 1986–87 and 1988–89 longitudinal panels. The variables used in this study are defined in Table 2.

The sample used in this analysis was limited to individuals who had been employed in 1987 or 1989 but who had worked at no more than one job during the year and who had experienced only one period of

Table 2

Variable Names and Definitions

Variable	Definition
WAGE	Worker's pre-injury weekly wage.
BENEFITS	Worker's expected temporary total disability benefits.
Married Male	1,0—Worker is a married male.
Married Female	1,0—Worker is a married female.
Single Female	1,0—Worker is a single female.
KIDS	Number of worker's children.
ENGLISH	1,0—Worker's mother tongue is English.
VISMIN	1,0—Worker is a member of a visable minority.
TENURE	Worker's tenure in pre-injury job.
TENURESQ	Square of pre-injury job tenure.
TOTHOURS	Total number of hours worked in pre-injury job.
AGE (20-24)	1,0—Worker is from 20 to 24 years of age.
AGE (25-34)	1,0—Worker is from 25 to 34 years of age.
AGE (35-44)	1,0—Worker is from 35 to 44 years of age.
AGE (45-54)	1,0—Worker is from 45 to 54 years of age.
ELEM	1,0—Worker's highest level of education is primary school.
HGHSCH	1,0—Worker's highest level of education is high school.
SPS	1,0—Worker's highest level of education is some post-secondary education.
TRADE CERT	1,0—Worker's highest level of education is a certificate from a trade school.

unemployment. Household members who were younger than 20 years old or older than 65 in the first year of the panel were also excluded from the study, as were self-employed persons and those living outside Canada or in the Northwest and Yukon Territories in the second year of the panel. Agricultural workers were also dropped from the sample because these workers are not covered by workers' compensation in several provinces. Pooling observations from both longitudinal panels resulted in a data set of 52,353 observations.

Dependent Variable

The following question from the LMAS, '[Last year] did . . . receive income from any of the following sources? . . . c) Workers' Compensation?' was used to construct the dependent variable in our study.[8] Following Krueger (1990), we identified household members as compensation claimants if they received workers' compensation benefits in year *t* but not in year *t* - 1. It was assumed that those members had suffered an industrial accident in year *t*. Household members who were

---

8 Krueger (1990) used a similar question from the 1983-85 Current Population Survey of the US Bureau of Labor Statistics to identify persons in that data set who had suffered a compensable occupational injury.

benefit recipients in year t - 1 were eliminated from the sample.[9] Using this 0–1 dependent variable, the probability of a compensable injury was estimated with a weighted maximum likelihood logit, where the weights are an inverse measure of the household member's probability of being included in the survey sample.

Unfortunately, our measure appears to underestimate substantially the true incidence of compensation claims in Canada. Table 3 presents claims incidence estimates for each region and province based on responses to the 1987 LMAS question relating to the receipt of workers' compensation benefits by an employed household member. Four different claim rates based on the LMAS are shown, two of which use the number of employees as a denominator (columns I and II) and two of which use the number of hours worked as a denominator (columns III and IV).

In addition, the figures in columns I and III assume that all individuals who reported that they had received compensation benefits in 1987 had also suffered a compensable occupational injury in that year. The numbers reported in columns II and IV assume that only individuals who had reported receiving benefits in 1987, but not in 1986, had suffered a compensable injury in 1987. For both sets of estimates, the denominator was provincial or regional employment where an individual was counted as employed if he or she had held a job at any time during 1987.

Table 3 also provides claim-rate estimates calculated from the administrative records of the various provincial compensation boards. As can be seen, these estimates exceed (they are about twice) those based on the LMAS. The data in Table 3 also indicate that there is less variation across jurisdictions for the LMAS estimates than for figures based on the administrative records of the workers' compensation boards.

There are a number of possible explanations for the disparity between claim rates derived from administrative records and those calculated from the LMAS. First, since the LMAS is based on a household survey where the respondent furnishes information on all household members, the data may be affected by reporting errors. Specifically, the

---

9 It is likely that household members who reported workers' compensation income in both years received compensation in year t for injuries sustained in year t - 1. Inclusion of those individuals could bias the results of the regression analyses. Of course, by dropping this group of household members from the study, workers who may have suffered compensable injuries in both years may be excluded. This exclusion could similarly bias results. The former event (that workers received compensation during both years for a single injury that occurred in year t - 1) is believed to be more likely than the former (that workers suffered different injuries in both year t and year t - 1); therefore, such workers were excluded from the sample.

Table 3

Claim Rate Comparisons, 1987, by Province and Region

		LMAS estimates[2]			
		Claims per thousand employees		Claims per million person-hours	
Province	Actual claims[1]	I	II	III	IV
Newfoundland	49.44	24.66	19.30[3]	16.97[3]	13.28[3]
Prince Edward Island	39.77	—[4]	—[4]	—[4]	—[4]
Nova Scotia	33.52	28.23	22.69	18.55	14.91
New Brunswick	40.14	17.44[3]	12.10[3]	11.77[3]	8.17[3]
Atlantic Region	39.40	22.72	17.53	15.30	11.81
Manitoba	45.75	18.04	15.20	12.45	10.49
Saskatchewan	34.69	14.83[3]	11.11[3]	11.82[3]	8.86[3]
Alberta	35.98	17.81	12.33	11.71	8.11
Prairies	38.00	17.21	12.77	11.91	8.84
Québec	74.27	26.23	20.38	17.58	13.66
Ontario	43.77	24.58	17.82	15.43	11.19
British Columbia	50.71	21.30	14.45[3]	12.57	8.53[3]
Canada	50.71	23.21	17.20	15.03	11.14

Source: Actual claim rates—Data on the number of accepted lost-time claims were taken from Statistics Canada (annual). Average annual employment figures were taken from Statistics Canada (monthly). Columns I-IV were calculated by the authors using data from the Labour Market Activity Survey (see text).
[1] Claim rates calculated by dividing the number of lost-time compensation claims by average annual employment, for persons 15 years and older.
[2] To obtain estimates for columns I and III, workers were counted as having suffered a compensable work injury if they indicated that they had received workers' compensation benefits in 1987, but not in 1986.
[3] Estimates have a high sampling variability. The coefficients of variation of associated estimates exceeds 16.6 percent.
[4] Sampling variability of estimates exceeds publication standards of Statistics Canada.

respondent's information about the compensation status of another household member may not be accurate. In addition, the injured worker may be unaware that he or she has received compensation benefits. This is particularly likely in Québec, where the employer continues to pay the injured worker at 90 percent of pre-injury wages for the first two weeks of time lost due to an occupational injury. Finally, some workers may have suffered more than one compensable lost-time injury during each year. The LMAS estimates count multiple claims by the same worker as one claim, while administrative records count each claim separately.

Independent Variables

The probability that a worker will suffer a compensable injury is estimated as a function of the worker's pre-injury wages, expected compensation benefits, and a number of demographic and job characteristics. These variables are discussed below. Summary statistics (means and standard deviations) for these variables appear in Table 4.

WAGE, which served as a measure of the worker's pre-injury weekly earnings, was computed by multiplying the reported hourly wage by hours worked in a normal week.[10] In accord with previous theoretical analyses (see, for example, Krueger 1990), it was expected that *WAGE* would be negatively related to the probability of a compensation claim since the opportunity cost of a job-related accident rises as the wage income increases.

The measure of expected workers' compensation benefits, *BENEFITS*, was determined differently for workers from 'gross wage' and 'net wage' provinces. In the former jurisdictions, *BENEFITS* is equal to 75 percent of *WAGE*, subject to minimums and maximums. For workers in net-wage provinces, annual net wages were computed by subtracting federal and provincial income taxes, contributions to the Canada or Québec Pension Plan, and deductions for Unemployment Insurance from gross annual wages.[11] Gross annual wages are equal to the multiplicand of the weekly wage and the number of weeks usually worked in a year. As previously discussed, it was expected that the level of compensation benefits would be positively related to the probability that the worker will suffer a compensable injury.

The estimated model contains several demographic variables, including the worker's age, education, gender, marital status, and number of children (*KIDS*).[12] In addition, dummies were used to indicate whether or not the household member belongs to a visible minority (*VISMIN*) or is an anglophone (*ENGLISH*) as opposed to a francophone or allophone. To the extent that males are employed, on average, in

10 Since the LMAS does not report weekly hours of work, the latter was derived from three other measures of time worked: the number of weeks per month, the number of paid days per week, and the number of paid hours per day that the household member usually worked in the reference period.

11 Federal and provincial taxes are calculated on the basis of the individual's wages at the time of injury. The LMAS does not provide information concerning nonlabour income. However, this is not problematic since compensation benefits are based on wage income. Tax deductions were imputed to household members according to their marital status and their relationship to the head of household. The marital deduction and deductions for children under the age of 16 were imputed to married heads of household, while deductions for children only were imputed to single heads. These imputations assume that the spouse and children do not work.

12 Age and education were measured by series of dummy variables. Sample observations were grouped into four age groups: 20 to 24 years, 25 to 34 years, 35 to 44 years, and 45 to 54 years. The omitted age category includes persons who are aged 55–65 years. Similarly, binary variables were used to indicate level of education as follows: up to eight years of education (*ELEM*), some high school or a high school diploma (*HIGHSCL*), a certificate from a trade school (*TRADE CERT*), or some post-secondary education (*SPS*). The omitted education category includes individuals who have earned a university degree.

Table 4

Weighted Sample Means and Standard Deviations[1]

	Total sample		Gross-wage provinces		Net-wage provinces	
Variable	Mean	Standard deviation	Mean	Standard deviation	Mean	Standard deviation
Compensation claim	0.199E-1	0.140	0.198E-1	0.139	0.202E-1	0.141
WAGE	513.7	320.7	514.7	323.3	509.4	309.1
BENEFITS	315.4	123.5	307.6	115.6	350.2	148.9
Married male	0.390	0.488	0.391	0.488	0.386	0.487
Married female	0.332	0.471	0.332	0.471	0.331	0.471
Single female	0.137	0.344	0.137	0.343	0.140	0.347
KIDS	1.13	1.14	1.13	1.13	1.12	1.16
ENGLISH	0.583	0.493	0.539	0.499	0.784	0.412
VISMIN	0.631E-1	0.243	0.585E-1	0.235	0.833E-1	0.276
TENURE	420.8	411.5	408.4	425.2	375.1	394.6
TOTHOURS	150.9	46.7	150.8	41.4	151.6	48.3
AGE (20-24)	0.132	0.338	0.134	0.341	0.120	0.325
AGE (25-34)	0.320	0.467	0.320	0.467	0.320	0.466
AGE (35-44)	0.273	0.446	0.271	0.445	0.282	0.450
AGE (45-54)	0.180	0.384	0.179	0.383	0.183	0.387
ELEM	0.897E-1	0.286	0.951E-1	0.293	0.657E-1	0.248
HGHSCH	0.427	0.495	0.423	0.494	0.447	0.497
SPS	0.108	0.311	0.105	0.307	0.123	0.329
TRADE CERT	0.205	0.404	0.208	0.406	0.192	0.394
Sample size	52,558		38,479		13,874	

more dangerous jobs than females, it was expected that males would be more likely than females to initiate a workers' compensation claim. For similar reasons, educated workers may be less likely to initiate a workers' compensation claim than less educated workers. Since economic theory offers little direction with regard to the expected impact of age, marital status, number of children, minority status, and language, no predictions were made for these variables.

A number of job characteristic variables were also included in the model specification. Work experience has a potentially complex relationship with the probability of a compensation claim. Conventional wisdom holds that experienced workers are less likely to have an occupational injury than less experienced workers, suggesting a negative relationship between work experience and claim probability. In addition, there is a well-known concave relationship between work experience and earnings. To the extent that the loss of future earnings is an opportunity cost for compensation claimants, it is expected that a non-linear, inverse relationship exists between experience and the probability of a workers' compensation claim. To measure the influence of work experience, two variables were included: *TENURE*, the number of weeks between the week that the household member began working at his or her job and the end of the survey year, and *TENURESQ*, a quadratic term or the square of *TENURE*.[13]

The logit model also contains a variable, *TOTHOURS*, that measures exposure to the risk of work injury, which is directly related to hours of work. *TOTHOURS* is defined as the number of hours the individual usually works in a month.[14] Since risk varies by industry and occupation, our full specification included 43 industry and 8 occupation dummies to control for these sectoral differences.

Finally, a dummy variable was used to indicate whether the data came from the 1986–87 or the 1987–88 longitudinal panel, and provincial dummies to control for differences (other than variations in benefits for temporary total disability) in the characteristics of compensation programs across Canadian jurisdictions were included.

Results

Table 5 presents results for two logit-regression models estimating the probability of a workers' compensation claim. The specifications differ from one another in that the model in column II includes three variables, (*TENURE*, *TENURESQ*, and *TOTHOURS*), not found in the model reported in column I.

These data offer some empirical support for the hypothesis that claim frequency is affected by worker behaviour. *BENEFITS* is positively and significantly related to the probability of transition into workers' compensation in both specifications. This corroborates predictions that workers are more likely to initiate compensation claims as benefit levels increase. The next to last line of Table 5 indicates that benefit elasticities ranged from 0.363 to 0.410.[15] This is comparable with elasticity estimates of 0.4 to 0.6 found by studies that examined aggregate American data, as well as those found by Krueger (1990), which ranged from 0.428 to 0.741 and were estimated using micro-level data and a methodology similar to ours.

13 For the 1986–87 panel, the end of the year was 31 December 1987, while for the 1988–89 panel, the end of the year was 31 December 1989.

14 This measure was constructed using the data described in footnote 10.

15 Elasticities were computed according to the following formula:

$$\eta = \frac{X_b}{p} \cdot \frac{\exp(X\beta)}{[1 + \exp(X\beta)]^2} \, \beta_b \, ,$$

where p is the probability of a compensation claim, X_b is *BENEFITS*, and β_b is the maximum likelihood coefficient associated with *BENEFITS*.

Table 5

Logit Regression Estimates Predicting the Transition into Workers' Compensation[1]

Variable[2]	Model I	Model II
WAGE	-0.293E-3 (0.282E-3)	-0.397E-3(0.289E-3)
BENEFITS	0.231E-2***(0.701E-3)	0.204E-2*** (0.72E-3)
Married male	0.165* (0.9983E-1)	0.171* (0.993E-1)
Married female	-0.130E-1 (0.121)	-0.427E-3 (O.121)
Single female	-0.278* (0.152)	-0.282* (0.153)
KIDS	-0.214E-1 (0.301E-1)	-0.202E-1 (0.301E-1)
ENGLISH	-0.184** (0.842E-1)	-0.178** (0.843E-1)
VISMIN	-0.473E-1 (0.145)	-0.666E-1 (0.145)
TENURE	—	0.286E-3 (0.232E-3)
TENURESQ	—	-0.236E-6 (0.152E-6)
TOTHOURS	—	0.240E-2***(0.921E-3)
AGE (20-24)	0.434*** (0.148)	0.354** (0.156)
AGE (25-34)	0.345*** (0.126)	0.266** (0.134)
AGE (35-44)	0.118 (0.132)	0.496E-1 (0.143)
AGE (45-54)	0.812E-1 (0.133)	0.441E-1 (0.134)
ELEM	1.14*** (0.204)	1.11*** (0.204)
HIGHSCL	1.19*** (0.182)	1.16*** (0.182)
TRADE CERT	0.885*** (0.203)	0.869*** (0.204)
SPS	1.03*** (0.181)	1.02*** (0.181)
Benefit elasticity	0.410	0.363
Log likelihood	-4693.2	-4688.5

***Statistically significant at the 0.01 level (Two-tailed test).
**Statistically significant at the 0.05 level (Two-tailed test).
*Statistically significant at the 0.10 level (Two-tailed test).
[1] Standard errors are within parentheses.
[2] Dummies for industry, occupation, province, and the panel year from which the observation was drawn (1986–87 or 1988–89) were also included in each specification, but are not reported in this table.

On the other hand, while the relationship between *WAGE* and the probability of compensation is negative in both specifications, it is not statistically significant in either. The lack of statistical significance may be due to a positive correlation between *WAGE* and risk, that is, higher paid jobs may be more risky than lower paid jobs. The positive relationship between risk and wage overwhelms the hypothesized incentive effects of wages on claim behaviour.

Males, younger, married, and less-educated workers are more likely to initiate a compensation claim and receive benefits than are females, older, single, and more-educated workers. Anglophones are less likely to receive compensation benefits than francophones or allophones. Furthermore, as expected, the probability of compensation is positively related to the hours normally worked in a month (*TOTHOURS*). However, the coefficients for *TENURE* and *TENURESQ* were not significantly different from zero, suggesting that claim probability is not related to work experience. Similarly, the number of children (*KIDS*) and visible minority status did not affect claim probability.

'Net' Versus 'Gross' Wage Provinces

As discussed previously, in four provinces indemnity benefits are paid as a proportion of gross (before-tax) wages, while in the other six, benefits are paid as a proportion of net (after-tax) wages. In order to determine if this difference in calculating indemnity benefits has any effect on the relationship between benefit levels and the probability of a compensation claim, the sample was partitioned accordingly and the models re-estimated. The results are presented in Table 6.

Likelihood ratio tests reveal that the split-sample model is superior to a model that restricts the coefficients to be identical in net- and gross-wage provinces. Overall, the economic model appears to perform better for gross-wage provinces than for net-wage provinces. Wages have a consistently negative relationship with the probability of transition into workers' compensation for gross-wage provinces. While wages are negatively related to claim probability in one of the two specifications for net-wage provinces, this relationship is not statistically significant in either model. In addition, while the coefficient for *BENEFITS* is always positive, as expected, it is statistically significant only in the simpler model specification for net-wage provinces. For gross-wage provinces, *BENEFITS* is statistically significant in both models.

These outcomes may reflect real differences in the incentive effects of wages and benefits between net- and gross-wage provinces. However, they are more likely to reflect differences in measurement error between the two samples. As previously indicated, the calculation of net wages, and, therefore, compensation benefits, involves the determination of federal and provincial income taxes. To estimate the latter, it was necessary to make a number of simplifying assumptions concerning exemptions for dependents, due to the absence of such information in the LMAS data. To the extent that these assumptions are incorrect, net wages are incorrectly measured, as are compensation benefits, in net-wage provinces.

There are other differences between the regression results for the two subsamples. In particular, *TENURE* and *TENURESQ* appear to have the opposite effect on claim probability in gross- and net-wage provinces. Contrary to expectations, claim probability increases at a decreasing rate with greater work experience in net-wage provinces.

Table 6

Logit Regression Estimates Predicting Probability of a Workers' Compensation Claim, by Type of Compensation Benefit[1]

Variable[2]	Net-wage provinces (N= 38,479)		Gross-wage provinces (N= 13,874)	
	Ia	IIa	Ib	IIb
WAGE	0.482E-5	-0.672E-4	-0.193E-2**	-0.217E-2***
	(0.287E-3)	(0.303E-3)	(0.754E-3)	(0.777E-3)
BENEFITS	0.179E-2**	0.133E-2	0.461E-2***	0.498E-2***
	(0.801E-3)	(0.849E-3)	(0.140E-2)	(0.143E-2)
Married male	0.171	0.178	0.120	0.140
	(0.117)	(0.118)	(0.186)	(0.187)
Married female	0.115	0.127	-0.868***	-0.843***
	(0.137)	(0.138)	(0.274)	(0.274)
Single female	-0.323*	-0.331*	-0.227	-0.220
	(0.181)	(0.181)	(0.284)	(0.285)
KIDS	-0.447E-1	-0.434E-1	0.859E-1	0.905E-1
	(0.356E-1)	(0.356E-1)	(0.560E-1)	(0.560E-1)
ENGLISH	-0.181*	-0.172*	0.245	0.251
	(0.100)	(0.996E-1)	(0.157)	(0.157)
VISMIN	0.561E-1	0.436E-1	0.387	0.391
	(0.171)	(0.171)	(0.275)	(0.275)
TENURE	—	0.679E-3**	—	-0.115E-2***
		(0.278E-3)		(0.416E-3)
TENURESQ	—	-0.481E-6***	—	0.640E-6***
		(0.185E-6)		(0.246E-6)
TOTHOURS	—	0.238E-2**	—	0.175E-2
		(0.110E-2)		(0.159E-2)
AGE (20-24)	0.497***	0.433**	0.894E-1	0.152E-1
	(0.171)	(0.182)	(0.299)	(0.315)
AGE (25-34)	0.353**	0.264*	0.251	0.243
	(0.148)	(0.157)	(0.241)	(0.261)
AGE (35-44)	0.113	0.191E-1	0.894E-1	0.139
	(0.155)	(0.159)	(0.128)	(0.265)
AGE (45-54)	0.117	0.661E-1	0.892E-1	0.510E-1
	(0.156)	(0.157)	(0.258)	(0.265)
ELEM	1.09***	1.05***	1.47***	1.45***
	(0.234)	(0.235)	(0.437)	(0.437)
HIGHSCL	1.19***	1.15***	1.24***	1.24***
	(0.208)	(0.208)	(0.399)	(0.398)
TRADE CERT	0.819***	0.791***	1.18***	1.17***
	(0.236)	(0.236)	(0.425)	(0.424)
SPS	0.976***	0.959***	1.24***	1.27***
	(0.207)	(0.207)	(0.398)	(0.397)
Benefit elasticity	0.313	0.233	0.172	0.186
Log likelihood	-3442.8	-3437.0	-1199.1	-1194.3

*** Statistically significant at the 0.01 level (Two-tailed test).
** Statistically significant at the 0.05 level (Two-tailed test).
* Statistically significant at the 0.10 level (Two-tailed test).
[1] Standard errors are within parentheses.
[2] Dummies for industry, occupation, province, and the panel year from which the observation was drawn (1986–87 or 1988–89) were also included in each specification, but are not reported in this table.

However, *TENURE* has the expected concave relationship with claim probability in the gross-wage provinces, with claim probability decreasing with greater work experience but at an increasing rate. Given the well-known relationship between wages and earnings, it is possible that the work-experience variables are capturing some of the effects of benefits in the net-wage provinces.

The results further indicate that claim probability is unrelated to age in the gross-wage provinces, while younger workers are more likely to initiate a compensation claim in net-wage provinces. The probability that anglophones will initiate a compensation claim is lower in net-wage provinces, but there is no statistically significant relationship for this variable in the gross-wage sample. Interestingly, none of the gross-wage provinces has a large population of francophone speakers, although two of the net-wage provinces (Québec and New Brunswick) do. The relationship between *TOTHOURS* and claim probability is positive, as expected, in both samples. However, this relationship is not statistically significant for the gross-wage sample. Finally, in gross-wage provinces, married females are less likely to receive workers' compensation benefits than single males, while single females have a lower claim probability than single males in net-wage provinces.

Conclusion

Results presented in this chapter indicate that raising workers' compensation benefits affects employee behaviour by increasing the likelihood of a compensation claim. While several previous researchers using American data have reached similar conclusions, this is the first study of Canadian workers that showed such a relationship. As previously mentioned, Lanoie (1992b) found that the claims rate in Québec was positively related to the replacement rate, but the latter variable confounds benefits and wages. This study also indicated that benefit-elasticity measures are similar to those estimated by American studies. Finally, this study showed that the probability of transition into a workers' compensation claim is related to a number of demographic and job characteristics, including age, education, gender, marital status, job tenure, and the number of hours typically worked in a week.

References

Association of Workers' Compensation Boards of Canada. 1987. Benefit comparisons as of January 1, 1987. Mimeographed.

Bartel, Ann and Lacy G. Thomas. 1985. Direct and indirect effects of regulation: A new look at OSHA's impact. *Journal of Law and Economics* 28:1–25.

Bruce, Christopher J. and Frank J. Atkins. 1993. Efficiency effects of premium-setting regimes under workers' compensation: Canada and the United States. *Journal of Labor Economics* 11:S38–S71.

Butler, Richard J. 1983. Wage and injury rate response to shifting levels of workers' compensation. In *Safety and the work force: Incentives and disincentives in workers' compensation*, edited by John D. Worrall, pp.61–86. Ithaca, NY: ILR Press.

Butler, Richard J. and John D. Worrall. 1983. Workers' compensation benefit and injury claims rates in the seventies. *Review of Economics and Statistics* 65:580–89.

Chelius, James R. 1973. An empirical analysis of safety regulation. In Supplemental studies for the *National Commission on State Workmen's Compensation Laws*, vol. 3, edited by Monroe Berkowitz pp.53–66. Washington, DC: US Government Printing Office.

———. 1974. The control of industrial accidents: Economic theory and empirical evidence. *Law and Contemporary Problems* 38:700–729.

———. 1977. *Workplace safety and health: The role of workers' compensation*. Washington, DC: American Enterprise Institute.

———. 1982. The influence of workers' compensation on safety incentives. *Industrial and Labor Relations Review* 35:235–42.

———. 1983. The incentive to prevent injuries. In *Safety and the work force: Incentives and disincentives in workers' compensation*, edited by John D. Worrall. Ithaca, NY: ILR Press.

Chelius, James R. and Karen Kavanaugh. 1988. Workers' compensation and the level of occupational injuries. *Journal of Risk and Insurance* 55:315–23.

Diamond, Peter A. 1977. Insurance theoretic aspects of workers' compensation. In *Natural resources, uncertainty and general equilibrium systems*, edited by A.S. Blinder and P. Friedman, pp.67–89. New York: Academic Press.

Fortin, Bernard and Paul Lanoie. 1992. Substitution between unemployment insurance and workers' compensation. *Journal of Public Economics* 49:287–312.

Krueger, Alan B. 1990. Incentive effects of workers' compensation insurance. *Journal of Public Economics* 41:73–99.

Lanoie, Paul. 1991. Occupational safety and health: A problem of double or single moral hazard. *Journal of Risk and Insurance* 58:80–100.

———. 1992a. Safety regulation and the risk of workplace accidents in Québec. *Southern Economic Journal* 58:950–65.

———. 1992b. The impact of occupational safety and health regulation on the risk of workplace accidents: Québec, 1983–87. *Journal of Human Resources* 27:643–60.

Oi, Walter Y. 1974. On the economics of industrial safety. *Law and Contemporary Problems* 38:669–99.

Rea, Samuel A., Jr. 1981. Workmen's compensation and occupational safety under imperfect information. *American Economic Review* 71:80–93.

Ruser, John W. 1985. Workers' compensation insurance, experience rating, and occupational injuries. *Rand Journal of Economics* 16:487–503.

———. 1991. Workers' compensation and occupational injuries and illnesses. *Journal of Labor Economics* 9:325–50.

Statistics Canada. Monthly *Labour force*. Cat. no. 71-001. Ottawa.

———. Annual. *Work injuries*. Cat. no. 72-208. Ottawa.

Thomason, Terry. 1992. The administration of workers' compensation in Ontario and Québec. Paper prepared for the Queen's-University of Ottawa Economic Projects.

Thomason, Terry and John F. Burton. 1993. Economic effects of workers' compensation in the United States: Private insurance and the administration of compensation claims. *Journal of Labor Economics* 11:S1–S37.

Table A.1

Workers' Compensation Claim Rates, Claims Involving Lost-Time Injuries, 1982–1990[1]

Province	1982	1983	1984	1985	1986	1987	1988	1989	1990	slope[2]
Newfoundland	44.89	45.40	47.26	50.25	48.18	49.44	52.16	53.18	51.58	0.99
PEI	33.31	33.90	30.51	35.74	37.94	39.77	45.09	45.37	46.38	2.00
Nova Scotia	39.94	38.11	35.64	37.91	37.01	33.52	30.65	37.26	33.96	-0.68
New Brunswick	40.07	38.90	39.29	35.24	37.82	40.14	43.28	46.07	42.98	0.77
Maritimes	40.70	39.70	38.96	39.58	39.72	39.40	40.13	43.99	41.36	0.29
Manitoba	40.88	38.69	45.44	47.24	48.34	45.75	35.58	43.41	42.31	-0.02
Saskatchewan	35.77	35.73	36.01	37.37	35.21	34.69	24.96	31.13	30.55	-0.99
Alberta	39.88	33.80	34.12	36.81	37.00	35.98	28.54	36.89	31.43	-1.12
Prairies	39.23	35.34	37.18	39.36	39.26	38.00	29.41	37.20	33.76	-0.80
Québec	61.88	61.47	65.38	70.22	75.53	74.27	72.66	72.16	66.69	1.17
Ontario	34.93	35.56	39.61	42.64	43.31	43.77	42.88	40.61	37.36	0.54
BC	55.64	52.90	49.81	50.12	48.15	50.71	42.98	56.87	58.25	0.94
Canada	45.04	44.11	46.57	49.44	50.75	50.71	47.65	49.77	46.58	0.47

Source: Data on the number of accepted lost-time claims were taken from Statistics Canada (annual). Average annual employment figures were taken from Statistics Canada (monthly).
[1] Claim rates calculated by dividing the number of lost-time compensation claims by total average annual employment, for persons 15 years and older.
[2] Slopes of trend regressions estimating the workers' compensation claim rate.

First Spells of Work Absences Among Ontario Workers

William G. Johnson, Richard J. Butler and Marjorie Baldwin

Most persons who are injured at work recover in a few weeks. For a few workers, however, the effects of their injuries cannot be completely corrected by medical care. If the effects of the injuries are not totally disabling, the workers are said to be permanently and partially impaired.[1] Workers with permanent partial impairments are of special interest because they account for a disproportionately large share of the cost of workers' compensation plans. The workers also present an extremely difficult problem for workers' compensation plans and disability insurers, who want to separate work absences caused by impairments from absences caused by moral hazard or by a weak demand for labour. Identifying the effect of a partial impairment on an individual's ability to work is very difficult, and most disability insurers, including public programs, such as Social Security Disability Insurance, do not cover partial impairments.

Workers' compensation plans, certain of the US Veteran's Administration programs, and some private disability policies are the only sources of insurance against disablement caused by permanent partial impairments. These insurers have traditionally avoided the problem of evaluating the effects of impairments on the ability to work by 'scheduling' benefits according to a worker's average wage and the type and severity of his or her impairment. The schedules, or 'meat charts,' tend

Note: The authors gratefully acknowledge the support of the Workers' Compensation Board of Ontario, for the collection of the data used in this study. The opinions expressed in this article are those of the authors and have not been endorsed by the Board.

1 Although the two terms 'impairment' and 'disability' are often used synonymously, the World Health Organisation (1980) makes important distinctions between them. An impairment is a psychological or anatomical loss or some other abnormality. A disability is any restriction on, or lack of, ability to perform an activity in the manner or within the range considered normal. The relevant activity, for the study of injured workers, is working for wages. Thus, the term disability is used to identify workers whose injury limits their activities at work

to overcompensate workers with less severe injuries and undercompensate more severely injured workers who incur large wage losses (Johnson, Cullinan and Curington 1979; Johnson and Curington 1986).

The Ontario Workers' Compensation Board (WCB) has attempted to eliminate the inequities of scheduled benefits by introducing benefit payments based on work disability, that is, work absences attributable to the effects of injuries, and the associated wage losses. The study reported in this chapter is an extension of the data collection and research efforts that were initiated by the WCB, then under the direction of Robert Elgie and Alan Wolfson, as part of its wage-loss benefit initiative.

The study, using data from the *Ontario Workers' Compensation Board Survey of Workers with Permanent Impairments*, focuses on the first post-injury absence from work, providing a basis for comparison with previous research on the subject.[2] Before presenting the model used in this study, and discussing the data and variables analyzed, previous research on single spells of post-injury work absences is summarized. Study results and conclusions are reported in the final two sections of the chapter.

Previous Research

Research on post-injury work absences has typically estimated the probability that injured workers would be re-employed during a specified time period. Most studies conclude that workers' compensation benefits provide small, but significant, work disincentives. Estimates of the elasticities of duration of absence from work with respect to benefits are smaller than those obtained in studies of the disincentive effects of nondisability plans, such as unemployment insurance.

Fenn (1981) estimated the determinants of the duration of first episodes of work absences caused by injuries or illnesses in the United Kingdom. Because Fenn's data include all illnesses and injuries, his results cannot be directly compared to the US studies, which are based on work injuries. Fenn found that disability benefits, expressed as a proportion of the time-of-onset wage, that is, the 'replacement rate', reduced the probability of returning to work. Age and severity of impairment also reduced workers' chances of resuming employment after a serious illness or injury. Persons living in households with other employed adults were less likely to return to work, presumably

---

2 Butler, Johnson and Baldwin (1995) report the results of an analysis of the determinants of multiple spells of work and work absences among Ontario workers.

because of alternate sources of income in the household. Impairments were more likely to disable workers whose jobs were physically demanding.

Johnson, Cullinan, and Curington (1979) studied workers' compensation clients, in five states, with permanent partial impairments. The workers, who had been injured in 1970, were interviewed in 1975 to obtain information on their post-injury employment and incomes.[3] Most of the workers who returned to work did so during the 12 months following their accidents. Nearly one-fifth of the workers who had returned to work were not employed in 1975. Most of those not employed had been out of the labour force for one to several years. This study referred to these persons as 'marginal' workers. The marginal workers were older, more likely to be women, and more likely to be black than the workers with stable post-injury work histories.

Ginnold's (1979) study of Wisconsin workers with permanent partial impairments caused by 1968 accidents found a similar pattern. Twenty-five percent of the workers who returned to jobs after being injured were not employed in 1976. Most of these workers identified their injuries as the reason they were not working. Neither of the two studies that described this pattern of post-injury withdrawal from work analyzed the influences that lead to this result.

Johnson (1983) used the 1970 accident data from New York to investigate the disincentive effects of workers' compensation benefits on post-injury labour force participation. The New York workers were paid scheduled benefits and, as expected, labour force participation was relatively insensitive to the benefit amounts. The elasticity of the labour force participation rate relative to benefits was 0.088 in 1971. In later years, the participation rate was even less sensitive to the benefit rate. For all the years studied, a 10 percent increase in the average workers' compensation benefit would have reduced labour force participation rates by slightly more than one-half of one percent.

Butler and Worrall (1985) studied first work absences of Illinois men who received workers' compensation benefits for back conditions. They found that a 10 percent increase in benefits increased the length of absence from work by 0.23 weeks. Durations also increased with injury severity, with the presence of a spouse and for workers who were represented by a lawyer. Butler and Worrall (1991) also investigated the effects of different levels of workers' compensation benefits on the

3 The states were: California, Florida, New York, Washington and Wisconsin. Unfortunately, data on employment and wages were collected for 1970, 1971, 1974, and time of interview. Because the survey was the first of its kind, it was predicated on the assumption that very few workers would experience multiple spells of work absences as the result of their injuries.

duration of claims in 12 states. Again, they found that claim duration was positively correlated with benefits.

First work absences among permanent partial beneficiaries of workers' compensation were analyzed by Johnson and Ondrich (1990), using data from the five-state study of 1970 workplace accidents.[4] Their results were consistent with the earlier studies: the pre-injury wage rate had a significantly negative effect and the benefit rate a significantly positive effect on duration of absence from work. Their estimates of the benefit elasticities were, however, higher, ranging in value from 1.114 to 1.161 for different specifications of the model. Johnson and Ondrich also reported that the type of impairment was more important than its severity in determining length of absence from work. The worker's ability to compensate for the effects of the injury (represented by education, experience, and the physical demands of the pre-injury job) was another important influence on returns to work. The durations of work absences were, all else being equal, longer for women and blacks than for other workers.

The US studies were published in scholarly journals and governmental reports. Studies of work absences among injured workers in Ontario were, for the most part, conducted for the WCB staff. In 1981, the WCB conducted a survey of nearly nine thousand pensioners. The pensioners estimated the influence of their injuries on their post-injury employment. Approximately one-fourth of the pensioners were out of work solely because of their injuries (Johnson and Baldwin 1993). Approximately one-sixth of the workers felt that their injuries were partially responsible for their being out of work. One-third of the persons who were not working attributed their work absences to causes other than the effects of their injuries. Workers with injury-related absences tended to be more severely impaired, older, and to have earned lower wages than other workers. Women were more likely than men to report an injury-related absence from work.

In 1983, the WCB surveyed pensioners who received 43(5) supplements to their pensions. The 43(5) survey was designed to obtain data on the work histories and wage losses of partially disabled workers whose supplementary benefits were related to their wage losses.[5] The data from the 1983 sample are unique because they contain information on post-injury work histories for as long as 16 years. Approximately one-fourth of the workers returned to a job within 12 months

4 Their data exclude the states of California and Washington.
5 The results of an analysis of the 43(5) survey are presented in an appendix to Paul Weiler's report to the Minister of Labour. See William G. Johnson, Appendix, in Weiler (1986).

of being injured. The proportion of workers who were employed reached a maximum approximately four to five years after the accident date and declined thereafter. The first work absences among the 43(5) pensioners are longer than the durations observed for workers with relatively severe permanent partial impairments in the United States. The US data show, for example, that more than two-thirds of the workers were re-employed by the twelfth month following their accidents. Employment rates for the two groups are comparable in the fifth year, however, suggesting that US workers return sooner, but are also less likely than the 43(5) pensioners to remain employed.

The studies summarized have either been restricted to single spells or did not adequately describe the long-term effects of injuries on employment. The research does, however, identify important influences on return to work that may also have long-term effects. Characteristics that significantly affect returns to work following the first absence are

Gender: men are more likely to return to work than women.

Age: the probability of return to work is lower at older ages.

Impairment: the probability of return is lower for more severe impairments.

Minority status: blacks are less likely to return to work than whites.

Education and skills: low levels of skill and below average years of education are associated with lower probabilities of return to work.

Marital status: married men and not married women tend to follow the same pattern of labour force participation following an injury, not married men and married women share a different pattern.

Wages: the higher the wage that an injured worker can earn, the higher the probability of his or her returning to work.

Workers' compensation benefits: the higher the benefit payment, the lower the probability of return to work. The evidence is mixed, however, and cannot be given the same confidence as the research on the factors listed above. Obviously, the difference between wages and workers' compensation benefits is especially important if the benefits end when the worker is employed. Scheduled benefits should have a smaller effect on work absences.

Medical rehabilitation: workers who receive rehabilitation services have a higher probability of returning to work, all else being equal, than workers who do not.

These characteristics are the basis for our model of the determinants of first post-injury returns to work.

Method

In the estimation of the duration of work absences, y is a random variable indicating the time absent from work after an injury and the probability density of these nonwork spells is written as $f(y|\theta,\alpha)$ and the distribution function as $F(Y|\theta,\alpha)$. θ is the location parameter of the distribution and α is a vector that includes the shape and scale parameters. A distinction is made between the location parameter and other parameters of the distribution because it is assumed that, as in virtually all empirical studies,[6] differences among injured workers affect only the location parameter. Differences among workers may or may not be correlated with observable characteristics, such as age or union membership.

If demographic characteristics did not matter, and all workers were subject to the same stochastic forces generating the duration of claims, then a *structural duration distribution without heterogeneity* would be estimated. It is assumed that this follows either an exponential or Weibull distribution. When there is no heterogeneity, it is assumed that the location parameter, θ, is a constant (say b), and does not vary with the economic or demographic characteristics of the claimant. The densities have the following forms (the exponential being a special case of the Weibull where $a = 1$):

Weibull: $\quad f(y) = ay^{a-1} \exp(-(y/b)^a)/b^a$ (1)
Exponential: $f(y) = \exp(-(y/b))/b$

Heterogeneity Controls for Observable Characteristics is introduced by making the logarithm of the ith worker's location parameter b a linear function of those observable characteristics so that

$$b_i = \exp(X_i\beta) \tag{2}$$

where X_i is a vector including the worker's age, union membership, compensation benefits, and so forth, and β are parametric weights assumed to be constant across workers. Heterogeneity allows the location parameter for the distribution of nonwork spells to vary from worker to worker, and thus allows heterogeneity in the structural distribution of claims.

---

6 A notable exception is the Butler and Worrall (1993) study, in which the parameters of the duration distribution are a function of demographic and economic variables.

Data Set

The largest survey of injured workers ever completed was conducted by the Ontario WCB between 12 June 1989 and 30 June 1990. The target group consisted of all injured workers scheduled for a physician examination for permanent partial disability assessment. Thus, the data consist of a census of injured workers rather than a sample.

The survey instrument included questions on demographics and characteristics of the time-of-injury job, wages and work from date of injury to date of interview, and amounts and sources of workers' incomes.[7] The survey data were supplemented with WCB administrative data on the worker's impairment, residence, and work history.

The characteristics of the workers who were interviewed are described in Table 1. The characteristics are limited to those included in the model. The workers are generally representative of a typical labour force population. The average age is 41 and more than three-quarters of the injured workers are married. The benefit-wage ratio is higher for women than for men because, on average, women's wages are lower, but there is very little difference between the sexes in educational attainment or in the percentage of workers who are members of labour unions.

Table 1

Means for the Sample of Ontario Workers[1]

	Males	Females	Total
N	6289	2401	8690
Censored	.25 (.43)	.29 (.45)	.26 (.44)
Observed spell length	435.57 (561.12)	442.24 (497.47)	437.41 (539.78)
Age	40.96 (12.05)	41.30 (10.93)	41.05 (11.75)
Married	.79 (.41)	.71 (.45)	.77 (.42)
Fractures	.11 (.31)	.06 (.24)	.10 (.30)
Strains	.14 (.35)	.20 (.40)	.16 (.36)
Union member	.58 (.49)	.55 (.50)	.57 (.50)
Northeast	.12 (.33)	.06 (.24)	.11 (.31)
High school or college education	.33 (.47)	.35 (.48)	.33 (.47)
Benefit-wage ratio	.66 (.13)	.76 (.12)	.69 (.14)
Manufacturing	.34 (.47)	.36 (.48)	.34 (.47)

[1] Standard deviations are in parentheses.

7 The survey instrument was designed by Professor Johnson in cooperation with Richard Allingham, Sandra Sinclair, and staff members of the Ontario WCB.

Empirical Results

Estimated coefficients for the model that accounts for heterogeneity are reported in Table 2 (the exponential distribution) and Table 3 (the Weibull distribution). The coefficients of the demographic variables are easy to interpret. Each coefficient measures the percentage change in the mean duration given a unit change in the associated independent

Table 2

Duration of First Absences: Exponential MLE Estimates[1]

	Males	Females	Total
Intercept	6.367 (.60)	5.731 (1.11)	6.072 (.52)
Age	.019 (.01)	.017 (.01)	.018 (.01)
Married	-.232 (.24)	.148 (.32)	-.033 (.19)
Fractures	.059 (.30)	-.260 (.63)	-.104 (.26)
Strains	.046 (.27)	-.106 (.36)	-.085 (.21)
Union member	-.248 (.19)	-.368 (.30)	-.287 (.16)
Northeast	.220 (.26)	.466 (.61)	.265 (.24)
High school or college education	-.353 (.20)	-.124 (.32)	-.285 (.17)
Benefit-wage ratio	-.440 (.70)	.191 (1.13)	-.155 (.55)
Manufacturing	-.234 (.19)	-.041 (.31)	-.189 (.16)
Log-likelihood	34526.28	12634.34	47180.65
χ^2-male/female	—	—	40.08

[1]Standard errors are in parentheses.

Table 3

Duration of First Absences: Weibull MLE Estimates[1]

	Males	Females	Total
Intercept	5.844 (.65)	5.338 (1.69)	5.658 (.82)
Age	.024 (.01)	.020 (.02)	.022 (.01)
Married	-.187 (.38)	.181 (.44)	-.033 (.28)
Fractures	-.067 (.44)	-.315 (.90)	-.124 (.38)
Strains	-.109 (.40)	-.110 (.51)	-.088 (.31)
Union member	-.293 (.28)	-.407 (.43)	-.337 (.23)
Northeast	.256 (.39)	.504 (.81)	.355 (.35)
High school or college education	-.355 (.30)	-.148 (.45)	-.296 (.25)
Benefit-wage ratio	.00 (.00)	.510 (1.70)	.196 (.86)
Manufacturing	-.286 (.29)	-.018 (.43)	-.219 (.24)
a	.722 (.11)	.745 (.18)	.728 (.09)
Log-likelihood	34051.00	12512.23	46588.49
χ^2-male/female (11 d.f.)	—	—	50.52

[1] Standard errors are in parentheses.

variable. The coefficient of .019 for the age variable for men, for example, indicates that the average duration of a jobless spell increases by 1.9 percent with a one year increase in age.

Parameters of the distributions were estimated by maximum likelihood employing a nonderivative secant method which is the non-derivative default method in SAS's *PROC NLIN* procedure. One disadvantage of the *NLIN* procedure is its extremely conservative estimates of standard errors. Comparisons to the estimates from other nonlinear or optimization software packages suggest that *NLIN*'s estimates can be more than five times as high. Thus, most of the coefficients that are discussed in this section are, in fact, statistically significant. Model χ^2 statistics (not reported here) indicate that the demographic variables are jointly significant at better than the 1 percent level.

The signs and magnitudes of many of the demographic variables remain fairly consistent between the exponential and Weibull distributions, despite the unlikely pattern of durations (they continuously decline throughout) intrinsic to the exponential distribution. In particular, age and living in the northeast significantly increase mean duration, while union membership, higher levels of educational attainment, and being in the manufacturing sector significantly decrease mean duration. Marital status has different effects for men and women.

A positive correlation between age and the duration of work absences has been observed in almost every study of work injury. Similar effects have been estimated for the relationship between age and the disabling effects of impairments that result from illnesses and non-work injuries.[8] The capacity to recover physically from the effects of injuries declines with age, but older workers may be better able to compensate for the physical limitations associated with an impairment because of their experience with the demands of their usual job.

Membership in a labour union reduces the duration of first post-injury jobless spells by 20 to 40 percent. This finding disagrees with the results of the US studies that found that work absences were longer among unionized workers (Butler and Worrall 1985, 1993; Johnson and Ondrich 1990). The differences between the Ontario results and the US results may reflect differences in the extent to which lawyers represent workers' compensation claimants. Borba and Appel (1987) demonstrated that union members were represented by attorneys much more frequently than nonunion workers. Their finding is consistent with the fact that some US labour unions retain law firms whose duties include representation of any union member who desires legal help with a workers' compensation claim.

8 For estimates of the contribution of age to work disability from all causes, see Chirikos and Nestel (1984), Berkowitz and Johnson (1974).

Ontario workers' compensation much more closely resembles the no-fault ideal than does workers' compensation in any of the US jurisdictions. The absence of insurers to contest claims and the provision of administrative remedies have made recourse to attorneys relatively rare. The effect of union membership on returns to work in Ontario appears to reflect unions' attempts to help their injured members return to work. A recent comparison of returns to work among a subset of the workers analyzed for this study supports the importance of the role of labour unions in helping injured workers to find jobs or to assist in arranging accommodations for workers in their pre-injury jobs (Johnson and Baldwin 1993). Although 66 percent of the workers were unionized, only 49 percent of the workers who did not return to work were unionized. More than one-quarter of the workers who moved to new jobs after being injured did so with the help of their labour union.

The benefit-wage ratio is not a significant influence on the duration of work absences among men. In the exponential model, the benefit-wage ratio significantly increases lengths of work absences among women.[9]

Marital status is another important influence on the durations of first spells of work absences. Married men have shorter durations than single men, while married women have longer durations than single women. Spells of joblessness of married men are approximately 20 percent shorter than spells for single men; the mean duration of joblessness for married women is from 15 to 18 percent longer than it is for single women. These results parallel observed differences in the labour force participation rates of noninjured workers by sex and marital status.

Differences between the sexes in the effects of workers' compensation benefits and marital status on the duration of work absences may be attributable to the presence or absence of a second wage income in a household. Spouses' wages were not measured, but most married women can count on the wages of an employed husband while a smaller proportion of employed married men have wives who also work for wages.[10] The income effect is reinforced by the fact that women, employed or not, produce a much larger proportion of household services than men.

One can speculate that married women, who do the majority of household work whether or not they are employed, can mix house-

9 The benefit-wage ratio was not a significant influence on the duration of absence for men or women in the Weibull distribution.
10 Fenn's (1981) results for the UK show that the presence of a second adult wage earner in a worker's household reduces the probability of returns to work. Johnson and Ondrich's (1990) estimates of the relationships between marital status/sex and returns to work also follow the pattern for the Ontario workers.

hold work with recuperation much better than men and, therefore, experience a less rapid decline in reservation wages as the healing process continues. In other words, for women, the combination of the value of household work and workers' compensation benefits slows the rate at which reservation wages decline with increases in health.

The sex-related differentials in the length of jobless spells imply that continued increases in the labour force participation of married women will increase the cost of work injuries, all else being equal. Workers' compensation programs may want to consider whether their current approaches to the rehabilitation of injured workers are designed to address the determinants of work absence durations among married women.

One of the important questions that must be considered in modeling work absences is the extent to which the estimates are affected by duration dependence. In this context, duration dependence means that the longer an injured worker is absent from work, the less likely he or she is to return to work. That is, the rate of exit from a workers' compensation claim falls for workers with longer claims. In the Weibull distribution, duration dependence is indicated by the size of the a coefficient: $a = 1$ implies no duration dependence, $a < 1$ implies duration dependence. Our results indicate that in the men's (and combined) sample, the a coefficient is significantly different from one at the 1 percent level, while in the women's sample, it is significantly different from one at the 10 percent level (one-tailed tests). In other words, the likelihood of a return to work declines as the duration of work absence increases.

The results on duration dependence may be of special interest to workers' compensation programs considering the adoption of the Ontario wage-loss approach to permanent partial disability claims. Most practitioners are familiar with the belief in the beneficial effects of 'early intervention' (the provision of rehabilitative services soon after injury) for workers who will have difficulty returning to work. Early intervention was, in fact, mandated by Bill 162 in 1989, which created the Ontario wage-loss system. There is, however, little empirical support for a belief in early intervention. Our results support the notion that the longer the work absence the less likely injured workers are to return to work. The results are consistent with Johnson and Baldwin's (1993) conclusion that a good proxy for whether or not injured workers will have long-term employment problems is return to work within 90 days of being injured.

Conclusion

The results reported here are, with the notable exception of the effect of union membership, remarkably similar to results obtained for workers with permanent partial disabilities in other years in several states in the US. These comparisons are possible because the study concentrated on completed first spells of absence following a workplace injury. The results support the conclusion that, despite important differences between the organization of workers' compensation in Ontario and the United States, the same characteristics exert similar effects on the duration of first work absences among both Canadian and US workers. The similarity suggests that the results of this study and our study of multiple spells of work absences (Butler, Johnson and Baldwin 1995) among Ontario workers can be generalized to the United States.

The first spell of absence provides an inadequate description of the effects of workplace injuries on employment and wages; the study of multiple spells of work absence shows that a single nonwork spell followed by stable employment is characteristic of only two-fifths of those who return to work. Approximately one-third of those who return to work leave their job because of the effects of their injuries and are not employed again. This result echoes findings from US studies reported in the 1970s. There is, however, a much larger group of workers who return to work and then experience multiple episodes of injury-related work absences. Some of these workers eventually return to stable employment, but many do not. The reasons for the differences in the ultimate outcomes of the effects of workplace injuries can only be understood by a careful analysis of all the spells of injury-related work absences.

References

Berkowitz, Monroe and William G. Johnson. 1974. Health and labor force participation. *Journal of Human Resources* 9:117–28.
Borba, Philip S. and David Appel. 1987. The propensity of permanently disabled workers to hire lawyers. *Industrial and Labor Relations Review* 40:418–29.
Butler, Richard J. and John D. Worrall. 1985. Work injury compensation and the duration of nonwork spells. *Economic Journal* 95:714–24.
———. 1991. Gamma duration models with heterogeneity. *Review of Economics and Statistics* 73:161–66.
———. 1993. Workers' compensation costs and heterogeneous claims. In *Workers' compensation insurance: Claim costs, prices and regulation*, edited by David Durbin and Philip S. Borba, pp.25–50. Boston: Kluwer Academic Publishers.
Butler, Richard J., William G. Johnson, and Marjorie Baldwin. 1995. Measuring success in managing work disability: Why return to work doesn't work. *Industrial and Labor Relations Review*, forthcoming.

Chirikos, Thomas and Gilbert Nestel. 1984. Economic determinants and consequences of self-reported work disability. *Journal of Health Economics* 3:117–36.

Fenn, Paul. 1981. Sickness duration, residual disability and income replacement: An empirical analysis. *Economic Journal* 91:158–73.

Ginnold, Richard. 1979. A follow-up study of permanent disability cases under Wisconsin workers' compensation. In *Research report of the Interdepartmental Workers' Compensation Task Force*, vol. 6, pp.79–94. Washington, DC: US Government Printing Office.

Johnson William G. 1983. The disincentive effects of workers' compensation insurance. In *Safety and the work force: Incentives and disincentives in workers' compensation*, edited by John D. Worrall, pp.138–53. Ithaca, NY: ILR Press.

Johnson, William G. and Marjorie Baldwin. 1993. Returns to work by Ontario workers with permanent partial disablities. A report to the Workers' Compensation Board of Ontario. Toronto: The Board.

Johnson, William G. and William P. Curington. 1986. Wage losses and workers' compensation benefits 1970–1980. In *Research papers of the NYS Temporary Commission on Workers' Compensation and Disability Benefits*. Albany, NY.

Johnson,, William G. and Jan Ondrich. 1990. The duration of post-injury absences from work. *Review of Economics and Statistics* 72:578–86.

Johnson, William G., Paul R. Cullinan, and William P. Curington. 1979. The adequacy of workers' compensation benefits. In *Research report of the Interdepartmental Workers' Compensation Task Force*, vol. 6, pp.95–122. Washington, DC: US Government Printing Office.

Weiler, Paul C. 1986. *Permanent partial disability: Alternative models for compensation*. Toronto: Ontario Ministry of Labour.

World Health Organisation. 1980. *International classification of impairments, disabilities, and handicaps*. Geneva: The Organisation.

Moral Hazard, Optimal Auditing and Workers' Compensation

Georges Dionne, Pierre St-Michel and Charles Vanasse

Moral hazard has been investigated often during the last two decades. Two types of moral hazard have been defined. The first relates to self-prevention activities affecting probabilities of accidents, while the second relates to the activities after the accident occurs that affect the distribution of losses associated with an accident. Drèze (1961), Arrow (1963), Kihlstrom and Pauly (1971), Marshall (1976), Shavell (1979), Holmström (1979) and Dionne (1982) focused on the first type, where the occurrence of an accident is known to the insurer and the insured, but neither the action of the insured nor the state of nature is observed. The insured's action affects, *ex ante*, the probabilities of accidents and the provision of insurance reduces (in general) the insured's incentives to be careful. See Arnott (1992) and Winter (1992) for recent reviews of the literature.

The existence of the second type of moral hazard was first suggested by Spence and Zeckhauser (1971) who showed that an optimal contract between a principal (insurer) and an agent (insured) depends on the ability of the principal to monitor the state of nature, the action taken by the agent, and the output of the consumption good. (See also Dionne, 1981, 1984a, 1984b). Townsend (1979) investigated in detail the case where the occurrence of an accident is known only by the agent unless costly verification is made. One method of such costly verification is auditing done by independent auditors or by the principal.

Townsend (1979) restricted his formal analysis to nonrandom auditing to determine auditing strategies. He showed that the optimal insurance contract involves auditing all cost reports above a certain level

Note: Martine Allaire, François Gagnon, Andrée Morin, Christian Rocque, and Gilles Therrien have contributed to this research. Comments by G. Larocque, T. Thomason, and M. Grace improved the interpretation of the results. Financial support by the Commission de la santé et la sécurité du travail du Québec (CSST) and the Fédération française des sociétés d'assurances is acknowledged. The opinions expressed in the paper are those of the authors and do not necessarily reflect the position or policies of the CSST.

and not auditing any lower cost reports. More recently, Mookherjee and Png (1989) extended Townsend's model in order to characterize optimal contracts when random audits are permitted (see also Townsend 1988). Their model investigated simultaneously the two types of moral hazard mentioned above. The agent first chooses, *ex ante*, an unobservable action that affects the probability of an accident and then reports to the principal his or her realized (privately observed) income or type of accident to the insurer. The insurer audits the report at a certain cost.[1] Their main result is that to reduce expected auditing costs without distorting the insured's incentives to make false reports, all audits must be random.

Few researchers have investigated moral hazard in empirical research,[2] even though several empirical studies have analyzed the effects of changes in insurance compensation on accident rates or on recovery time (especially Butler, 1983; Butler and Worrall, 1983, 1985; Chelius, 1982; Doherty, 1979; Fenn, 1981; Ruser, 1986; Viscusi and Moore, 1987; Worrall and Appel, 1982; Worrall, Appel and Butler, 1987; Leigh and Sheetz, 1988; Lanoie 1988, 1989; Cousineau, Lacroix and Girard, 1989; Moore and Viscusi, 1992). The first study that explicitly analyzed the incentive to shirk was conducted by Staten and Umbeck (1982). They were concerned by the effect of variation of information costs on absence from work. Their study was recently extended by Dionne and St-Michel (1991) who conducted an explicit analysis of the effects of a change in insurance coverage. They used different types of diagnoses to separate the variation of length of absence from work due to moral hazard from total variation. They showed that, in the presence of moral hazard, variation in the length of the recovery period associated with an increase in insurance coverage is greater for injuries which are difficult to diagnose (or to observe), such as back-related injuries, than for injuries that are easy to diagnose, such as fractures, contusions, or amputations. If the insurer had possessed full information concerning the insured's health status, variations in recovery periods for the two injury types would have been identical.

---

1 See Melumad and Mookherjee (1989) on the delegation of the auditing policy when the principal is unable to commit to all significant policy variables. Here, it is implicitly assumed that the principal can commit himself to all policy variables, and, more explicitly, that the agents have information on the principal's auditing activities. The commitment problem is simplified with nonrandom auditing. See Dionne and Viala (1992) and Bond and Crocker (1993) for recent models with nonrandom auditing.

2 See, however, Boyer and Dionne (1989) and Dionne and St-Michel (1991). The type of *ex post* moral hazard considered here and in Dionne and St-Michel (1991), can be interpreted in some circumstances as claims evasion, claims build-up, or even insurance fraud (Bond and Crocker, 1993; Weisberg and Derrig, 1991; Dionne, Gibbens and St-Michel, 1993, Derrig and Kraus, 1992).

The objective of this chapter is to present additional empirical evidence concerning the effect of moral hazard on the length of absence from work. A new data set has been created from claims initiated with the Commission de la santé et de la sécurité du travail du Québec (CSST). The sample contains about 1,150 work-related injuries which occurred in 1987 and involved some temporary disability.

Three principal characteristics distinguish this study from that of Dionne and St-Michel (1991). First, unlike the previous study, there was no change in the insurance plan during the period of analysis. Therefore, variation in insurance coverage between individual workers is not the result of a structural change in the insurance plan, but arises from differences in real insurance coverage mainly due to differences in insurance profiles or to differences in access to tax exemptions associated with the workers' compensation program in 1987. Second, we are able to control for several additional variables that were obtained from a survey of injured workers and that affect the duration of disability benefits. Finally, in this chapter, individual gross income is considered as an endogenous variable and the models are estimated with two-stage least squares.

The first section of the chapter presents a theoretical model that first describes the two types of moral hazard and then shows how changes in insurance coverage can affect optimal consumption behaviour (or the optimal number of days of compensation) of workers for a given auditing scheme. The next section presents the detailed methodology developed by Dionne and St-Michel (1991) to isolate the effect of the second type of moral hazard on the length of absence from work due to occupational injury. A brief description of the workers' compensation program in Québec is followed by the description of the data set. Finally, econometric results are given. A short conclusion interprets the results and discusses their policy implications.

Theory

When both types of moral hazard are present, the insurer's problem is to calculate, *ex ante*, the values of the decision variables (a, I_i, P_i, p_i) that maximize the expected utility of the worker

$$\sum_{i=1}^{n} \pi_i(a) \left[p_i U (Y_i + I_i - P_{ii}) + (1 - p_i) U(Y_i + I_i) \right] - G(a)$$

under the following constraints:

$$p_i U (Y_i + I_i - P_{ii}) + (1 - p_i) U(Y_i + I_i) \geq p_h U(Y_i + I_h - P_{hi})$$
$$+ (1 - p_h) U(Y_i + I_h) \tag{1}$$

$$\sum_{i=1}^{n} \pi_i(a) \left[p_i U (Y_i + I_i - P_{ii}) + (1 - p_i) U(Y_i + I_i) \right] - G(a)$$

$$\geq \sum_{i=1}^{n} \pi_i(a) \left[p_i U (Y_i + I_i - P_{ii}) + (1 - p_i) U(Y_i + I_i) \right] - G(a') \tag{2}$$

for all a and $a' \in A$, where a is efficient and A is the set of all possible actions,

$$\sum_{i=1}^{n} \pi_i(a) \left[- I_i - p_i (E_i - P_{ii}) \right] = 0 \tag{3}$$

$$Y_i + I_i - P_{ii} \geq 0, \ Y_i + I_i \geq 0, \ 0 \leq p_i \leq 1, \ 0 \leq \pi_i(a) \leq 1, \tag{4}$$

$$\sum_{i=1}^{n} \pi_i(a) = 1,$$

where,

U is the von Neuman-Morgenstern utility function of wealth, where $U'(.) > 0$, $U''(.) < 0$ and $U(0) = 0$ which arbitrarily rules out large penalties;

G is the cost of effort in utility terms, $G'(a) > 0$, $G''(a) > 0$;

L_i is the number of leisure days in state i;

Y_i is the income in state i; $Y_i = w(\overline{L} - L_i)$ where w is the wage rate and $\overline{L}$ is the total number of working days available in a given period;

I_i is the insurance coverage net of premium, $I_i \gtrless 0$;

$\pi_i(a)$ is the probability of state i; it is a function of the insured's level of care activity[3] (a);

p_i is the probability that the insured's report of accident will be audited when L_i is reported;

P_{hi} is the penalty when L_h is found reported instead of L_i;[4]

P_{ii} is the reward when L_i is reported to be true;

E_i is the auditing cost;

$L_h \geq L_i$ and $I_h \geq I_i$, since L_h corresponds to exaggerating the number of leisure days, while L_i corresponds to truth telling.

---

3 A more general model would also consider that π_i is a function of the employer's level of safety. However, this generalization of the above problem to the double moral hazard literature (Cooper and Ross, 1985; Lanoie, 1989) is not essential for our purpose.

4 It is important to note that, here, the probability of finding a false report when there is a false report is equal to one (see Parsons 1989a and 1989b, on imperfect state verification). However, Mookherjee and Png (1989) claim that their results, obtained from a similar model, can be extended to 'the case where there are 'small' errors of auditing' (p. 414).

Equation (1) is a self-reporting constraint, while equation (2) is an effort constraint. The third constraint indicates that the principal cannot have positive expected profits, which is a reasonable assumption for a regulated public insurer. The last constraint summarizes technical relationships that are necessary to obtain a feasible solution. When the second type of moral hazard is absent, one can see that the above problem is the standard principal-agent problem (Grossman and Hart 1983): (1) set $p_i \equiv 0$, and (2) notice that the first constraint is useless since L_i is observable.

Introducing the second type of moral hazard implies that the feasible solution should require the agent to report L_i truthfully. The first constraint indicates that he or she prefers to report L_i truthfully when L_i is the true realized state. Mookherjee and Png (1989) obtained some important results from a similar model. They showed that $p_i < 1$ for all L_i that are audited, which means that reports must be audited randomly. Moreover, the maximum penalty can be set such that $Y_i + I_h - P_{hi} = 0$ and truthful reports must be rewarded, i.e., $P_i < 0$. Finally, only the report that corresponds to the lower accident cost does not have to be audited.

The above results clearly indicate that the usual insurance contracts for workers' compensation in effect in many states or provinces are not optimal when the second type of moral hazard (or claims evasion, build-up, or even fraud) is present. In many insurance plans, the insurer does not allocate any resources to verify the insured's health status, even when the diagnoses are difficult to verify by the physician or the insurer. Another characteristic is that partial insurance coverage alone is not appropriate to reduce the ill effect of the second type of moral hazard, although it is optimal for the first type. The intuition of this result is the following: partial insurance coverage alone introduces some uncertainty, *ex ante*, and therefore creates incentives for a level of care equal to (*a*). This is the traditional trade-off between risk bearing and incentives. When, *ex-post*, the insured has to report his or her type of accident, such a trade-off is no longer present in the traditional principal-agent model. Therefore, when the second type of moral hazard is present, a second mechanism is necessary to obtain optimal resource allocation. Random audited reports with penalties and rewards reintroduce the desired trade-off and achieve lower auditing costs than those corresponding to a nonrandom mechanism.

However, partial insurance influences the consumption of leisure days when insurance is not a pure lump-sum indemnity conditional on the state of health, but when total payment varies with the number of days absent from work as in many workers' insurance plans. When L_i is not perfectly observable and when there is no mechanism to detect a false declaration, an increase in the insurance coverage (or real insurance coverage, net of tax) may lead to the consumption of additional leisure time. In other words, variation in the coinsurance rate not only affects (a), but also the number of leisure days when there is no appropriate mechanism to detect a false declaration. This is the definition of the second type of moral hazard used in this chapter.[5]

Empirical Hypotheses

In this section of the chapter, a method of measuring the effect of moral hazard on consumption is presented. The difficulty inherent in obtaining an econometric measure of moral hazard stems from the fact that the amount of information regarding the consumer's true state of health is limited to what the insurer knows. In other words, the researcher has no more information than the insurer. One way to solve this information problem is to isolate different types of diagnoses in order to predict variation in consumption related to variation in insurance coverage (see Kniesner and Leeth, 1989, for a method based on simulation).

Table 1 presents a summary of the method proposed in Dionne and St-Michel (1991). All things being equal, following the same variation (in percentage) of insurance coverage for each case, let ΔMIJ (for $J = E$, D) and ΔMAJ (for $J = E$, D) represent the variation (in percentage) in the number of days of compensation for two types of injuries (major and minor) and for two types of diagnoses (easy and difficult). MI and MA represent, respectively, minor and major injuries and E and D designate, respectively, easy and difficult diagnoses.

Following a change in the insurance rate, under asymmetrical information, we should observe:

$CASE$ 1 (identical severity and different degrees of observability):

$\Delta MID > \Delta MIE$ and $\Delta MAD > \Delta MAE$,

whereas in

$CASE$ 2 (different categories of severity with identical degrees of observability):

$\Delta MIE = \Delta MAE$ and $\Delta MID = \Delta MAD$.

---

5 However, overconsumption (i.e., consumption unrelated to the true state of the world or claims evasion, build-up, and fraud) is not necessarily generated by the insured. In fact, intermediaries in the principal-agent relationship play a very important role in several specialized markets since they can be motivated to modify the distribution of losses at the expense of the insurer, with or without the agent's cooperation. In these circumstances auditing activities concern the verification of intermediaries' reports. Examples of intermediaries are automobile mechanics and physicians (Dionne, 1984b, Dionne, Gibbens and St-Michel, 1993). We limit our interpretation to the role of the agent and consider the physicians as neutral intermediaries in the principal-agent relationship.

Table 1

Variation in the Number of Days of Compensation Due to a Change in the Insurance Coverage

	Easy diagnosis $(J = E)$	Difficult diagnosis $(J = D)$
Minor injuries (MI)	ΔMIE	ΔMID
Major injuries (MA)	ΔMAE	ΔMAD

A classification based on the degree of severity or degree to which an injury is observable is quite arbitrary. In fact, the degree of severity is the most arbitrary of the two. For example, a severe contusion, i.e., a minor injury (MI), could result in a longer recovery period than a minor concussion, which is classified as a major injury (MA). Moreover, these cases cannot easily be classified according to the level of disutility the injury produces. In order to make up for this imprecision, the distinction between MI and MA must be as clear as possible.

Severity is measured by the average length of absence from work. The comparison of average recovery times is based on the type of injury, since it is a classification variable which best describes the medical and diagnostic nature of the injury. From the longest average recovery time to the shortest, injuries included in the study are:[6] fracture, sprain, amputation without permanent partial disability (WPPD), lower back pain, friction burn, and contusion.

Injuries can be classified into two groups based on severity and type, as follows: major injuries (MA), such as fracture and sprain; minor injuries (MI), such as amputation WPPD, lower back pain, contusion, and friction burn.

Injuries are also categorized according to difficulty of diagnosis. This classification is based on information obtained from the medical literature.[7] Injuries are classified from the easiest ($J = E$) to the most difficult ($J = D$) to diagnose, as follows: contusion, amputation WPPD, fracture and friction burn ($J = E$); and sprain and lower back pain ($J = D$). Table 2 summarizes the above classification.

It is important to note that lower back pain and sprain are categories which include diagnoses both related and unrelated to back injury. The empirical analysis of the data will take this distinction into account

---

6 Several types of injuries were grouped together to simplify the presentation. A detailed list is available on request.

7 See Burton (1985), Hadler (1989), Leigh (1989), Moretz (1987), as well as Spitzer et al. (1987) for a detailed discussion on the medical, legal, and economic aspects of occupational lower back injuries.

Table 2

**Classification of Occupational Injuries by Degree
of Severity and Relative Difficulty of Diagnosis**

Severity of injury	Easy diagnosis $(J = E)$	Difficult diagnosis $(J = D)$
Minor injuries (*MI*)	contusion, amputation WPPD, and friction burn	lower back pain
Major injuries (*MA*)	fracture	sprain

(i.e., related/unrelated to back injury) by cross-matching injury type with the site of injury. Particular attention is focused on back pain because it has been identified in the medical literature as being very difficult to diagnose (see, for example, Spitzer et al. 1987).

Estimation of Moral Hazard

Empirical Model

The estimation of moral hazard is conducted in two major steps. First, it must be verified whether or not an increase in insurance coverage is significant in the estimation of the demand for days of compensation. Second, it must be shown that variations associated with difficult diagnoses are greater than those associated with other diagnoses.

The first step, therefore, is to estimate the effect of variation in insurance coverage on the number of days of compensation. The model includes control variables such as age, sex, gross annual income, as well as economic sector, union, type of job, and accident period. The type of injury is also included among the variables. Therefore, the model is the following:

$Days = f (INS, AGE, INCOME, GENDER, SECTOR, MIE, MIDB,$
$\quad\quad\quad MIDNB, MAE, MADB, MADNB, JOBTYPE, UNION, PERIOD,$
$\quad\quad\quad CONS, RELAPSE)$

These variables are defined in Table 3.

The second step examines how insurance coverage (insurance profile) affects the estimated coefficients of the diagnoses. It is assumed that, without asymmetrical information, insurance coverage will have no effect on these coefficients since they only represent variation explained by differences in medical characteristics.

Table 3

Variable Names and Definitions

Variable	Definition
Days	Natural logarithm of the number of days that the claimant received temporary total disability benefits.
INS	1,0: Insurance profile—a measure of the extent of the claimant's insurance coverage—equal to 1 if the claimant has one of the following four characteristics: (1) has a spouse in the labour force, (2) has at least one dependent, (3) worked part-time, and (4) has an annual family income less than that projected by the CSST and used for compensation.
AGE	Natural logarithm of claimant's age at the time of injury.
GENDER	1,0: Claimant's gender (male = 1).
INCOME	Natural logarithm of claimant's gross annual income.
SECTOR	Vector of 1,0 variables indicating the industrial sector in which the claimant worked: Primary, Construction, Transportation, Commerce, Administration, Others, and Manufacturing.
JOBTYPE	Vector of 1,0 variables indicating the nature of the claimant's employment: Occasional, On call, Seasonal, and Yearly basis.
UNION	1,0: Claimant belongs to a labour union (member = 1).
PERIOD	Vector of 1,0 variables indicating the date on which the injury occurred: 1st - 4th trimesters.
MIDB	1,0: lower back pain—back injury.
MIDNB	1,0: lower back pain—nonback injury.
MAE	1,0: fractures.
MIE	1,0: contusion, amputation without permanent partial disability or friction burn.
MADB	1,0: sprains—back injury.
MADNB	1,0: sprains—nonback injury.
RELAPSE	1,0: the claimant has more than one event for that file number (more than one = 1).
CONS	1,0: Consumption profile—indicates the claimant's propensity to extend the duration of disability benefits for reasons other than the type of moral hazard associated to insurance profile—equal to 1 if the claimant has one of the following characteristics: (1) the claimant knows that workers' compensation is more generous than unemployment compensation, (2) the claimant considered several physicians before making a final choice, and (3) the claimant does not consider his or her job to be interesting.

In the presence of moral hazard, however, insurance coverage should significantly increase the values of the estimated coefficients of diagnoses that are difficult to verify when there is no formal auditing mechanism that prevents overconsumption. To verify the presence of moral hazard in our data set, the following model was estimated:

$$Days = ß_0 + ß_1 \, MIDB + ß_2(MIDB * INS) + ß_3 \, MIDNB + ß_4 (MIDNB * INS)$$
$$+ ß_5 (MAE) + ß_6 (MAE * INS) + ß_7 (MADB) + ß_8 (MADB * INS)$$
$$+ ß_9 \, MADNB + ß_{10} (MADNB * INS) + \text{other explanatory}$$
variables + error term,

where *INS* is used for insurance profile and where *MIE* and *MIE*INS* are included in the constant term, $ß_0$, the reference group of the dichotorized variables.

After these coefficients are estimated, statistical testing is conducted to determine, on the one hand, if they are significant and, on the other, if they are mutually significantly higher or lower. This testing is based on the empirical hypotheses discussed previously. They are summarized in the following way:

CASE 1: $ß_2 > 0$, $ß_4 > 0$ $\Delta MID > \Delta MIE$,
      $ß_8 > ß_6$, $ß_{10} > ß_6$ $\Delta MAD > \Delta MAE$.

CASE 2: $ß_8 = ß_2 = ß_{10} = ß_4$ $\Delta MAD = \Delta MID$,
      $ß_6 = 0$ $\Delta MAE = \Delta MIE$.

Coefficients $ß_2$, $ß_4$, $ß_8$ and $ß_{10}$ are for injuries with a difficult diagnosis ($ß_2$ and $ß_8$ are for back-related injuries). There will be moral hazard if they are significantly higher than the others.

Description of the Québec Workers' Compensation Plan and Data

The workers' compensation program in Québec is primarily a public plan. It is administered by a state monopoly, the Commission de la santé et de la sécurité du travail du Québec. Supplementary private insurance is available for those who believe that insurance coverage provided by the public plan is insufficient. The public plan provides benefits equal to 90 percent of net income up to a maximum that is defined by the claimant's gross annual earnings. For individuals earning more than the maximum, benefits are calculated by assuming that the workers' gross annual earnings are equal to the maximum. In 1987, the maximum gross earnings covered by workers' compensation was $35,500.

Compensation is exempted from income tax. There is no waiting period and the worker chooses his or her treating physician. The Commission does not audit information communicated by workers, although a medical report is necessary to get workers' compensation benefits. In addition, the employer may contest the treating physician's conclusions concerning the nature and extent of work disability.

Data used in the study were collected from claims initiated in 1987.

These data were restricted to work-related injuries involving temporary total disability. The files in the sample were closed. Claims involving self-insured employers were not included in the sample. Finally, the recovery period excludes vocational rehabilitation.

The sample of injured workers was randomly selected from a population of 210 thousand files. It contains 1,471 work-related injuries which occurred between 1 January and 31 December 1987 inclusively. To increase our understanding of different factors that may influence the number of compensation days, a sample survey was administered by an independent firm. Information was obtained on the type of job, union status, the accident period and, more important, the insurance profile of the injured worker.

For the purpose of the analysis, only 1,162 files were used since many of the selected files did not contain information on all variables, particularly on variables gathered from the survey. Moreover, some files did not correspond to a diagnosis retained for this study or there simply was not enough medical information to make a classification. Table 4 describes the main statistics of the sample.

Of the victims, 84 percent are men, and 57.6 percent are under the age of 35. Moreover, 67.4 percent of workers who suffered work-related injuries have a gross annual income lower than $25,000, and more than 6 percent have an income higher than $35,500, which is the maximum a worker receives to have workers' compensation benefits equal to 90 percent of lost income. Those with incomes higher than $35,500 receive benefits that are equal to less than 90 percent of net income. Overall, 35.2 percent of claims come from the manufacturing sector. Eighty-one percent of the injured workers have full-time, full-year jobs and 63.2 percent are members of a union. Accidents occur more frequently in the second half of the year (55 percent).

Injured workers received, on an annual basis, average compensation benefits equal to $14,585 with a maximum of $23,138.64, which is the amount awarded to an individual with three dependents, who has a gross income greater than or equal to $35,500. The average annual number of days of compensation is 26.

More than 48 percent of the diagnoses are minor (fractures, contusions, and amputations without permanent partial disability) easy diagnoses; 9.4 percent are lower back pain and 34.5 percent sprains. The last two categories include diagnoses that are both related and unrelated to back injury.

Finally, the insurance profile variable (INS) has a frequency of 60.5 percent while the consumption profile (CONS) has a frequency of 37.6 percent. As mentioned in the introduction, there was no structural change in the insurance plan during the period of analysis. Insurance

Table 4

Observed Frequencies

	Frequency	Percentage		Frequency	Percentage
Age			Diagnostic (continued)		
Under 25 years old	291	25.0	Lower back pain	43	3.7
25-34	379	32.6	(no back)		
35-44	257	22.1	Fractures	88	7.6
45-54	164	14.1	Sprain (back)	226	19.4
55 and above	71	6.1	Sprain (no back)	175	15.1
(Average: 34.50 years)					
			Gross annual income		
Gender			Under $15,000	231	19.9
Male	976	84.0	$15,000 - $20,000	339	29.2
Female	186	16.0	$20,000 - $25,000	213	18.3
			$25,000 - $30,000	177	15.2
Economic sector			$30,000 - $35,500	131	11.3
Primary	40	3.4	$35,500 and up	71	6.1
Construction	111	9.6	(Average: $21,476)		
Transportation	341	29.3			
Commerce	159	13.7	Number of days of compensation		
Administration	85	7.3	Under 25 days	893	76.9
Manufacturing	409	35.2	25-50	107	9.2
Others	17	1.5	50-75	55	4.7
			75-100	26	2.2
Type of job			100-150	39	3.4
Occasional	76	6.5	150-200	17	1.5
On call	46	4.0	200-250	5	0.4
Seasonal	99	8.5	250-300	6	0.5
Yearly basis	941	81.0	300 days or more	14	1.2
			(Average: 25.94 days)		
Union (Member = 1)	734	63.2			
			Annual amounts of compensation		
Accident period			Under $10,000	182	15.7
1st trimester	238	20.5	$10,000 - $15,000	461	39.7
2nd trimester	283	24.4	$15,000 - $20,000	328	28.2
3rd trimester	324	27.9	$20,000 - $23,138.64	191	16.4
4th trimester	317	27.3	(Average: $14,585)		
Diagnostic			Insurance profile	703	60.5
Contusion,	564	48.5			
amputation, WPPD and friction burn			Consumption profile	437	37.6
Lower back pain	66	5.7			
(back)			Relapse	68	5.9

coverage varies among individuals in the sample for many reasons. The insurance profile variable (*INS*) is a measure of insurance coverage or the extent to which benefits replace lost income. Specifically, the variable indicates those individuals who are most likely to have real insurance coverage greater than 90 percent of their net salary. Classification of a claimant in the 'insurance profile' category was based on four criteria: (1) the claimant's spouse is in the labour force, (2) the claimant has at least one dependent, (3) the claimant worked on a part-time basis prior to injury, and (4) the claimant's true income is less than the income projected by the CSST and used for compensation. The dichotomous variable is equal to 1 when a worker has at least one of the above characteristics and zero otherwise.

The insurance profile measures variation in insurance coverage due to methods used by the CSST to compute the claimant's gross annual income, which are the basis of compensation benefits. The rationale for the first two criteria is based on the observation that (1) the CSST does not include income from the claimant's spouse or from other dependents to determine gross earnings for purposes of determining benefits and (2) income taxes are progressive, i.e., the effective marginal tax rate increases as taxable income increases. If the claimant's family income includes income from other sources (i.e., the claimant's spouse or other dependents), the tax rate used to compute benefits is lower than the rate used to compute pre-injury taxes. (Recall that compensation benefits are based on the claimant's income net of taxes, so that benefits increase as the applicable tax rate declines.) If not, then the tax rate used to calculate benefits is equal to the rate used to determine pre-injury taxes. As the 'benefit' tax rate increases relative to the pre-injury rate, the ratio of benefits to pre-injury wages declines.

The third criterion is motivated by the fact that the CSST places a floor on the gross annual income used to compute compensation benefits. In no case may the gross annual income used to compute benefits be less than the gross annual income determined on the basis of the minimum wage in effect when the injury occurred. The income of part-time workers is more likely to be below this floor (the gross annual income determined on the basis of the minimum wage) than the income of full-time employees. Consequently, insurance coverage for part-time workers is more likely to be higher than the coverage for full-time workers.

Finally, the fourth criterion is based on the observation that the CSST may project gross annual earnings to be higher than a claimant's actual earnings for reasons other than those covered by the first three criteria, e.g., the claimant is a seasonal worker or the claimant is working for more than one employer. If the claimant is working for more than one employer, his or her income replacement indemnity is based on the job with the most remunerative income that he or she is no longer able to perform, even if the claimant was injured while working at the lower paying job.

Table 5 presents the average number of days of compensation by diagnosis and insurance profile. One can observe that individuals with greater insurance coverage who satisfy one of the four criteria determining *INS*, the insurance profile variable, consume disability benefits

Table 5

Average Days of Compensation, Insurance Profile and Types of Injury

Diagnostic	All individuals (1)	Individuals with insurance profile (2)	Individuals without insurance profile (3)	Diff. (2-3)/3
Contusions, amputations WWPD, friction burn	14	15	13	+15%
Lower back pain (back)	25	31	12	+158%
Lower back pain (no back)	15	17	13	+31%
Fractures	80	82	75	+9%
Sprains (back)	43	50	30	+67%
Sprains (no back)	19	19	19	0%
Total	26	30	21	+43%

Average number of days of compensation according to the consumption profile
With insurance profile: 27.75
Without insurance profile: 24.85

for a longer period than individuals with less insurance coverage. However, when the average length of compensation by diagnosis is compared, the variation is not necessarily proportional. Only a multivariate regression analysis can identify the significant variation due to moral hazard.

Statistical Results

Tables 6 and 8 present regression results for the number of days of compensation, while Table 7 reports gross annual income.[8] These results are comparable with those obtained by Dionne and St-Michel (1991) even if the latter study had fewer variables in the regression specification and considered gross annual income to be exogenous. The results for the control variables, age and sex, are consistent: age positively affects duration while gender is not statistically significant. Moreover, gross annual income is not significant in the equations reported in Tables 6 and 8, while it was significant in the previous study. Differences are observed in economic sector variables, but they are not significant. It is interesting to observe that duration of claims filed by workers with seasonal jobs are significantly greater than those filed by other workers, a result predicted by many researchers who have documented that workers' compensation benefits are more generous

8 Two additional variables were used as instruments: $SCOL_i$ which is the degree of scolarity for $i = 1, 2, 3, 4$ where 1 is for primary, 2 for secondary, 3 for CEGEP and 4 for university; and Experience which measures the total number of years of experience in the labour market.

Table 6
Regression # 1
Ln (Days of Compensation) as a Function of Explanatory Variables[1]
(Two-Stage Least Squares)(Québec, 1987)

Explanatory variable	Coefficient	T-ratio	Explanatory variable	Coefficient	T-ratio
Intercept	-3.8842	-0.607	Accident period		
Age (ln)	0.4518	1.823*	1st trimester	0.1129	1.010
Gender (Male = 1)	-0.2154	-0.815	2nd trimester	0.0858	0.801
Income (ln)	0.4186	0.553	4th trimester	-0.0054	-0.054
Economic sector			*MIDB*	0.4939	2.991**
Primary	0.0789	0.362	*MIDNB*	0.1530	0.763
Construction	-0.1973	-1.352	*MAE*	1.8628	12.311***
Transportation	0.0366	0.377	*MADB*	0.9060	8.570***
Commerce	0.2334	1.233	*MADNB*	0.3477	3.028***
Administration	-0.2530	-1.574	Insurance profile (*INS*)	-0.1065	-0.679
Others	0.2804	0.891	Consumption profile	0.1377	1.567
Type of job			(*CONS*)		
Occasional	-0.0294	-0.162	*RELAPSE*	1.5248	9.556***
On call	0.0820	0.379	R^2		.2616
Seasonal	0.4321	2.770***	*F*		16.781
Yearly basis (omitted)			*n*		1162.
Union (Member = 1)	-0.1917	-0.970			

* Significant at 90 percent. ** Significant at 95 percent. *** Significant at 99 percent.
[1] Manufacturing and 3rd trimester are omitted.

Table 7
Regression # 1a
Ln (Gross Annual Income) as a Function of Explanatory Variables[1]
(Québec, 1987)

Explanatory variable	Coefficient	T-ratio	Explanatory variable	Coefficient	T-ratio
Intercept	8.5469	44.742***	*MIDB*	-0.0185	-0.419
Age (ln)	0.2072	3.595***	*MIDNB*	-0.0015	-0.029
Gender (Male = 1)	0.3101	10.320***	*MAE*	0.0421	1.074
Economic sector			*MADB*	0.0407	1.503
Primary	-0.0264	-0.454	*MADNB*	0.0421	1.423
Construction	0.0596	1.619	Insurance profile (*INS*)	0.1768	8.083***
Transportation	-0.0417	-1.657*	Experience	0.0045	2.597***
Commerce	-0.1976	-6.058***	Education		
Administration	-0.0028	-0.064	*SCOL2*	0.1011	3.081***
Others	0.0355	0.424	*SCOL3*	0.1151	2.719***
Type of job			*SCOL4*	0.2698	4.397***
Seasonal	-0.0880	-2.355***	Consumption profile	-0.0551	-2.644***
Occasional	-0.1320	-3.252***	(*CONS*)		
On call	-0.1266	-2.454***	*RELAPSE*	-0.0230	-0.541
Union (Member=1)	0.2271	10.343***	R^2		.3782
Accident period			*F*		27.150
1st trimester	0.0329	1.129	*n*		1162
2nd trimester	-0.0393	-1.416			
4th trimester	0.0235	0.872			

* Significant at 90 percent. ** Significant at 95 percent. *** Significant at 99 percent.
[1] Manufacturing, yearly basis, 3rd trimester, *MIE* and *SCOL1* are omitted.

Table 8
Regression # 2
Ln (Days of Compensation) as a Function of Explanatory Variables[1]
(Two-Stage Least Squares)(Québec, 1987)

Explanatory variable	Coefficient	T-ratio	Explanatory variable	Coefficient	T-ratio
Intercept	-4.7555	-0.741	MIDB	0.0974	0.333
Age (ln)	0.4329	1.742	MIDNB	0.0053	0.018
Gender (Male = 1)	-0.2249	-0.850	MAE	1.5626	6.281***
Income (ln)	0.5263	0.693	MADB	0.4867	2.834***
Economic Sector			MADNB	0.4283	2.371***
Primary	0.0641	0.293	Insurance profile (INS)	-0.3053	-1.724*
Construction	-0.2241	-1.531	MIDNB*INS	0.2627	0.655
Transportation	0.0322	0.332	MIDB*INS	0.6022	1.697*
Commerce	0.2443	1.288	MAE*INS	0.4624	1.523
Administration	-0.2573	-1.598	MADNB*INS	-0.1146	-0.510
Others	0.2269	0.719	MADB*INS	0.6493	3.113***
Type of job			RELAPSE	1.5564	9.726***
Occasional	0.0028	0.016	Consumption profile	0.1522	1.727*
On call	0.0978	0.451	(CONS)		
Seasonal	0.4594	2.936**	R^2		.2693
Union (Member = 1)	-0.2143	-1.082	F		14.384
Accident period			n	1162	
1st trimester	0.1006	0.897			
2nd trimester	0.0840	0.782			
4th trimester	0.0106	0.105			

* Significant at 90 percent. ** Significant at 95 percent. *** Significant at 99 percent.
1 Manufacturing, yearly basis and 3rd trimester are omitted.

than unemployment insurance compensation. In Québec workers' compensation benefits are exempted from income tax, while unemployment benefits are not.[9] Union member status does not significantly affect the length of recovery. Coefficients for injury type have similar patterns in both studies.

The coefficient for the insurance-profile variable (INS) in Table 6 is not statistically different from zero, which implies that workers, who satisfy at least one of the four characteristics that define this variable, do not have a longer recovery time. However, it is not clear that the variation is the same for all diagnoses. In fact, the insurance-profile variable has two effects: a negative wealth effect and a positive moral hazard effect. Although we control for income, the number of dependents and part-time components of the insurance-profile variable may

9 For example, a worker without dependents and with an annual income of $22,021 has a net unemployment benefits/net income from work ratio of .718 and a workers' compensation benefits/net income from work ratio of .953 which is greater than .90 because adjustments are made for the monetary costs of going to work (Guindon, 1988). See also Fortin and Lanoie (1992) on this issue.

reduce the duration of compensation for all injuries, while the moral hazard effect may increase duration. In fact, the above empirical hypothesis suggests that larger variations should be observed for diagnoses that are difficult to verify. A second regression was conducted to separate these two effects and to analyze the relative moral hazard components of different diagnoses.

Table 8 shows that the only insurance-diagnosis pairs with a positive and significant coefficient involve injuries that are difficult to diagnose (lower back pain and sprains with back-related injuries). The results of the different tests (available) confirm the presence of moral hazard for these two pairs. Moreover, the coefficient of insurance profile is negative and significant when interaction variables are present, which suggests that only the wealth effect remains. Finally, both *RELAPSE* and Consumption Profile (*CONS*) have a positive effect on the number of days of compensation. As mentioned above *RELAPSE* controls for many events for a given file while Consumption Profile (*CONS*) controls for those workers who extend the duration of disability benefits for reasons other than the type of moral hazard studied in this chapter. A positive sign for these variables is intuitively acceptable. Results from the income equation (Table 7) are similar to those obtained in other studies: age and sex have positive coefficients while seasonal, occasional, and on-call jobs have negative ones. Moreover greater work experience and higher levels of education are positively related to income levels.

Our results confirm the existence of moral hazard for lower back pain (back) and sprains in the sample studied. It has been shown that the change in the workers' compensation insurance profile (*INS*, insurance coverage) increased the recovery period to a greater degree for injuries that are difficult to diagnose (back-related) than for other injuries. The coefficient of the insurance profile is negative and statistically significant when changes in severity-diagnosis pairs are controlled, which implies that the differences in insurance benefits include a significant negative wealth effect for those claimants who have dependents and work part time.

Summary and Conclusion

An empirical test to measure the significance of moral hazard in the Québec workers' compensation program has been proposed. The analysis was limited to the definition of moral hazard related to the incentive for the agent to misrepresent the occurrence of the realized income or accident. The public plan is based on two characteristics, which are standard in many other programs in North America: 1) it offers partial insurance coverage (a maximum of 90 percent of net income) for labour income lost due to occupational injuries, although many workers may have higher effective insurance coverage rates when income tax considerations and private insurance programs are taken into account; 2) it does not audit the information communicated by the agent, although a medical report is necessary to receive compensation benefits.

The statistical results show that the length of the recovery period increases with an increase in insurance coverage for back-related injuries, lower back pain, and sprains, but does not increase for all other injuries.

The statistical results have important policy implications. As was discussed in the theoretical part of the paper, partial insurance coverage is not a sufficient tool for optimal resource allocation when both forms of moral hazard are simultaneously present. Selective auditing procedures were shown to be optimal in this circumstance. This conclusion is particularly strong when the insurance system provides reimbursement that is proportional to the monetary value of leisure days (or days of absence) as do many workers' insurance plans. The empirical procedure developed in this study permits the identification of diagnoses for which this particular resource allocation problem is significant and, therefore, can be used to set an optimal auditing strategy. The empirical results show that priority should be given to back-related injuries because auditing is costly.

References

Arnott, R.J. 1992. Moral hazard and competitive insurance markets. In *Contributions to insurance economics*, edited by G. Dionne, pp.325–59. Boston: Kluwer Academic Press.

Arrow, K.J. 1963. Uncertainty and the welfare economics of medical care. *American Economic Review* 53:941–73.

Bond, E.W. and K.J. Crocker. 1993. Hard ball and the soft touch: The economics of optimal insurance contracts with costly state verification and endogenous monitoring costs. Working paper, Department of Economics, Pennsylvania State University.

Boyer, M. and G. Dionne. 1989. An empirical analysis of moral hazard and experience rating. *Review of Economics and Statistics* 71:128–34.

Burton, John F., Jr. 1985. Disability benefits for back disorders in workers' compensation. In *Arthritis in society: The impact of musculoskeletal disease*, edited by N.M. Hadler and L.D. Gillings, pp.89–103. London: Butterworths.

Butler, Richard J. 1983. Wage and injury rate response to shifting levels of workers' compensation. In *Safety and the work force: Incentives and disincentives in workers' compensation*, edited by John D. Worrall, pp.61–86. Ithaca, NY: ILR Press.

Butler, Richard J. and John D. Worrall. 1983. Workers' compensation benefit and injury claims rates in the seventies. *Review of Economics and Statistics* 65:580–89.

———. 1985. Work injury compensation and the duration of nonwork spells. *Economic Journal* 95:714–24.

Chelius, James R. 1982. The influence of workers' compensation on safety incentives. *Industrial and Labor Relations Review* 35:235–42.

Cooper, R. and T.W. Ross. 1985. Product warranties and double moral hazard. *Rand Journal of Economics* 16:103–113.

Cousineau, J.-M., R. Lacroix and A.-M. Girard. 1989. Occupational hazard and wage compensating differentials. Université de Montréal, Montréal. Mimeographed.

Derrig, R.A. and L.K. Krauss. 1992. First steps to fight workers' compensation fraud. Working paper, Insurance Fraud Bureau of Massachusetts.

Dionne, G. 1981. Moral hazard and search activity. *Journal of Risk and Insurance* 48:422–35.

———. 1982. Moral hazard and state-dependent utility function. *Journal of Risk and Insurance* 49:405–22.

———. 1984a. Search and insurance. *International Economic Review* 25:357–67.

———. 1984b. The effects of insurance on the possibilities of fraud. *Geneva Papers on Risk and Insurance* 9:304–322.

Dionne, G. and P. St-Michel. 1991. Workers' compensation and moral hazard. *Review of Economics and Statistics* 83:236–44.

Dionne, G. and P. Viala. 1992. Optimal design of financial contracts and moral hazard. Working paper no.9219, Economics Department, Université de Montréal.

Dionne, G., A. Gibbens, and P. St-Michel. 1993. An economic analysis of insurance fraud. Working paper no.9310, Economics Department, Université de Montréal.

Doherty, N. 1979. National insurance and absence from work. *Economic Journal* 89:50–63.

Drèze, J.H. 1961. Les fondements logiques de l'utilité cardinale et de la probabilité-subjective. In *La Décision*, Colloques Internationaux du Centre National de la Recherche Scientifique, Paris, 25–30 Mai 1960, pp. 73–87. Paris: Editions du Centre National de la Recherche Scientifique. (English translation published in *Essays on economic decisions under uncertainty*. Cambridge, MA: Cambridge University Press, 1987.)

Fenn, Paul. 1981. Sickness duration, residual disability, and income replacement: An empirical analysis. *Economic Journal* 91:158–73.

Fortin, Bernard and Paul Lanoie. 1992. Substitution between unemployment insurance and workers' compensation. *Journal of Public Eonomics* 49:287–312.

Grossman, S.J. and O.D. Hart. 1983. An analysis of the principal-agent problem. *Econometrica* 51:7–45.

Guindon, D. 1988. Une approche au problème de simultaneité des *gaps* sur le marché des biens et du travail: Une application à l'estimation des taux d'activité et des taux de chomage. Cahier de recherche, Direction des études structurelles, Ministère des Finances du Québec.

Hadler, N.M. 1989. Disabling backache in France, Switzerland, and the Netherlands: Contrasting sociopolitical constraints on clinical judgement. *Journal of Occupational Medicine* 31:823–31.

Holmstrom, B. 1979. Moral hazard and observability. *Bell Journal of Economics* 10:74–91.

Kihlstrom, R. and M. Pauly. 1971. The role of insurance in the allocation of risk. *American Economic Review* 61:371–79.

Kniesner, T.J. and J.D. Leeth. 1989. Separating the reporting effects from the injury rate effects of workers' compensation insurance: A hedonic simulation. *Industrial and Labor Relations Review* 42:288–93.

Lanoie, Paul. 1988. Occupational safety and health: The problem of double moral hazard. Economics Department, Université Laval. Mimeographed.

———. 1989. The impact of occupational safety and health regulation on the incidence of workplace accidents: Québec 1982–1987. Economics Department, Université Laval. Mimeographed.

Leigh, J.P. 1989. Specific illnesses, injuries, and job hazards associated with absenteeism. *Journal of Occupational Medicine* 31:792–97.

Leigh, J.P. and R.M. Sheetz. 1988. Prevalence of back pain among full-time US workers. Working paper, Department of Economics, San Jose State University.

Marshall, J.M. 1976. Moral hazard. *American Economic Review* 66:880–90.

Melumad, N.D. and D. Mookherjee. 1989. Delegation as commitment: The case of income tax audits. *Rand Journal of Economics* 20:139–64.

Mookherjee, D. and I. Png. 1989. Optimal auditing insurance and redistribution. *Quarterly Journal of Economics* 104:205–28.

Moore, M.J. and W.K. Viscusi. 1992. Social insurance in market contexts: Implications of the structure of workers' compensation for job safety and wages. In *Contributions to insurance economics*, edited by G. Dionne, pp.399–422. Boston: Kluwer Academic Press.

Moretz, S. 1987. Back injuries: Diagnosis is difficult. *Occupational Hazards* 49:47–49.

Parsons, D.O. 1989a. Social insurance with imperfect state verification. Working paper, Ohio State University.

———. 1989b. Self-screening mechanisms in targeted public transfer programs. Working paper, Ohio State University.

Ruser, J.H. 1986. Workers' compensation insurance, experience rating, and occupational injuries. *Rand Journal of Economics* 16:487–503.

Shavell, S. 1979. On moral hazard and insurance. *Quarterly Journal of Economics* 93:541–62.

Spence, M. and R. Zeckhauser. 1971. Insurance, information and individual action. *American Economic Review* 61:380–87.

Spitzer, W.O. et al. 1987. Scientific approach to the assessment and management of activity-related spinal disorders: A monograph for clinicians. Report of the Québec task force of spinal disorders. *Spine, European Edition* 12, Supplement 1:1–59.

Staten, M.E.E. and J. Umbeck. 1982. Information costs and incentives to shirk: Disability compensation of air traffic controllers. *American Economic Review* 73:1023–37.

Townsend, R. 1979. Optimal contracts and competitive markets with costly state verification. *Journal of Economic Theory* 22:265–93.

———. 1988. Information constrained insurance: The revelation principle extended. *Journal of Monetary Economics* 21:411–50.

Viscusi, W.K. and M.J. Moore. 1987. Workers' compensation: wage effects, benefit inadequacies, and the value of health losses. *Review of Economics and Statistics* 69:249–61.

Weisberg, H.I. and R.A. Derrig. 1991. Fraud and automobile insurance: A report on bodily injury claims in Massachusetts. *Journal of Insurance Regulation* 9:497–541.

Winter, R.A. 1992. Moral hazard in insurance contracts. In *Contributions to insurance economics*, edited by G. Dionne, pp.61–96. Boston: Kluwer Academic Press.

Worrall, John D. and David Appel. 1982. The wage replacement rate and benefit utlization in workers' compensation insurance. *Journal of Risk and Insurance* 49:361–71.

Worrall, John D., David Appel, and Richard J. Butler. 1987. Sex, marital status, and medical utilization by injured workers. *Journal of Risk and Insurance* 54:27–44.

Experience Rating of Workers' Compensation Insurance Premiums and the Duration of Workplace Injuries

Boris Kralj

Experience rating is a workers' compensation pricing scheme which attempts to more closely associate what an employer pays in workers' compensation insurance premiums with the employer's actual accident claims record. Over the last decade, most Canadian jurisdictions have recognized that establishing workers' compensation premium rates using the traditional collective or pooled risk approach results in economic disincentives for occupational health and safety. The pooled risk mechanism provides very little, if any, incentive for individual firms to allocate resources to activities that reduce workplace hazards or the progress of claimants' recovery from injury. With experience rating, the insurance premium of *each individual firm* may be higher or lower than the basic rate for the *industry group* to which it belongs. This is in contrast to a purely collective liability scheme in which all employers in a particular industry group pay the same premium, per $100 of payroll, based on the accident experience of the group as a whole.

The basic goal of experience rating is to modify firm-specific behaviour toward improving workplace safety through a price mechanism, specifically through the application of a refund or surcharge to the basic workers' compensation annual premium. Firms with below average accident claim cost records pay lower premiums than firms with above average accident experience. In effect, experience rating represents a regulatory mechanism which taxes a firm on the basis of its safety record. By charging employers something for relatively poor performance, an economic incentive for safety is added to the other incen-

Note: The author is indebted to the Workers' Compensation Board of Ontario (WCB) for providing access to data. The opinions expressed in this paper are those of the author and do not necessarily reflect the position or policies of the WCB. The constructive and helpful comments of Richard Butler and John F. Burton, Jr. are gratefully acknowledged. The usual caveat applies.

tives that may be present.[1] The primary objective of experience rating is to reduce accident frequency and severity (duration of disability). Concurrently, experience rating attempts to introduce more equity in the way workers' compensation costs are allocated among employers.

Workers' compensation experience rating is available in some form to at least some industry groups in nine out of twelve Canadian jurisdictions.[2] The majority of these programs have been set up or have undergone major revision in the last decade. Although available for some time in the United States, experience rating is a relatively new feature of Canadian workers' compensation. In Ontario, over 70 percent of employers are in industries that are experience rated; experience rating in Ontario has been elective (by industry) rather than mandatory as in most other jurisdictions. In 1992, the Ontario Workers' Compensation Board (WCB) operated two separate experience-rating programs, the New Experimental Experience Rating (NEER) program and the Council Amended Draft-7 (CAD-7) program. Both of these programs were introduced in 1984.

Duration on benefit is clearly a significant factor determining the overall cost of the workers' compensation system. In 1991, about 13 million work days were lost in Ontario due to work related accidents. The vast majority of these days were lost due to injuries that resulted in temporary total compensation (92 percent). Total award costs for temporary total compensation exceeded $900 million in 1991. In that same year, the average daily claim cost for temporary compensation was approximately $75. The estimated lifetime cost of the average temporary total compensation claim was about $5,400. As illustrated in Figure 1, average claim duration has been increasing steadily over the past decade. At the same time accident frequency rates, defined as the number of lost-time injuries (LTIs) per 100 employees, has been relatively stable. In fact, since 1987, the accident frequency has decreased while average claim duration and cost have not only increased but accelerated.

A number of employer responses to experience rating, such as the provision of light duty/modified work and rehabilitation programs to

1 The philosophical underpinning of experience rating is common to most insurance schemes. Homeowners will be familiar with questions concerning the nature of the construction of their house and the distance to the nearest fire hydrant on their applications for household fire insurance protection. Automobile owners know that their past accident and driving conviction records, as well as the type of car they drive, will influence the rate they must pay for automobile insurance coverage. Individuals purchasing life insurance are often required to submit to a medical examination, and their previous health history becomes an important part of the calculation of their premium. Each of these provides an example of experience rating at work in rate setting.

2 Including British Columbia, Alberta, Saskatchewan, Manitoba, Ontario, Québec, Newfoundland, New Brunswick, and the Yukon.

Figure 1
Accident Frequency Rate and Average Claim Duration in
Ontario, 1980-1990

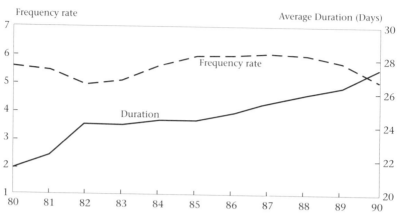

injured workers, can be expected to affect the duration of disability and workers' compensation system costs (see Krueger 1990 and Kralj 1994). Therefore, in this chapter, the impact of the introduction of workers' compensation premium experience rating on the duration of claims is examined. Specifically, the duration on disability benefits of accident claims reported in the Ontario construction industry at two points in time are analyzed. First, during a period when individual employers were experience rated, and second, during a period when construction firms paid workers' compensation insurance rates that were determined by the traditional pooled or collective risk approach. As a result, a comparison of duration on disability benefits of injury claims at those two points—before and after the introduction of the CAD-7 experience-rating program in the construction industry—will provide a test of the effect of experience rating on claim duration. Details concerning the CAD-7 experience-rating program formula are provided in an Appendix.

The research reported in this chapter is only the fourth investigation of the impact of experience rating of workers' compensation insurance premiums on injury duration, and the first conducted in the Canadian context utilizing micro-level claim data.

Hypothesis to be Tested and Literature Summary

For any level of output, an experience-rated firm will have stronger incentives to undertake a program to reduce accident claim costs than will an otherwise identical firm whose insurance premiums are not experience rated. The major hypothesis investigated is that experience-rated firms will be more likely to undertake initiatives such as the provision of modified work, light duty and rehabilitation programs, and monitoring of injured workers' recovery progress than nonexperience-rated firms. As a result, experience-rated firms will experience relatively shorter disability claim duration spells and corresponding claim-cost reductions. They are expected to implement such activities because the relatively lower claim costs are translated, through the experience-rating formula, into lower insurance premiums and hence lower labour costs. In other words, experience-rated employers bear a higher marginal cost of claims, compared to nonexperience-rated firms whose premiums are not adjusted according to individual claim costs.

Economic research on the workers' compensation system as a whole has been relatively scarce compared to research examining other major social programs, such as unemployment insurance. Despite the pervasiveness of workers' compensation experience rating across the United States and Canada, the effects of these programs on employer behaviour have received little attention from empirical researchers. This is somewhat surprising given the public policy implications. There are only ten published studies of the impact of experience rating.[3] The vast majority of these studied the effect of experience rating on injury incidence and only three examine the Canadian experience. Three studies investigated some aspect of the relationship between experience rating and disability duration.[4]

Chelius and Kavanaugh (1988) were the first to consider the effect of insurance premium rate-setting methods on claim duration. They studied, within a quasi-experimental setting, the impact of a switch in workers' compensation insurance coverage—from insurance purchased from a private insurance carrier to self-insurance by the employer—on injury rates and severity (duration on temporary disability benefits).[5] They collected data on two New Jersey community colleges on a quarterly basis for the period from 1979 to 1984. Ordinary least squares estimation of a duration equation revealed a negative and statistically sig-

3 These include Hyatt and Kralj (1995), Bruce and Atkins (1993), Lanoie (1992), Moore and Viscusi (1990), Ruser (1985, 1991), Kniesner and Leeth (1989), Chelius and Kavanaugh (1988), Worrall and Butler (1988), and Chelius and Smith (1983). The first three studies utilize Canadian data.

4 The vast majority of disability duration studies focus on the impact of benefit levels. For example, Fenn (1981), Butler and Worrall (1985), Worrall and Butler (1985), Johnson and Ondrich (1990), Gardner (1991), Dionne and St. Michel (1991) and Meyer, Viscusi and Durbin (1990). In the majority of studies the estimated elasticities of duration with respect to benefits range from +0.18 to +0.90. For a more complete summary, refer to Smith (1992).

5 Employers who are self-insured pay for the entire cost of claims, so that self-insured employers are fully (100 percent) experience-rated.

nificant relationship between a period of self-insurance and claim duration. While this result was statistically significant it is nevertheless based on a relatively small sample of only 54 observations.

Krueger (1990) utilized a micro-level data set consisting of approximately 27 thousand temporary total disability claims from administrative records in Minnesota to study the determinants of disability spell duration. Based on ordinary least squares estimation of a semi-logarithmic model he found that injured workers of self-insured (or perfectly experience-rated) firms tend to return to work sooner than workers of imperfectly experience-rated firms who suffer similar injuries. Specifically, Krueger's results indicate that the average duration of claims for self-insured firms is 10 percent shorter than claim duration for non-self-insured employers.

Lanoie (1992), utilizing average industry level data from Québec, found no support for the hypothesis of a negative relationship between experience rating and claim duration. Lanoie attempted to gauge the effect of experience rating at the aggregate industry level; he concluded that the experience rating of workers' compensation premiums had a *positive* and statistically significant effect on claim duration.[6] He provided no explanation for this unexpected result.

Descriptive Statistics and Analysis

The eleven rate groups that are covered by the CAD-7 program (construction industry) comprise approximately 45 thousand firms who together employ over 200 thousand workers. The vast majority of covered firms are quite small; only about 1 percent of them employ 50 or more workers. As indicated in Table 1, workers' compensation assessment rates for these industries vary substantially from a low of $5.99 per $100 of assessable payroll for Mechanical and Electrical Contractors to a high of $23.28 per $100 of assessable payroll for the Wrecking industry. In 1990, over 14,000 lost-time accidents were reported for the construction sector.

In 1992, 26,317 construction sector employers received CAD-7 program rebates averaging $2,265, and 7,075 employers paid an average surcharge of $2,321. It is projected that, in 1993, the CAD-7 experience-rating program will redistribute approximately $71 million in assessment revenue. About $20 million will be collected in premium surcharges from construction industry employers with relatively poor accident records and approximately $51 million will be redistributed to

---

6 Lanoie's experience-rating measure was the number of rate groups used to determine employer assessments for each industry.

Table 1

CAD-7 Program Summary Information

Rate group	No. of firms[1] Total	No. of firms[1] Large[2]	Number of workers[1]	Assessment rate[3]	Number of LTIs[3]
736 Road builders	1,015	42	10,581	6.60	477
744 Sidewalks	363	1	1,498	8.23	109
753 Sewers	2,344	60	16,403	12.25	1,114
761 Tunnelling	12	0	105	11.73	8
809 Steel erection	144	3	879	23.26	122
827 Heavy installation	822	16	4,643	10.10	456
836 Breakwaters, canals	183	3	927	10.69	84
854 General construction	7,942	150	49,731	9.68	3,409
859 Wrecking	84	3	291	23.28	23
864 Mechanical & electrical contractors	29,313	238	115,083	5.99	7,973
873 Painting & decorating	2,912	6	7,330	8.64	496
Total	45,134	522	207,471	n.a.	14,271

[1] Based on 1989 data.
[2] Firms employing 50 or more workers.
[3] Based on 1990 data. LTI—lost-time injury.

employers with relatively good accident records through premium refunds.

Table 2 reports some basic information on construction industry LTI accident claims prior to the introduction of the CAD-7 experience-rating program (i.e., 1983) and after the program was introduced (i.e., 1988). The post-CAD-7 claims exhibit longer average duration than the pre-CAD-7 claims. The average number of days on temporary total disability benefits increased by almost two days or 6 percent. Since the mean of the untransformed data is susceptible to large changes due to a few observations, two other measures of the central tendency of the duration distribution are presented: the median and the mean of the natural logarithm. The median claim duration increased by three days while the mean of the logarithm of duration increased by 0.11 between 1983 and 1988.

The composition of claims—the claims mix—also changed between 1983 and 1988. In particular, contusion, crushing, bruise claims, and hearing loss claims constituted a larger share of total injuries in 1988 than in 1983. On the other hand, the proportion of fractures and back claims decreased.

The total number of workdays lost to temporary total disability in the construction sector increased from 386,000 to 581,000 between 1983 and 1988.

To account for potential changes in the composition of accident claims after the introduction of experience rating, it is desirable to con-

Table 2

Construction Industry Claim Duration and Composition, Pre-CAD-7 and Post-CAD-7

	Pre-CAD-7 (1983)	Post-CAD-7 (1988)	Difference
Claim duration (Days)			
Mean	33.22	35.15	+ 1.93
Median	17	20	+ 3.00
Mean of natural log	2.76	2.87	+ 0.11
Composition of claims(%)			
Part of body injured			
Head	7.9	8.4	+ 0.5
Neck	0.1	2.0	+ 1.9
Upper extremities	23.6	21.9	- 1.7
Back	29.6	24.9	- 4.7
Trunk (excl. backs)	6.1	9.3	+ 3.2
Lower extremities	21.7	21.4	- 0.3
Multiple parts	6.5	7.2	+ 0.7
Other	4.5	4.9	+ 0.4
Nature of injury			
Burn	2.3	1.7	- 0.6
Contusion, crushing, bruise	11.2	18.3	+ 7.1
Cut, laceration, puncture	12.4	12.3	- 0.1
Fracture	7.4	4.4	- 3.0
Scratch, abrasion	3.5	1.8	- 1.7
Sprains, strains	28.9	27.5	- 1.4
Hearing loss	2.5	14.4	+11.9
Other	31.8	19.6	-12.2
Number of claims (LTIs)	11,626	16,534	+ 4,908
Total workdays lost	386,000	581,000	+195,000

trol for covariates in estimating the response of the duration of disability to the change in the rate-setting scheme.

Estimation of the Empirical Model

Data Samples and Variables

The data used for the modelling exercise were collected from claims of the WCB. The analysis is based on claims involving lost-time temporary total disability in the construction sector. Two samples of claims were randomly selected. The first sample consists of 2,312 work-related LTIs which occurred in 1983—before the introduction of the CAD-7 experience-rating program on 1 January 1984. The second sample contains 2,095 cases of work-related LTIs occurring in 1988, the most recent consistent data available representing the post-experience-rating period.

Data from various WCB administrative files were pooled to construct the final database. These data contain a rich collection of information. Specifically, they allow control for injured worker characteristics such as age, gender, occupation, years of work experience with the accident employer, weekly compensation benefits received, geographic region, time of year injured (season), part of body injured, and nature of injury. In addition, information on the size of the accident employer was collected. Variables utilized in the modelling exercise are defined in Table 3.

The vast majority of injured workers in the overall sample are male (98.6 percent) and the average age of claimants is 33 years. The mean tenure of injured workers with their accident employer is just under 2 years and the average size (estimate by person-years) of the accident employer is 40. Moreover, the average weekly workers' compensation benefit received is $346 for the whole sample. Workers' compensation in Ontario pays compensation equal to 90 percent of pre-accident net

Table 3

Duration Modelling Variable Definitions

Name	Description
CAD-7 program	Dichotomous variable equal to 1 if the accident took place after the introduction of the CAD-7 experience-rating program (i.e., 1 January 1984).
Firm size	Size of accident employer (person years).
Age	The age of the injured worker at time of accident (years).
Experience	Injured workers tenure with accident employer prior to accident (years).
Weekly benefit	Weekly workers' compensation benefits received by injured worker (current $). In Ontario injured workers on temporary total disability benefits receive 90 percent of net pre-accident earnings.
Female	Dichotomous variable equal to 1 for female injured workers.
Married	Dichotomous variable equal to 1 for married injured workers.
Occupation	Dichotomous variable equal to 1 for white-collar injured workers.
Region	Dichotomous variable equal to 1 for workers reporting injury in the Toronto area.
Season	A vector of dichotomous variables identifying whether the accident occurred in the first, second, third (omitted), or fourth quarter of the year.
Part of body	A vector of dichotomous variables identifying the part of the body injured: wrist, hand, back, shoulder, knee, ankle, foot, leg, chest, arm, multiple parts, other trunk, other lower extremities, and head/neck (omitted).
Nature of injury	A vector of dichotomous variables identifying the nature of the injury suffered: burn, contusion/crushing and bruise, fracture, sprain/strain, freezing, hearing loss, other and cuts/lacerations and punctures (omitted).

earnings (i.e., earnings after deduction of income tax, Canada Pension Plan and Unemployment Insurance contributions) up to a specific ceiling to workers who are temporarily and totally disabled. These benefits are not subject to taxation. Furthermore, back injuries and sprains/strains are the most common injuries suffered by workers, 22 percent and 30 percent respectively. Finally, the average duration for the overall sample is 34.6 days, 33.3 days of the 1983 sample of claims and 36.1 days for the 1988 claim sample.

The dependent variable is the logarithm of the number of calendar days the claimant received temporary total (TT) disability benefits measured within a 90-day window. In other words, any spell on TT in excess of 90 days is artificially censored to be 90. This calendar-day duration measure counts all days between two dates including weekends.

Statistical Results

Artificial censoring of the data, an institutional constraint, does not pose great econometric difficulties as the degree of censoring is relatively mild—only about 5 percent of the data are censored. As a result, ordinary least squares estimation can be carried out without seriously biasing the estimates. These results, along with variable sample means and standard deviations, are shown in Table 4.

Unexpectedly, despite the theoretical prediction of an inverse relationship between the introduction or degree of experience rating and duration on benefit, the estimated coefficient of the CAD-7 experience-rating program variable is positive and statistically significant at the 6 percent level.[7] Specifically, the introduction of experience rating in the Ontario construction industry *increased* duration on benefit by 8.4 percent (i.e., exp(0.0807) – 1 = 0.084].[8] This finding of a positive relationship between experience rating and claim duration is consistent with results from Lanoie (1992) and contrary to Krueger's (1990) findings.

The coefficient of the age variable indicates that age has a positive and significant effect on the duration on total temporary disability benefits. This result is similar to findings obtained by Dionne and St-Michel (1991), Butler and Worrall (1983) and Krueger (1990). The esti-

7 A model specification which included interaction terms was also estimated. Specifically, the interaction of the weekly benefits variable with the experience rating variables (i.e. weekly benefit x firm size x CAD-7) proved to be positive and statistically significant (coefficient and t-statistic of 0.0000027 and 3.1 respectively).

8 For a semi-logarithmic formulation, the coefficient on each of the continuous independent variables can be interpreted as the proportional change in duration resulting from a unit change in a specific independent variable. However, this interpretation is only strictly true for infinitesimal changes in the independent variable as noted by Thornton and Innes (1989). For a semi-logarithmic equation of the type $\ln Y = \alpha + \beta X$ the correct way to calculate a proportional change in Y from a non-infinitesimal change in X is $[\exp(\beta \Delta X) - 1]$ where β is the OLS regression coefficient. For a unit change in X, the special case of a dummy variable, the expression becomes $[\exp(\beta) - 1]$.

Table 4

Ordinary Least Squares Duration Equation Estimates, Total Sample [Dependent variable=ln(days on TT benefits)]

Explanatory variable	Model specification[1] (1)		(2)		Mean	Standard deviation
Intercept	0.7851	(6.79)	0.7704	(6.67)		
Firm characteristics						
CAD-7 program			0.0807	(1.86)	0.475	0.499
Firm size	-0.0004	(2.01)	-0.0004	(1.98)	39.92	89.86
Worker characteristics						
Age	0.0163	(9.99)	0.0167*	(10.1)	33.03	12.75
Experience	-0.0109	(2.18)	-0.0112	(2.25)	1.793	3.639
Weekly benefit	0.0023	(11.5)	0.0022*	(10.1)	346.0	104.2
Female	0.2276	(1.31)	0.2225	(1.28)	0.014	0.117
Married	0.0461	(1.07)	0.0603	(1.38)	0.612	0.487
Occupation						
White collar=1	-0.2280	(1.39)	-0.2291	(1.41)	0.015	0.121
Region						
Toronto=1	0.2320	(5.36)	0.2357*	(5.44)	0.253	0.435
Season [Quarter 3][3]						
Quarter 1	0.0524	(0.94)	0.0494	(0.88)	0.190	0.392
Quarter 2	0.0259	(0.50)	0.0240	(0.46)	0.231	0.421
Quarter 4	0.1995	(3.96)	0.2054*	(4.07)	0.273	0.446
Part of body [head/neck][3]						
Wrist	0.4359	(3.51)	0.4273*	(3.44)	0.032	0.175
Hand	0.1473	(1.31)	0.1377	(1.27)	0.048	0.214
Back	0.4774	(5.18)	0.4827*	(5.23)	0.223	0.417
Shoulder	0.5457	(4.50)	0.5396*	(4.45)	0.036	0.185
Knee	0.6152	(6.06)	0.6160*	(6.06)	0.054	0.226
Ankle	0.2369	(2.15)	0.2364	(2.14)	0.050	0.217
Foot	0.0371	(0.31)	0.0283	(0.24)	0.040	0.196
Leg	0.2033	(1.70)	0.2145	(1.80)	0.050	0.218
Chest	-0.0054	(0.04)	-0.0049	(0.04)	0.026	0.160
Arm	0.3216	(2.80)	0.3261*	(2.84)	0.048	0.214
Multiple parts	0.6339	(6.41)	0.6333*	(6.39)	0.081	0.273
Other trunk	0.6185	(4.95)	0.6221*	(4.99)	0.027	0.161
Other lower extremities	-0.0884	(0.47)	-0.0844	(0.44)	0.014	0.118
Not known	-0.2185	(1.41)	-0.2193	(1.41)	0.032	0.175
Nature of injury [cuts/lacerations and punctures][3]						
Burn	0.1662	(1.18)	0.1687	(1.19)	0.018	0.133
Contusion/crushing and bruise	-0.0295	(0.38)	-0.0395	(0.50)	0.154	0.361
Fracture	1.3335	(15.3)	1.3432*	(15.4)	0.062	0.242
Scratch	-1.1291	(8.77)	-1.1155*	(8.63)	0.027	0.163
Sprain/strain	0.2554	(3.09)	0.2546*	(3.08)	0.296	0.456
Freezing	-0.9948	(4.04)	-1.0261*	(4.10)	0.011	0.102
Hearing loss	0.6907	(7.32)	0.6646*	(6.95)	0.086	0.280
Other	0.4133	(5.24)	0.4286*	(5.41)	0.216	0.411
No. of observations	4407		4407			
R-squared	0.2284		0.2290			

* Significant at the 1 percent level.
[1] Absolute value of t-statistic is shown in parenthesis. The results include correction for heteroscedasticity, Breusch-Pagan Chi-Square(34) = 122.8 for specification (1) and 125.6 for specification (2).
[2] Mean of dependent variable = 2.80669.
[3] Reference group.

mates suggest that white-collar workers have shorter claim durations than other workers. However, the occupation variable was not statistically significant. In addition, the injured worker's marital status and gender were statistically nonsignificant variables.

Employees who work for larger employers have shorter claim durations than injured workers employed by smaller establishments. Similarly, employees who have longer tenure with the accident employer have shorter claim durations. Workers who suffered injuries in the last three months of the year experience duration spells that are about 23 percent longer than workers with injuries reported in the third quarter of the year. This finding may reflect the seasonal employment cycle observed in the construction sector.

Relative to head/neck injuries, workers suffering back injuries have claim durations that are 62 percent longer. Workers with sprain/strain injuries experience claim durations about 29 percent longer than those with cuts/lacerations and punctures.

The elasticity of duration of claims with respect to workers' compensation benefits is estimated, at the sample mean, to be 0.76 (i.e., 0.0022 x 346). This implies that a 10 percent increase or decrease in benefit levels would increase or decrease the average duration of temporary total work injuries in the construction industry by 2.6 days. As noted previously, other studies of the duration of work disability have estimated benefit elasticities in the range of +0.18 to +0.9.

Discussion of Findings

The findings indicate that the implementation of the CAD-7 experience-rating program in Ontario's construction industry has not led to the hypothesized decrease in claim duration. In fact, the results reveal that it has increased duration. Lanoie (1992) reached the same conclusion using aggregate, industry-level data from Québec. However, he provided no explanation for the finding, noting that 'There is no clear reason as to why the experience rating variable has a positive sign' (Lanoie 1992, 657).

It should be remembered that the CAD-7 experience-rating program formula, used to calculate premium refunds and surcharges, gives equal weight to the frequency of LTIs and claims cost. No-lost-time injury (NLTI) claims are not included in the experience-rating calculation and do not impact the amount of the refund or surcharge. Therefore, employers have an incentive not only to prevent the occurrence of LTIs through real safety improvements but also to fail to report them or to misreport them as NLTIs. If employers are responding to these incentives, a change will be evident in the reported levels of accidents (frequency rate) as well as in the mix or composition of reported claims.

Figure 2 depicts the accident frequency rate, defined as the number of LTIs per 100 employees, and the NLTI claim ratio for the construction industry for the period 1980 through 1990. The NLTI claim ratio is defined as the number of NLTI claims divided by the sum of NLTI and LTI claims. The accident frequency rate has decreased noticeably, from 10.4 to 7.7, since the implementation of experience rating in 1984. At the same time the NLTI ratio has increased dramatically.

The increase in the NLTI series may be indicative of one or both of the following effects. First, a 'conversion'of LTI claims to NLTI claims either through deliberate misreporting of claims by employers or through health and safety initiatives that reduce the severity of injuries that occur. Second, a rise in this series can come about through nonreporting of LTI accidents. The aggregate data depicted in Figure 2 reflects the net effect but unfortunately does not allow identification of the individual components.

It can be argued that relatively mild or less medically severe injuries are the best candidates for being 'converted' or prevented by employers. As a result, it is the relatively more severe injuries—those with longer durations—that are reported as LTIs and become a part of the employer's experience-rating record. Consequently, the average duration at the aggregate industry level increases due to the implementation of experience rating.

Once an LTI is registered on a firm's experience record, the individual, experience-rated employer has an incentive to limit claim costs by encouraging injured workers to return to work by providing a modified or light workload and implementing initiatives such as medical and vocational rehabilitation programs.

Figure 2
Ontario Construction Industry Accident Frequency Rate and NLTI Ratio, 1980-1990

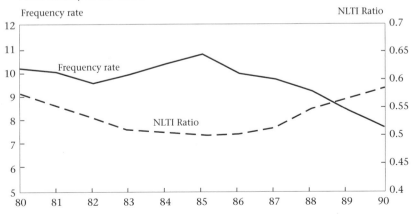

Given the above discussion, one can hypothesize that experience-rated firms may concentrate their efforts on returning more severely injured employees—those with relatively long claim durations and higher costs—back to work and off compensation benefits, rather than on those employees who are less severely disabled. To test this hypothesis the OLS duration model for various subsamples of claims representing workers with injuries with varying degrees of severity have been re-estimated. These results are presented in Table 5. For convenience, column (1) replicates the estimates for the full sample. Column (2) reports estimates of the same equation for a subset of injured workers with claim duration of 21 days or greater, while column (3) reports estimates using workers with claim durations of 28 days or greater and finally column (4) reports estimates using workers with claim durations of 35 days or more.

Table 5

OLS Duration Equation Estimates: Claim Subsamples
[Dependent variable = ln(days on temporary total disability benefits)]

	Parameter Estimates (t-statistic)			
Explanatory variable	Full sample (1)	21 days or more (2)	28 days or more (3)	35 days or more (4)
Intercept	0.7704*	3.5430*	3.8250*	4.0614*
	(6.67)	(46.9)	(56.7)	(69.3)
Firm characteristics				
CAD-7 program	0.0807	-0.0237	-0.0314	-0.0376*
	(1.86)	(1.02)	(1.58)	(2.24)
Firm size	-0.0004*	-0.0003*	-0.0002*	-0.0002*
	(1.98)	(3.00)	(2.86)	(2.69)
Worker characteristics				
Age	0.0167*	0.0009	0.0007	0.0007
	(10.1)	(1.01)	(0.97)	(1.10)
Experience	-0.0112*	-0.0040	-0.0018	-0.0033
	(2.25)	(1.43)	(0.80)	(1.58)
Weekly benefit	0.0022*	0.0011*	0.0008*	0.0006*
	(10.1)	(8.71)	(8.00)	(7.08)
Female	0.2225	0.0050	0.0151	-0.0318
	(1.28)	(0.06)	(0.22)	(0.49)
Married	0.0603	-0.0137	-0.0190	-0.0182
	(1.38)	(0.58)	(0.95)	(1.09)
Occupation	yes	yes	yes	yes
Region	yes	yes	yes	yes
Season	yes	yes	yes	yes
Part of body	yes	yes	yes	yes
Nature of injury	yes	yes	yes	yes
R-squared	0.229	0.137	0.121	0.110
Sample size	4407	2157	1886	1679

* Significant at the 5 percent level. The results also include correction for heteroscedasticity.

Experience-rating incentives affect claim durations of more severe injuries as economic theory predicts. The introduction of experience rating has *decreased* the disability spells of these relatively more severely injured workers by 3.7 percent.

Appendix

CAD-7 Program Formula

CAD-7 was introduced on 1 January 1984 to employers in the eleven rate groups that make up the construction sector. Premium rebates and surcharges are determined by considering both the accident costs and frequency rates of the individual firm relative to the industry average. Construction industry employers believe they can prevent accidents, but that the severity of accidents depends on random chance. In other words, they can control the frequency of accidents, but not, to any great extent, the cost of accidents. Under the CAD-7 formula, equal weighting is given to accident costs and accident frequency.

The refund or surcharge that CAD-7 employers receive is based on the product of their performance index (*PI*), expected cost index (*EC*), and the rating factor (*RF*). The *performance index* is the arithmetic average of the cost (*CI*) and frequency indices (*FI*). It is therefore a measure of both the number and the severity of accidents that occur in an employer's workplace. The performance index ranks a firm's accident performance on a scale from unity to negative two. If the performance index score is between zero and positive one, the firm receives a refund. If the score is between zero and negative two, the firm pays a surcharge. Thus, the refund/surcharge calculation is given by:

Refund/Surcharge = $RF*PI*EC$,

where

$PI = \frac{1}{2}(FI + CI)$

The *frequency index* is determined by comparing the actual number of compensable lost-time injuries recorded by a firm during the two most recent years to the number of compensable lost-time injuries that the employer was expected to have over the same period. No-lost-time accidents are not included in the frequency calculations. A firm that has not had any injuries over the relevant two years will have a frequency index score of unity. If the firm's actual number of injuries is the same as it's expected number of injuries, the index score will be zero. The lowest possible index score is limited to negative two.

The *cost index* is a comparison between a firm's total accident costs over the two most recent years and the total expected costs over the same period. Actual accident costs include expenditures on indemnity compensation, health care and vocational rehabilitation, as well as the capitalized value of pension awards (excluding industrial disease claims allowed after 1 January 1987). Costs are limited to accidents that have occurred in the previous five years. As with the frequency index, if a firm does not have any accident costs, the cost index score will be unity. If the firms actual costs are the same as its expected costs then the index score will be zero. The lowest possible index score is limited to negative two.

A firm's expected costs for a given year are equal to 20 percent of the assessment premium paid by the firm in the same year, plus 15 percent of the previous year's assessment, plus 11 percent of the assessment from the second previous year, plus 8 percent of the assessment from the third previous year, plus 6 percent of the assessment from the fourth previous year. A firm's assessment premiums can be used in this way because they reflect both the size of the firm's labour force, the firm's wage scale, and the average accident costs of the industry in which the firm operates.

The *rating factor* is applied to the product of the firm's performance index and expected costs to moderate the size of the refund or surcharge. The rating factor is designed so that small firms, generally those with six or fewer employees, face refunds and surcharges that are about 15 percent of what they would otherwise be. Larger firms, generally those with 25 or more employees, are rated so that they face full refunds and surcharges. For medium sized firms, the rating factor rises in direct proportion (linear) to size determined by the estimated total number of hours worked by their employees.

CAD-7 has a maximum potential refund of 60 percent of the assessment premium for a large firm and a maximum potential surcharge of 120 percent. As a result, it is considered to be a relatively aggressive program. Since CAD-7 was introduced in 1984, no additional industries have requested it.

For a more detailed discussion of the CAD-7 experience-rating program, refer to Construction Safety Association of Ontario (1986).

References

Bruce, Christopher J. and Frank J. Atkins. 1993. Efficiency effects of premium-setting regimes under workers' compensation: Canada and the United States. *Journal of Labor Economics* 11:S38–S69.

Butler, Richard J. and John D. Worrall. 1983. Workers' compensation benefit and injury claims rates in the seventies. *Review of Economics and Statistics* 65:580–89.

———. 1985. Work injury compensation and the duration of nonwork spells. *Economic Journal* 95:714–24.

Chelius, James R. and Karen Kavanaugh. 1988. Workers' compensation and the level of occupational injuries. *Journal of Risk and Insurance* 55:315–23.

Chelius, James R. and R.S. Smith. 1983. Experience rating and injury prevention. In *Safety and the work force: Incentives and disincentives in workers' compensation*, edited by John D. Worrall, pp.128–37. Ithaca, NY: ILR Press.

Dionne, G. and P. St-Michel. 1991. Workers' compensation and moral hazard. *Review of Economics and Statistics* 83:236–44.

Fenn, Paul. 1981. Sickness duration, residual disability, and income replacement: An empirical analysis. *Economic Journal* 91:158–73.

Gardner, John A. 1991. *Benefit increases and system utilization: The Connecticut experience*. Cambridge, MA: Workers' Compensation Research Institute.

Hyatt, Douglas E. and Boris Kralj. 1995. The impact of workers' compensation experience rating on employer appeals activity. *Industrial Relations* 34:95–106.

Johnson, William G. and Jan Ondrich. 1990. The duration of post-injury absences from work. *Review of Economics and Statistics* 72:578–86.

Kniesner, T.J. and J.D. Leeth. 1989. Separating the reporting effects from the injury rate effects of workers' compensation insurance: A hedonic simulation. *Industrial and Labor Relations Review* 42:288–93.

Kralj, Boris. 1994. Employer responses to workers' compensation insurance experience rating. *Relations Industrielles* 49:41–61.

Kralj, Boris and Douglas E. Hyatt. 1990. Employer appeals of workers' compensation board decisions: The impact of experience rating. In *Teaching and research in industrial relations: Proceedings of the 27th conference of the Canadian Industrial Relations Association*, edited by Allen Ponak, pp.329–37. Calgary, AB: University of Alberta.

Krueger, Alan B. 1990. Workers' compensation insurance and the duration of workplace injuries. Working Paper no. 3253, National Bureau of Economic Research, Cambridge, MA.

Lanoie, Paul. 1992. The impact of occupational safety and health regulation on the incidence of workplace accidents: Québec 1983–87. *Journal of Human Resources* 27:643–60.

Meyer, B.D., W.K. Viscusi, and D.L. Durbin. 1990. Workers' compensation and injury duration: Evidence from a natural experiment. Working Paper no.3494, National Bureau of Economic Research, Cambridge, MA.

Moore, M.J. and W.K. Viscusi. 1990. *Compensating mechanisms for job risk*. Princeton, NJ: Princeton University Press.

Ruser, John W. 1985. Workers' compensation insurance, experience rating and occupational injuries. *Rand Journal of Economics* 16:487–503.

———. 1991. Workers' compensation and occupational injuries and illnesses. *Journal of Labor Economics* 9:325–50.

Smith, Robert S. 1992. Have OSHA and workers' compensation made the workplace safer? In *Research frontiers in industrial relations and human resources*, edited by D. Lewin, O.S. Mitchell and P.D. Sherer, pp.557–86. Madison, WI: Industrial Relations Research Association, University of Wisconsin.

Thornton, R.J. and J.T. Innes. 1989. Interpreting semi-logarithmic regression coefficients in labor research. *Journal of Labor Research* 10:443–47.

Worrall, J.D. and R.J. Butler. 1985. Benefits and claim duration. In *Workers' compensation benefits: Adequacy, equity and efficiency*, edited by J.D. Worrall and David Appel, pp.57–70. Ithaca, NY: ILR Press.

———. 1988. Experience rating matters. In *Workers' compensation insurance pricing*, edited by D. Appel and P.S. Borba, pp.81–94. Boston: Kluwer.

Development of a Schedule for Compensation of Noneconomic Loss: Quality-of-Life Values vs. Clinical Impairment Ratings

Sandra Sinclair and John F. Burton Jr.

The research reported in this chapter was undertaken at the Workers' Compensation Board (WCB) of Ontario to compare two possible measures of the extent of noneconomic loss suffered by workers with permanent consequences of work injuries: quality-of-life values based on the workers' assessments of the consequences of injuries, and clinical impairment ratings based on evaluations of the injuries by medical professionals.

The consequences of any injury or disease can be categorized as temporary or permanent, a distinction that has an important bearing on the types of benefits provided by workers' compensation programs (Burton 1992). The temporary disability period extends from the onset of the injury or the disease until maximum medical improvement (MMI) has been achieved; the permanent disability period is the time following MMI.

For most injured workers MMI represents full recovery. For those workers with relatively serious injuries, several permanent consequences are possible. The permanent consequences shown in Figure 1 are the focus of most of the debate concerning the design of permanent disability benefits in a workers' compensation program.

A permanent impairment is any anatomic or functional abnormality or loss that remains after MMI. Examples of permanent impairments are an amputated limb or an enervated muscle. The impairment probably causes the worker to experience functional limitations. Performance of physical activities, such as walking, climbing, reaching, and hearing may be limited; the worker's emotional and mental performance also may be affected. Permanent impairment and functional limitations are, in many workers' compensation programs, assessed simultaneously to produce what is termed a 'permanent impairment rating'; therefore, the term 'permanent impairment' is used to encompass the resulting functional limitations.

Figure 1
Permanent Consequences of an Injury or Disease

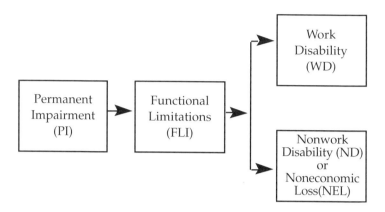

Permanent impairment can lead to disability, of which two types are recognized: work disability, the loss of earning capacity or the loss of actual earnings that results from the permanent impairment, and nonwork disability. The latter is known in Ontario as noneconomic loss. It includes the loss of the capacity to perform activities, such as recreational pursuits and household tasks, not undertaken in exchange for wages.

In Ontario, workers' compensation for the consequences of permanent impairment has, until recently, been based on a single-track, pension-award system whose underlying objective was the compensation of work disability; i.e., it replaced the lost wages suffered due to the ongoing effects of the impairment. The extent of wage loss was estimated based on the nature and degree of injury with reference to a disability rating schedule, a list of clinical conditions and the percentage of impairment associated with each condition. For example, in Ontario impairment ratings were determined with reference to the *Permanent Disability Rating Schedule* (Ontario Workers' Compensation Board 1972). Weekly benefits were equal to 90 percent of the worker's preinjury net wage multiplied by the impairment rating. For example, the total loss of a thumb received a 20 percent impairment rating, which meant that workers who lost their thumb (or use of their thumb) received weekly benefits equal to 90 percent of their preinjury wages multiplied by 20 percent. Benefits were paid on a regular basis for the rest of the worker's life. Thus, the percentage of impairment (or functional loss) was used as a proxy measure of wage loss, and the award was given regardless of the actual impact of the injury on income.

Such disability rating schedules have been used by compensation systems for many years to facilitate and standardize the process of determining the value of compensatory awards. The use of rating schedules and single-award compensation were presumably founded on the premise that within the relatively narrow spectrum of occupations covered by workers' compensation earlier in the century, a reasonably high correlation existed between the degree of physical impairment or functional loss and the extent of lost earnings. Studies in recent years (e.g., Berkowitz and Burton 1987) have shown that this correlation is low, and inequities in this approach have become apparent. Under the single-award approach, workers with similar degrees of impairment and pre-accident wages received similar permanent impairment awards, even if their post-accident income varied. Workers who returned to work received a lifetime pension for the permanent impairment in addition to their regular earned income, while those with similar impairments who were unable to return to gainful employment had only their permanent impairment pension as income. Temporary pension supplements were used in Ontario to redress the most serious cases of inequity, where the actual loss of earnings was significantly greater than would be anticipated from the nature and degree of injury. However, the supplements were not permanent and the approach was never fully satisfactory.

Bill 162, passed in July 1989, attempted to redress inequities in the Ontario system by introducing a dual award for the consequences of permanent impairment. It was recognized that permanent impairment caused by workplace injury or illness created two types of harm (see Figure 1): a reduction in the workers' capacity to enjoy their usual everyday life (noneconomic loss) and a reduction in their capacity to earn their usual income from work (work disability). The dual-award system introduced by Bill 162 included a future-economic-loss component specifically designed to compensate injured workers for their loss of earning capacity and a noneconomic loss component to compensate for the loss of enjoyment of nonworking life.

An assumed consequence of dual-award compensation for the effects of permanent impairment was a redistribution of benefits: workers with similar levels of impairment would receive a similar amount of noneconomic-loss compensation. In addition, workers with income loss, regardless of the degree of impairment, would receive an economic (future economic loss) award commensurate with their loss-of-earning capacity. With passage of Bill 162, Ontario became one of seven Canadian jurisdictions to introduce dual-award compensation for the effects of permanent impairment.

The Noneconomic-Loss Study

The noneconomic-loss study began in September 1988 when the changes to the workers' compensation program that resulted in Bill 162 were under consideration.

In reports for the Ministry of Labour and the Ontario Workers' Compensation Board, both Weiler (1980, 1986) and Burton (1986), supported continued use of a rating schedule to determine noneconomic-loss awards under the then-proposed dual-award system for Ontario, rather than examination of the actual consequences of impairment for each injured worker. Burton also recommended the American Medical Association's *Guides to the Evaluation of Permanent Impairment* (hereinafter the *Guides*)[1] in preference to other schedules he had reviewed, because of their superior operational characteristics. However, both Weiler and Burton identified a need for careful studies to examine the degree of correlation between the clinical rating values from the *Guides* and the actual nonwork disability or loss of enjoyment of life typically experienced by workers with particular impairments. This research study of noneconomic loss was designed by the Workers' Compensation Board to examine the relationship between the clinical measurement of impairment and the measurement of loss of enjoyment of life. The intent was to complete the research prior to the adoption by the Workers' Compensation Board of any schedule to determine noneconomic loss.

The specific purposes of the research were (1) to determine the appropriateness of using impairment values from the *Guides* for the loss of enjoyment of life for noneconomic-loss awards under the *Workers' Compensation Act*; (2) to use the research results to refine a schedule to measure more accurately the loss of enjoyment of life if important differences were found between the permanent impairment ratings from the *Guides* and the loss of enjoyment of life or quality-of-life values.

A Methodological Advisory Committee of international experts (Appendix A) in the fields of workers' compensation, health economics, quality-of-life measurement, and medicine was formed in late 1988. The Committee met frequently during the course of the research program to provide consultation and advice to the WCB research staff. Representatives of the Committee also participated in the presentation of the final research results to the Board of Directors of the Ontario Workers' Compensation Board in June 1991.

---

1 Burton (1986) referenced the 1984 2nd edition of the AMA *Guides*. Further references are to the 1990 edition.

In defining the purpose of a noneconomic-loss award, the concept of an award to compensate for the loss of enjoyment of life associated with permanent impairment was initially introduced in the United States by the National Commission on State Workmen's Compensation Laws in 1972 (National Commission 1972) and in Canada by Professor Weiler in 1980 (Weiler 1980). It has subsequently been adopted in several jurisdictions. However, this study apparently is the first to investigate the relationship between noneconomic-loss and rating-schedule values. All other jurisdictions that have adopted the dual-benefit approach have implicitly assumed that the rating schedules adopted by those jurisdictions provide appropriate values for the loss of quality of life.

Research Method

Quality-of-Life Values

While the measurement of quality of life (Q of L) has no precedent in the development of a workers' compensation benefits' schedule *per se*, the impact of injury on quality of life has been studied in a number of other areas where monetary valuation for a loss is the ultimate outcome. Certainly, in determining pain and suffering or general damage awards in the tort system, the concept of quality of life is an important one. The measurement of quality of life is also frequently employed in economic evaluations when examining the costs and benefits (or utility) associated with various treatment programs or health-care interventions (Drummond et al. 1987).

Quality of life is frequently measured by ascertaining the preferences of individuals or groups for particular health states or treatment outcomes. Determining the opinions or preferences of relevant populations for alternative health states is a measurement technique that has been used extensively in the development of quality of life measures in health-care, economic, and social-sciences research over the past 20 years.

The question of whose values should be considered when measuring loss of quality of life is recognized as an important issue. It has been acknowledged in research related to health care that the preferences or values of consumers of health-care services should be considered in making health-care decisions that will potentially affect them. In Ontario, the *Permanent Disability Rating Schedule* had repeatedly been criticized by the injured worker community for a number of reasons, including the lack of input from that community. For this research on the relative values of loss of enjoyment of life for different impairment conditions associated with workplace injury and disease, a survey of the opinions of injured workers who are permanently impaired was considered appropriate. However, since members of this population might also be the recipients of noneconomic-loss awards for future injuries or diseases, a potential for bias existed. Thus, a control group, representative of the general population of Ontario, was also included in the research design.

Rating-Schedule Values: The AMA Guides

The *Guides* measure permanent impairment. As used in the *Guides*, the term impairment means 'an alteration of an individual's health status that is assessed by medical means.' 'Impairment' is what is wrong with a body part or organ system and its function (American Medical Association 1990, 1). The *Guides* do not purport to measure the extent of disability associated with a particular impairment, but simply to assign a percentage rating, determined by physicians, to the degree of total body impairment resulting from a specific set of clinical observations.

The *Guides* are made up of 13 separate and independently developed 'guides' each of which represents a specific body system (e.g., the musculoskeletal system, the respiratory system, the cardiovascular system. The relative values for the various impairments reflect the collective judgment of independent groups of clinical specialists who prepared the various chapters of the *Guides*.[2]

The Noneconomic-Loss Survey

The noneconomic-loss survey, conducted between August 1988 and January 1991, involved the voluntary participation of approximately twelve thousand injured workers, plus three hundred individuals from the general population of Ontario who were matched to a subset of injured workers. Seventy-eight medical conditions covering a wide range of impairments were selected as subjects for videos. The benchmark conditions selected for the study were identified on the advice of experienced Workers' Compensation Board physicians responsible for conducting permanent impairment examinations. The selection criteria for the benchmark conditions were frequency of occurrence in Ontario workers' compensation permanent impairment cases and representativeness, both of type of injury or disease and severity of impairment, in the worker population with permanent impairment. As a result, the 78 benchmark conditions constituted impairments from a number of the 13 chapters in the *Guides*.

---

2 This procedure was confirmed in personal communication with the *Guides'* past editor, Alan J. Engelberg. The number of physicians involved in producing any one chapter was relatively small.

The videos portrayed the limitations and adaptations to lifestyle required of workers with the permanent impairment condition. A minimum of two workers per condition were portrayed in videos. A neutral commentator provided voice-over description as the workers discussed their condition with a therapist, and demonstrated their capacity to perform various daily-living tasks.

Each survey respondent spent one half-hour viewing four or six of the videos, randomly assigned, excluding videos depicting his or her condition. Respondents were asked to rate, on an 'opinion meter' scale, the loss of enjoyment of life they believed they would suffer if they had the condition portrayed. These ratings were on a scale of 0 to 100, with 0 representing normal health and 100 representing death.[3]

During the development of the final interview protocol, a number of specific methodological issues, including the effect of using video case studies instead of the written case profiles normally used in Q of L research, were examined in pilot studies. No statistically significant differences were shown between values elicited using the videos and values elicited by written descriptions of the same conditions.

Data Analysis and Research Findings

The primary focus of the analysis was to determine if, and under what circumstances, the quality of life or non-economic-loss values derived from survey participants (both injured workers and the general population control group) were different from the permanent impairment ratings from the *Guides* (AMA PI) for the 78 benchmark conditions. The survey data were examined to determine whether statistically significant differences exist between AMA PI values and the Q of L values from the two populations. A finding of consistent, significant differences between the two would lead to the conclusion that the AMA PI values are not appropriate proxy measures for determining noneconomic awards.

Group mean scores are the values commonly used in analyzing the outputs of quality-of-life measurement. Individuals vary greatly in their health-state preferences and these differences are not fully explained by

3 The end points of normal health ('for a person of your age') and death were selected primarily to ensure comparability of the Q of L values derived in this research with those of other researchers; these end points are those most commonly used by researchers to measure health-related quality of life. Also, these end points are well-defined and commonly and easily understood. Respondents readily identified individuals of their own age who enjoy good health—the positive end point of normal health. Many researchers consider the negative end point of death as more similarly conceptualized and more consistently valued than other negative states, such as coma or quadriplegia. Respondents' experience and preferences related to these types of conditions may vary considerably.

the usual demographic characteristics, such as age, socioeconomic status, religion, illness, and occupation. Nonetheless, group mean values for Q of L have been found to be remarkably stable regardless of the make-up of the group (Drummond et al. 1987). Thus, the imprecision and variability inherent in individual measurements are overcome by the use of group means. Mean respondent values from the survey for each of the benchmark conditions constitute the Q of L data used in the analysis. Table 1 shows the mean Q of L values for the 78 conditions from the injured worker and control group populations and the corresponding AMA PI value.

In interpreting the data from the non-economic-loss survey, it was recognized that there is no 'gold standard' against which to compare the correctness of the values for the purpose of measuring loss of enjoyment of life. AMA PI values and Q of L values are both subjective measures, derived from different perspectives, of the effects of the permanent consequences of injury or disease on an individual. Thus, there need not be any prior expectation that the AMA PI values and Q of L values will be the same. As well, the Q of L survey values and the AMA PI values measure different underlying concepts: noneconomic loss and impairment.

Analysis Across All Benchmark Conditions

The first analysis of the data involved investigating overall differences between the AMA PI values and the mean Q of L survey values from the two samples. Figure 2 is a graphic representation of the data for the injured-worker sample. In addition, the values from the two population samples were compared to determine if statistically significant differences existed between them. The results are shown in Table 2, and the findings from these analyses are summarized below.

- Injured-worker values of the loss of enjoyment of life are significantly higher than the associated AMA PI values for the majority of conditions. That is, workers consider the loss of enjoyment of life to be greater than the impairment value that would be assigned to the condition using the AMA *Guides*.
- Control-group values of the loss of enjoyment of life are also higher than the AMA PI values.
- Although *higher* than the AMA PI values, the control-group values are significantly *lower* than the injured-worker values for those conditions with a clinical impairment rating between 1 and 10 percent. That is, for less clinically severe conditions, the control group considers the value of the loss of enjoyment of life to be significantly lower than the matched injured-worker group.

Table 1

Comparisons of AMA PI Ratings with Mean Q of L Values for Various Videos from Injured Workers and A Control Group

Video title	AMA PI	Mean Q of L value Injured worker[1]	Control group[2]
Amp of part of tip of finger[3]	0	10 **	
Crushing to the finger[3]	0	12 **	
Single broken finger, Dom	1	16 **	15 **
Single broken finger, Non-Dom	1	13 **	11 **
Vibr induced white finger A	2	23 **	
Elbow injury Dom	3	30 **	25 **
Elbow injury Non-Dom	3	25 **	23 **
Broken wrist B, Non-Dom	3	22 **	
Broken wrist B, Dom	4	25 **	20 **
Shoulder injury B, Non-Dom	4	28 **	25 **
Shoulder injury B, Dom	5	29 **	23 **
Injury to wrist B, Dom	5	31 **	32 **
Amp of thumb, Non-Dom	5	20 **	23 **
Amp of part finger B, Dom	5	21 **	23 **
Dermatitis A	5	35 **	
Amp of thumb, Dom	5	25 **	30 **
Broken pelvis	5	57 **	70 **
Amp of part of finger B, Non-Dom	5	19 **	22 **
Broken heel bone	5	28 **	40 **
Injury to lower back D	6	52 **	
Amp of part of finger A, Non-Dom	6	21 **	25 **
Amp of part of finger A, Dom	7	22 **	
Broken wrist A, Dom	7	24 **	39 **
Broken wrist A, Non-Dom	7	25 **	
Shoulder injury D, Non-Dom	7	30 **	21 **
Shoulder injury D, Dom	7	30 **	30 **
Broken hip	7	36 **	38 **
Injury to knee joint	8	32 **	39 **
Several broken fingers B, Non-Dom	8	21 **	20 **
Broken bones in lower leg	8	35 **	41 **
Shoulder injury A, Non-Dom	8	38 **	38 **
Several broken fingers B, Dom	8	24 **	39 **
Broken ankle B	9	30 **	33 **
Injury to wrist A, Dom	9	32 **	37 **
Vibr induced white finger B	9	34 **	
Hearing loss A	9	38 **	
Shoulder injury A, Dom	9	36 **	32 **
Injury to knee cap	10	33 **	
Chronic pain A	10	63 **	
Dermatitis B	10	35 **	
Injury to lower back B	10	55 **	
Broken ankle A	11	37 **	41 **

(continued)

Table 1 (continued)

| Video title | AMA PI | Mean Q of L value | |
		Injured worker[1]	Control group[2]
Broken elbow, Non-Dom	11	27 **	
Injury to knee ligaments	11	34 **	35 **
Broken elbow, Dom	11	38 **	
Asthma A	13	46 **	
Shoulder injury C, Non-Dom	13	35 **	28 **
Shoulder injury C, Dom	14	39 **	36 **
Hearing loss B	16	37 **	
Amp of several fingers D, Non-Dom	16	35 **	37 **
Amp of several fingers D, Dom	17	37 **	36 **
Amp of several fingers C, Non-Dom	18	37 **	37 **
Amp of several fingers C, Dom	19	40 **	60 **
Chronic pain A	20	65 **	
Facial burn	20	54 **	
Injury to lower back A	20	53 **	
Injury to lower back C	20	60 **	
Amp of several fingers B, Non-Dom	23	39 **	46 **
Eye loss	24	43 **	
Amp of several fingers B, Dom	25	41 **	49 **
Amp of several fingers A, Non-Dom	29	43 **	55 **
Head injury B	30	64 **	
Head injury C	30	67 **	
Amp of several fingers A, Dom	31	45 **	57 **
Several broken fingers A, Non-Dom	33	38 **	50 **
Several broken fingers A, Dom	35	43 **	46 **
Below knee amp B	35	49 **	49 **
Below knee amp A	38	57 **	64 **
Heart attack	·45	65 **	
Below elbow amp B, Non-Dom	49	58 **	54 *
Amp of hand, Non-Dom	49	53 **	54 **
Below elbow amp A, Non-Dom	49	57 **	57 **
Above knee amp B	50	61 **	
Below elbow amp B, Dom	54	56 **	65 **
Amp of hand, Dom	54	56 **	51
Below elbow amp A, Dom	54	61 **	61 **
Asthma B	63	61 *	
Head injury A	75	78 *	

**Statistically significant difference exists between AMA PI and Q of L value at 1 percent level of significance.

*Statistically significant difference exists between AMA PI and Q of L value at 5 percent level of significance.

[1] Mean Injured Worker values shown here are based on the total sample of injured workers not the subset matched to the general population.

[2] Blank values for conditions for the Control Group column indicate these videos were not viewed by the general population sample.

[3] These conditions would have received a 0.4 percent PD award under the Ontario Permanent Disability Rating Schedule in use prior to Bill 162. The impairment is, however, not of significant clinical consequence to warrant a rating under the *AMA Guides*.

Figure 2
Plot of AMA Percentages Against Mean Q of L Values for
Injured Workers

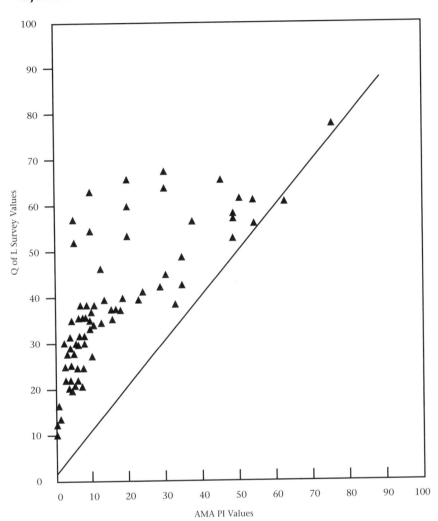

Table 2

Mean Values and Mean Differences between Control Group and Injured Workers[1] by Percentage of AMA Permanent Impairment Rating (AMA PI)

AMA PI rating	N	Mean value Injured workers (IW)	Control group (CG)	Difference (CG-IW)
1.0 - 5.0%	291	26.8	22.6	-4.2 **
5.1 - 10.0%	316	33.7	30.6	-3.1 *
10.1 - 25.0%	203	40.1	39.1	-1.0
25.1 - 100.0%	403	54.0	54.4	0.4

* Indicates a statistically significant difference at the 5 percent level of significance.
**Indicates a statistically significant difference at the 1 percent level of significance.
[1] Table 2 presents the results of analysis of the differences between the Q of L values for the general population control group and a matched subset of injured workers. (Injured-worker values in Table 1 are on the total injured-worker sample.)

- Injured-worker and control-group values are not significantly different in the mid- and high-AMA PI ranges.
- Occasions when the injured-worker Q of L values are not significantly different from the AMA PI values occur most frequently for those conditions where the clinical impairment rating is high. The Q of L values and the AMA PI values converge as the impairment ratings become more severe. Thus, there appears to be greater agreement between the severity of loss of enjoyment of life and the degree of permanent impairment for conditions considered more severe clinically.
- A 'sanctity-of-body' effect appears to exist even with the most minor clinical impairments. Sanctity of body refers to the observation that, regardless of the severity of the clinical measure of an impairment, a significant loss of quality of life is associated with it.[4]

Analysis by Body System

The Q of L values for the benchmark conditions and the relevant AMA PI values were mapped by relevant body systems, corresponding to chapters in the AMA *Guides*. This analysis, shown in Figure 3, led to the following findings:

- The data points on the 78 conditions readily subdivided into five groupings related to the body systems' chapters of the AMA *Guides*,

4 Several other researchers have noted a similar phenomenon, including Torrance (1982), Kaplan et al. (1979), and Wolfson et al. (1982), although for medical conditions not directly comparable to those considered in this study.

Figure 3
Plot of AMA Percentages Against Mean Q of L Values for Injured Workers by Body System Groupings

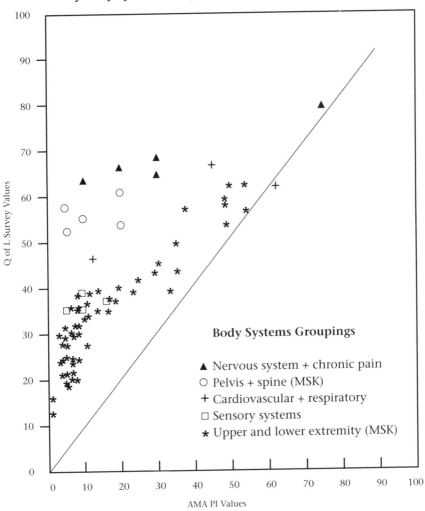

with musculoskeletal (MSK) subdividing into injuries of the extremities and injuries of the spine and pelvis.
- Some body systems have few data points (i.e., few benchmark conditions) and these are limited to a narrow range of AMA PI values (e.g., sensory systems, which includes visual and hearing impairments).
- Different relationships appear to exist between AMA PI and Q of L values depending on body system. For example, a 10 percent (AMA

PI) impairment of the musculoskeletal system and a 10 percent (AMA PI) impairment of the nervous system receive very different loss-of-enjoyment-of-life values, 32 percent and 62 percent respectively. This finding, termed the 'body system effect,' is apparent across most of the body systems included in the research.

- The body system effect appears to reflect, in part, the workers' view that those conditions where chronicity of pain was significant, (e.g., pelvis and spine MSK) have considerably greater impact on the quality of life than other conditions with similar AMA PI values (e.g., upper and lower extremity MSK).

Discussion of the Major Findings and Conclusions

The Systematic Tendency of the AMA Guides

Figure 2 provides a convenient way to assess the appropriateness of using the AMA PI values as a proxy for the loss of the enjoyment of life. If the AMA PI values were a perfect proxy for the Q of L survey results, all the triangles (each of which shows the correspondence between the AMA PI value and Q of L value for a particular medical condition) would fall exactly on the diagonal line. A more realistic test of the validity of using the AMA PI values as proxies for the loss of the enjoyment of life would require the triangles to fall relatively near the diagonal line, with about as many observations above as below it.

Neither of these tests of the appropriateness of using AMA PI values as a proxy for the loss of the quality of life is satisfied. Instead, with minor exceptions, the triangles lie well above the diagonal line, which means the AMA PI values systematically underpredict the loss of the quality of life that workers associate with the various permanent impairments. It should be emphasized that the data in Table 1 make clear that not only workers but the control group representative of the general Ontario population systematically reported losses of the quality of life that exceeded the AMA PI ratings for a wide range of impairments. We are unaware of any previous research establishing the systematic tendency of the AMA PI ratings to undervalue the loss of enjoyment of life associated with a large number of impairments encompassed by the AMA *Guides*.

The Body-System Effect

The apparent difference in the relationship of the Q of L values to AMA PI values by body system groupings, as denoted in Figure 3, is an interesting and significant research finding that also has not been previously identified. However, several factors indicate that caution is necessary in interpretating these data. Due to the small number of data points, other than in the upper and lower extremity grouping, it would be inappropriate to generalize this finding based on existing data. It would be inappropriate to assume the differences demonstrated across the body systems shown in Figure 3 were similar across the full range of AMA PI ratings for those body systems. Moreover, it would be inappropriate to assume that the body system effect operated for the body systems not represented in Figure 3.

The small number of data points does not, however, suggest that the effect seen here is random, since, in fact, there are a large number of observations contributing to the mean values shown. However, for each body system, the number of conditions portrayed in the videos is small, given the wide range in severity of impairments that may occur within a particular body system grouping. Also, a wider range of conditions fully representing each and every different body system was not included in the 78 benchmark conditions.

The Pain Effect

The video presentations of conditions associated with the Spine, Pelvis and Chronic Pain Syndrome (involving the back and extremities), show that pain stands out as a significant and ongoing component of these cases. Survey participants appear to have considered this aspect of the impairment as having a significant impact on the quality of life over and above the physical limitations suffered due to the nature of the condition. The effect of pain may have been differently perceived by the physicians estimating the AMA PI value of the cases; their clinical experience may have influenced them to view the pain element as a more episodic and integral component of impairment rather than a continuous and additional aspect of it. Thus the AMA PI ratings by physicians for these benchmark conditions are considerably lower than their Q of L values, apparently because the impact of pain on one's enjoyment of life is considered more important to the survey respondent than to the physician estimating a clinical impairment rating. However, there are too few data points to support this finding with complete confidence, and this is an area which warrants additional investigation.

The Sanctity-of-Body-Image Effect

There appears to be a 'threshold' effect at the lower end of the Q of L scale. Several videos in the upper and lower extremity grouping represent conditions with minimal clinical impairment and with clinical impairment values of 1 percent AMA PI or less. However, even these conditions result in significant Q of L values of between 10 and 16 percent. This difference may represent a 'sanctity of body image effect.' In addition, while the phenomenon appeared to be a component in the values of both the injured-worker sample and the control group, the Q of L values were significantly lower in the control group than in the injured-worker group for conditions with AMA PI impairment ratings of less than 10 percent AMA PI. Thus, it appears that the magnitude of this effect may be sensitive to variation across respondent groups. Nonetheless, the magnitude of the sanctity of body image effect reported in this study appears so marked for minimal impairments, even for the control group, that this concept requires further investigation.

Conclusion

Clearly, the Q of L measures from the survey are significantly different, both statistically and substantially, from the AMA PI values of similar conditions. We conclude that clinically determined impairment ratings are not the most appropriate proxy measure of the loss of enjoyment of life. From the results of this study, an interim Q of L scale for use in determining noneconomic loss awards could be developed for the upper and lower extremity conditions, with some adjustment for the sanctity-of-body-image effect. An interim Q of L scale might be considered a first step in the development of a series of scales based on the part-of-body effect, if further research corroborates the existence of this phenomenon.

An interim Q of L scale was suggested to the Board of Directors of the Workers' Compensation Board of Ontario in June 1991, when the noneconomic-loss research results were reported. While the WCB found the research results of considerable interest, the findings generated substantial debate. The cost implications of adopting the Q of L values to determine noneconomic-loss awards are significant, and using Q of L values as the primary approach to determining administrative awards in a system as large as the Ontario Workers' Compensation Board would be unique.

A process of consultation with the workers' compensation stakeholder community was subsequently undertaken to apprise interested parties of the research findings. No consensus could be reached among representatives of workers and employers on the appropriate use of the findings.

Thus, informed by the consultation process results and concerned about the financial and policy implications of moving to a quality of life scale, the Workers' Compensation Board decided to continue to use the AMA *Guides* clinical ratings to determine noneconomic-loss awards.

References

American Medical Association. 1990. *Guides to the evaluation of permanent impairment.* 3rd ed. rev. Chicago, IL: The Association.

Berkowitz, Monroe and John F. Burton Jr. 1987. *Permanent disability benefits in workers' compensation.* Kalamazoo, MI: Upjohn Institute.

Burton, John F. Jr. 1986. The role of the permanent disability rating schedule in the Ontario workers' compensation program. Report prepared for the Ontario Workers' Compensation Board. Mimeographed.

————. 1992. A primer on permanent disability benefits. In *Workers' compensation desk book,* edited by John F. Burton and T. Schmidle. Horsham, PA: LRP Publications.

Drummond, M.F., G.L. Stoddart, and G.W. Torrance. 1987. *Methods for the economic evaluation of health care programmes.* New York: Oxford University Press.

Kaplan, Robert M., James W. Bush and Charles C. Berry. 1979. Health status index: Category rating vs. magnitude estimation for measuring levels of well being. *Medical Care* 17:501–85.

National Commission on State Workmen's Compensation Laws. 1972. *The report of the National Commission on State Workmen's Compensation Laws.* Washington, DC: US Government Printing Office.

Ontario Workers' Compensation Board. 1972. *Permanent disability rating schedule.* Toronto: The Board.

Torrance, George W. 1982. Multiattribute utility theory as a method of measuring social preferences for health states in long-term care. In *Values and long term care,* edited by R. Kane and R. Kane. Lexington, MA: Lexington Books.

Weiler, Paul. 1980. *Reshaping workers' compensation for Ontario.* Toronto: Ontario Ministry of Labour.

————. 1986. *Permanent partial disability: Alternative models for compensation.* Toronto: Ontario Ministry of Labour.

Wolfson, A., A. Sinclair, C. Bombardier, and A. McGeer. 1982. Preference measurements for functional status in stroke patients: Inter-rater and inter-technique comparison. In *Values and long term care,* edited by R. Kane and R. Kane. Lexington, MA: Lexington Books.

Appendix A

Members of the Methodological Advisory Committee, Noneconomic Loss Study

Dr. Claire Bombardier* (Medicine, Clinical Epidemiology, Quality of Life Measurement)
Director, Clinical Epidemiology Program, University of Toronto
Director, Clinical Epidemiology Unit, Wellesley Hospital
Rheumatologist, Rheumatic Disease Unit, Wellesley Hospital

Prof. John F. Burton Jr.* (Workers' Compensation Research, Economics)
Director, Institute of Management and Labour Relations, Rutgers University, New Jersey

Prof. Anthony J. Culyer (Economics, Quality of Life Measurement)
Head of Department, Department of Economics and Related Studies, University of York, England

Prof. Robert Evans (Health Economics, Health Policy)
Professor of Economics, University of British Columbia
National Health Scientist, Health and Welfare Canada
Fellow and Director, Program in Population Health,
Canadian Institute for Advanced Research

Prof. William Johnson (Workers' Compensation, Economics, Disability Research)
Professor of Economics, School of Health Administration and Policy, College of Business, Arizona State University

Prof. George Torrance* (Health Economics, Measurement Methodology, Quality of Life Measurement)
Professor, Department of Clinical Epidemiology and Biostatistics, McMaster University

Prof. Paul Weiler (Workers' Compensation Research & Policy)
Professor of Law, Harvard Law School, Harvard University

*Core Member of the Committee.

Re-employment and Accommodation Requirements Under Workers' Compensation

Morley Gunderson, Douglas Hyatt and David Law

Re-employment and reasonable accommodation requirements are key components of recent workers' compensation reforms, such as those enacted in Ontario under Bill 162, which was passed in July 1989 and took effect in January 1990. That legislation requires employers to re-employ their injured workers and to accommodate their return to work where feasible.[1] These requirements are intricately related to other components of the recent Ontario reforms, including vocational rehabilitation and compensation for wage loss (Allingham and Sangster 1990).

In this chapter the re-employment and accommodation requirements are analyzed in their broader context and especially in relation to the other reforms that have occurred in this area. The objectives are fivefold, and each objective represents a section of the chapter: (1) to outline the possible rationale for the re-employment and accommodation requirements, (2) to place the re-employment and accommodation requirements under workers' compensation into their broader context, (3) to outline the re-employment and accommodation provisions of the Ontario *Workers' Compensation Act* in the context of other provisions of the Act, (4) to discuss the cost of accommodation, (5) to explore the extent to which employers may shift some of the costs back to injured workers. Mention is made throughout the chapter, of the jurisprudence that has arisen over the interpretation of the Act, instigated by both the Workers' Compensation Board and the Workers' Compensation Appeals Tribunal.

Note: Financial assistance of the Social Sciences and Humanities Research Council is gratefully acknowledged. The opinions expressed in this paper are those of the authors, and do not necessarily reflect the positions or policies of the Ontario Workers' Compensation Board.

1 While the phrase 'reasonable accommodation' has conventionally been used to describe that requirement, in fact the stronger phrase 'duty to accommodate' is appropriate since the accommodation generally is required unless it imposes 'undue hardship'. The standard is up to the point of undue hardship, not simply one of 'reasonableness' (Lepofsky 1992, 18).

Rationale for Re-employment and Accommodation Requirements

The present emphasis on re-employment and reasonable accommodation has been provoked by a variety of factors. It is consistent with recent antidiscrimination and human-rights initiatives that emphasize the accommodation of diversity and individual differences. It is also consistent with affirmative action and employment equity initiatives that stress the need for special considerations to compensate for unequal starting points and create equal opportunity for members of disadvantaged groups. 'Competitive handicaps' are often regarded as necessary to ensure a 'fair race,' and 'vertical equity' (i.e., the unequal treatment of unequals) is as important a concept of fairness as 'horizontal equity' (i.e., the equal treatment of equals).[2]

Re-employment and accommodation requirements are also consistent with newer vocational rehabilitation strategies. As indicated by Berkowitz (1990, 52):

Traditional rehabilitation has concentrated on altering the individual, by changing attitudes, by improving functioning capabilities, or by instilling new skills through training and education. Increasingly, rehabilitation professionals are beginning to recognize that it may be more efficacious to operate not on the individual, but on the environment. In addition to allowances for the worker or subsidies for the employer, it is possible to change the workplace to accommodate the worker's residual functioning capacities. . . . The idea of operating on the environment rather than the individual is thoroughly in accordance with the aspirations of the disability rights movement. Disability activists are quick to claim that they are not disabled, it is the environment that is disabled. In their view, improving societal attitudes, providing access to the job, providing accessible transportation and modifying the job to accommodate impairments will remove whatever handicaps are involved in a particular disabling condition.

Re-employment and accommodation requirements are also consistent with the emphasis in the field of vocational rehabilitation on the idea that it is preferable to integrate workers into 'real world' situations rather than provide assistance through sheltered workshops.[3] Such

2 Two issues of the first volume of the *Canadian Labour Law Journal* were devoted to issues surrounding the duty to accommodate in its many applications.
3 Abt Associates (1989); Hudson et al. (1988); Konig and Schalock (1991); Ontario Ministry of Labour (1985); Ontario Advisory Council for Disabled Persons (1990).

integration is also compatible with the view, held by many who provide social assistance, that it is preferable to empower recipients to earn their income rather than receive it as a transfer payment. Earned income promotes self-sufficiency and self-esteem, and integration into the workplace provides disabled workers with associated social interactions, as well as labour-market income.

Re-employment and accommodation requirements imposed on the employer on whose premises the accident occurred would also facilitate the injured worker returning to that specific employer. This can be important because empirical evidence indicates that workers who return to their accident employer do not experience any wage loss associated with the accommodation requirements, while injured workers who return to work for a new employer experience a wage loss of around 30 percent to compensate for the cost of the accommodation.

Re-employment and accommodation requirements imposed on the accident employer also may be both equitable, since the costs fall, in part, on the employer where the injury occurred, and more efficient because these requirements create an incentive for employers to reduce such injuries and the associated re-employment and accommodation costs.

In terms of the workers' compensation reforms in Ontario, re-employment and accommodation requirements may be seen as an important instrument to encourage the return to work of permanently disabled workers. This may be necessary to offset the monetary disincentive to return to work, given the high income replacement rate (approximately 90 percent of lost wages) that exists under the new system.

Viewed in a more negative light, the re-employment and accommodation requirements may be part of a broader strategy of governments to shift more of the cost of providing conventional government services, such as vocational rehabilitation and transfer payments, to employers. Faced with severe budget constraints, governments understandably may try to shift some of the fiscal burden.

Re-employment and Accommodation Requirements in Context

Whatever the rationale for the re-employment and accommodation requirements, they are an important component of recent workers' compensation reform in Ontario. In general, such re-employment requirements under workers' compensation are quite rare. In Canada, they exist only in Ontario and Québec. They are not features of workers' compensation in the United States, and while they exist in some European jurisdictions, they are often not enforced (Berkowitz 1990, 60).

Accommodation requirements under workers' compensation are related to the broader set of accommodation requirements that exists, usually as part of human rights or antidiscrimination legislation. That legislation often requires accommodation to the special needs of persons based on such factors as religion, gender, age, or any other factor enumerated in the legislation. Disability—no matter what its origin—is one of the enumerated factors in human rights legislation in all jurisdictions in Canada (Adell 1991). As well, human rights legislation pertains to accommodation in areas such as access to goods, services and facilities, and the workplace. Thus, accommodation requirements under workers' compensation are a subset of more general accommodation requirements—that subset being the workplace accommodation of injured workers who are returning to their pre-accident employer. Broader accommodation requirements exist for persons other than injured workers, and they apply to areas other than the workplace.

Relevant legislation, therefore, can exist as part of human rights and antidiscrimination law, as well as workers' compensation legislation. It will be shaped by regulations and guidelines that are often produced to help interpret general legal obligations. The accommodation requirements will also be determined by the associated jurisprudence from the courts and from decisions of human rights and workers' compensation boards and tribunals that interpret the relevant legislation and its accompanying regulations and guidelines. As well, arbitral jurisprudence[4] with respect to these issues can develop as arbitrators settle grievances over the interpretation of a collective agreement.

While it may appear that there is a plethora of information on accommodation requirements, this is relatively uncharted terrain. The notion of reasonable accommodation was not introduced into Canadian law until 1985, in the Supreme Court of Canada's decisions in *Bhinder* and in *O'Malley* (Lynk and Ellis 1992, 241), with illustrative criteria for determining what could be considered as undue hardship for meeting accommodation requirements not being enunciated until 1990 in the *Central Alberta Dairy Pool* case.[5] These Supreme Court decisions are

4 Discussed, for example, in Adell (1991), Ginsburg and Bickley (1992), Taras (1992) and Winkler and Thorup (1992).

5 These Supreme court cases, along with jurisprudence from human rights tribunals and from arbitrators, are discussed in Taras (1992) and in Winkler and Thorup (1992). The *Bhinder* decision essentially stated that the employer was not required to accommodate the special needs of a Sikh to wear a turban instead of a hard hat once the employer first established that the hard hat was a *bona fide* occupational qualification (BFOQ) of all workers for safety reasons. The *O'Malley* decision indicated that the employer was required to accommodate the requirement of a Seventh-Day Adventist not to work on Saturdays, since the employer was unable to establish a BFOQ. The *Alberta Dairy Pool* case also required the employer to accommodate the religious holidays of an employee, with the accommodation being required *prior* to the consideration of a BFOQ defence.

not only recent and rare, but they also addressed the issue of accommodation for religious reasons, not specifically for workplace disability. The statutory requirements in the area of reasonable accommodation are also relatively new and they do not explicitly exist in all jurisdictions (Molloy 1992; Winkler and Thorup 1992). They were explicitly added to the human rights laws for Ontario in 1986 (effective 1988), for the Yukon in 1986, and for Manitoba in 1988. Specific legal regulations detailing the requirements have not been outlined in those jurisdictions, although Ontario and Manitoba have issued guidelines. British Columbia and Alberta have also issued guidelines, although their statutes do not contain explicit accommodation requirements. Other jurisdictions simply prohibit discrimination on the basis of a variety of enumerated factors including disability, subject to a *bona fide* occupational qualification as a legitimate defence.

Reasonable accommodation requirements in Canada have not been guided much by precedence in the United States since accommodation requirements in that country were minimal until the *Americans with Disabilities Act* became effective in July 1992. That federal legislation imposed accommodation requirements up to the point of 'undue hardship.' Until then, however, the accommodation requirements in the United States generally pertained to religious discrimination cases and they usually imposed only *de minimus* efforts by employers rather than accommodation up to the point of undue hardship (Fasman 1992).

In such circumstances, it is understandable that considerable uncertainty prevails. What are the obligations of employers with respect to the accommodation and re-employment requirements? What are the cost implications of such accommodation? Who ultimately bears the costs, and to what extent are they shifted back to injured workers?

Provisions and Interrelationships of the Ontario Act

The re-employment and accommodation provisions under Ontario's workers' compensation system must be viewed, not only in the broader context of other legislative requirements and jurisprudence especially pertaining to accommodation, but also in the specific context of other provisions of the *Workers' Compensation Act* as well as the Ontario Human Rights Commission guidelines.

Re-employment and Accommodation Provisions

The re-employment and accommodation provisions are contained in section 54 of the Ontario *Workers' Compensation Act* (as amended by Bill 162 in 1989). The legislation, which covers employers with 20 or more employees, states:

Upon receiving notice from the Board that a worker is able to perform the essential duties of the worker's pre-injury employment, the employer shall offer to reinstate the worker in the position the worker held on the date of injury or offer to provide the worker with alternative employment of a nature and at earnings comparable to the worker's employment on that date. . . .

Upon receiving notice from the Board that a worker, although unable to perform the essential duties of the worker's pre-injury employment, is medically able to perform suitable work, the employer shall offer the worker the first opportunity to accept suitable employment that may become available with the employer. . . .

In order to fulfil the employer's obligations under this section, the employer shall accommodate the work or the workplace to the needs of a worker who is impaired as a result of the injury to the extent that the accommodation does not cause the employer undue hardship.

In essence, the employer must reinstate the injured worker to his or her former job or to a comparable job with comparable wages. The ability to perform the job is assessed *after* potential accommodations are considered.[6] Comparable wages are taken to be equal to at least 90 percent of pre-injury earnings.[7] If the worker is medically unable to do the previous or comparable job, then the employer must re-employ the worker to the first suitable job that becomes available with the employer. A suitable job is one 'which the worker has the necessary skills to perform, is medically able to perform and which does not pose a health or safety hazard to the worker or any co-worker.'[8] The employer must re-employ the injured worker as long as the worker returns to work within two years after the injury. For such purposes, the Board has interpreted the date of injury as the date at which it is determined that the person is 'unable to work.' The employer must maintain continuous employment for that worker for at least six months after his or her return. Termination can occur if it is necessary for the financial viability of the business, but such a case is usually difficult to make. Termination can also occur if it is directly related to inadequate performance of duties. In interpreting this standard, the Board uses the common law principle of 'just cause,' a relatively high standard for employers to meet.

The Board does not have the power to order the reinstatement of injured workers (Baker and Sones 1990). However, employers who do

6 Workers' Compensation Board policy document 07-05-08 (May 10, 1991).
7 Workers' Compensation Board policy document 07-05-09 (May 10, 1991).
8 Workers' Compensation Board policy document 07-05-10 (April 30, 1991).

not comply may be subject to a penalty up to the worker's earnings for the year preceding the injury. The Board may award the injured worker up to the amount the worker would have received for one year if the normal compensation arrangements had occurred. In effect, this is the worker's temporary disability payment, which is typically 90 percent of his or her lost earnings if the worker does not work. This compensation amount may be added to the employer's penalty, effectively implying that the employer's penalty may be equal to almost two years of the worker's earnings.

Relationship to Human-Rights Guidelines

Re-employment requirements are based on the presumption that reasonable accommodations have been made up to the point of undue hardship. In determining undue hardship, the Board has adopted the approach developed by the Ontario Human Rights Commission in their *Guidelines for Assessing Accommodation Requirements for Persons with Disabilities*.[9]

Those guidelines place fairly stringent obligations on employers before undue hardship is considered to have been reached—'undue hardship' obviously implies a higher standard than 'reasonable accommodation.' The guidelines state

Costs will amount to undue hardship if they are:
1 quantifiable;
2 shown to be related to the accommodation; and
3 (a) so substantial that they would substantially affect the essential nature of the enterprise, or
(b) so significant that they would substantially affect the viability of the enterprise.

The guidelines further indicate that cost estimates must be firmly documented, and they must be spread over the entire organization, not just the unit making the accommodation. The employer must make every effort to mitigate costs through outside sources of support or subsidies. Benefits from the accommodation should be subtracted to arrive at net costs. Costs should be amortized or depreciated as appropriate, and may require that the organization borrow the money, if necessary.

The guidelines indicate that the terms of a collective agreement may have to be modified as a part of the accommodation process. If a joint solution is not agreed upon, the employer must make the accommodation in spite of the agreement. While the guidelines indicate that the

9 Workers' Compensation Board policy document 07-05-07 (May 1, 1991).

terms of a collective agreement may have to be modified, the *Workers'*
Compensation Act itself specifically 'exempts' seniority provisions. This
is also consistent with the limited arbitral and human-rights jurisprudence that exists in this area (Adell 1991).

The extent of the accommodation requirements can perhaps be best
illustrated by the way they are traded off against another sacrosanct
principle in this area—the health and safety of workers. The guidelines
state

> Where the effect of such a [health or safety] requirement is to
> exclude a person with a disability from the workplace or service, it
> may be necessary to modify or waive the health or safety require-
> ment. Whether this will create undue hardship or not depends upon
> whether the remaining degree of risk outweighs the benefit of
> enhancing equality for persons with disabilities.

The trade-off is more likely to be allowed if the risk falls on the person for whom the accommodation is being made, and that person is
willing to assume the risk.

Relationship to Other Provisions of the Act

Prior to implementation of reforms to workers' compensation in
Ontario in 1989, workers with a temporary disability received compensation benefits equal to 90 percent of their lost earnings (the difference
between their post-injury and pre-injury earnings). Workers with a permanent disability—including those whose 'temporary' disability was
deemed permanent after sufficient time had passed for their maximum
medical improvement to be determined—were given a pension equal
to their pre-accident earnings multiplied by a disability rating that
reflected the Board's assessment of the extent to which the person was
disabled. The assessment was based on the so-called meat chart. Persons
with a permanent *total* disability would be considered 100 percent disabled, and their full income would be replaced, subject to a statutory
maximum. Persons with a permanent *partial* disability would have a
portion of their income replaced; the portion increased as the severity of
the worker's injury increased. The pension would be paid for life, irrespective of the person's subsequent work behaviour and earnings.

Problems with the former system included the fact that the 'temporary' compensation often went on for long periods. As well, the permanent disability rating depended on the severity of the injury and
not directly on the income loss that may result from the injury.

Bill 162 introduced a dual approach. The first component is a small
lump-sum award or noneconomic loss for physical and functional

loss—akin to 'pain and suffering' in personal injury awards. The award is based on a disability rating schedule, with the total amount being inversely related to the age of the individual, reflecting the number of years the person can expect to experience the noneconomic loss.

The second, and more important component, is the economic-loss component, designed to replace most of the lost earnings and earnings capacity that occurs as a result of the injury. There are two phases to the economic-loss component. The first phase involves 'temporary' compensation for 90 percent of the actual income loss that is incurred in the first year—possibly up to 18 months—after the injury. The Board then determines if the earnings loss is likely to be permanent. If so, the amount of compensation for permanent partial disabilities is equal to 90 percent of the expected 'future economic loss', calculated as the difference between the worker's earnings *capacity* and his or her pre-injury wage. The worker's earnings capacity may be equal to the actual post-injury wage, including zero earnings, if that is deemed appropriate by the Board. If it is not deemed appropriate, the individual may be assigned a wage based on what he or she reasonably could be expected to earn in suitable and available employment. This future-economic-loss calculation is made one year after the injury, with a first review three years after the injury, and a second review six years after the injury. Each assessment, however, involves calculating the expected future economic loss until the age of 65, not just until the next review. After the final review—six years after the injury—the worker's compensation will continue to be equal to 90 percent of his or her lost earnings capacity, irrespective of subsequent work behaviour and earnings.

Clearly, such a wage-loss system with a high income-replacement rate of 90 percent creates little *monetary incentive* to return to work, at least until the final review is made. In fact, it creates a monetary incentive for the worker to minimize 'earnings capacity' so as to increase the magnitude of the award. This is a natural by-product of the desirable insurance feature of replacing most of the worker's lost income. The *potential* adverse work-incentive effects of high income replacement was recognized by those who were influential in the recent Ontario reforms (Burton 1983, 34; Weiler 1986, 18). There is also empirical evidence from the United States indicating that, other things being equal, higher disability payments reduce the incentive to return to work and participate in the labour market. Hyatt (1992, 1993) reviews that evidence, and provides similar evidence for Ontario based on a sample of workers who were injured in 1988.

In part, because of the potential for the wage-loss system to reduce the monetary incentive to return to work, other features became an integral part of the system to facilitate and encourage the claimant's return to work. Those features include (1) vocational rehabilitation, (2) provisions whereby workers may be assigned an expected wage based on suitable and available jobs, (3) the expansion of experience rating of employers, (4) re-employment requirements placed on the employer where the injury occurred, and (5) reasonable accommodation requirements to facilitate that re-employment. The latter two requirements are the focus of this analysis.

The Cost Implications of Reasonable Accommodation

Employers have been concerned about the potential cost implications of reasonable accommodation, in part because of the uncertainty associated with the nature of accommodation requirements. This is one aspect of a growing concern about the cost of labour-market regulation or regulation more generally. In a world of increasing international competition and free trade, there is concern that costly regulation can make Canadian employers less competitive, resulting in loss of business and fewer jobs. As well, greater international capital mobility means that firms may base their plant location and investment decisions, in part, on the level of such regulatory costs.

Unfortunately, there is little systematic evidence, especially in Canada, of the cost of accommodation. Some earlier US evidence suggested an average cost per accommodation of $1,350.[10] This calculation may be biased upwards since it excluded accommodations for which there was no cost. However, it may also be biased downwards since it would not include potential accommodations that were not made because they were perceived to be too costly. The uncertainty of the cost is illustrated in a media report[11] that discussed the *Americans with Disabilities Act* of 1990: 'There is no estimate of the Act's total cost to business, but firms could spend an average of $100 per disabled employee.'

Survey evidence for Ontario indicates that only 12 percent of disabled workers require accommodation in forms that imply costs, such as special equipment, facilities, or arrangements (Abt Associates 1989). As well, some of the costs of accommodation may be offset by the work habits of disabled persons who tend to balance the negative effect of their disability through lower turnover, absenteeism, and accident rates, as well as higher productivity.[12] There is also some evidence that accommodation does not engender negative reactions from co-work-

10 This cost estimate is derived in Gunderson (1992) based on data provided in Berkeley Planning Associates (1982).
11 *USA Today*, July 26, 1990.
12 Nathanson (1977); U.S. Department of Labor (1984); and various studies reviewed in Collignon (1989).

ers, customers, or unions (Berkeley Planning Associates 1982). Obviously, there is empathy and understanding about what may appear to some as 'special treatment.' As well, it is possible that some of the accommodations benefit persons other than those with disabilities.

The cost of accommodation can also be offset by the wide range of support services available to assist employers in this area (Gunderson 1992). One survey, for example, identified 324 organizations in Canada that have facilitated supported employment for disabled persons (Annable 1989). Employment and Immigration Canada (1989) also operates the Job Accommodation Network to provide information on workplace accommodation (Krahn 1988).

The indirect cost of administrative and managerial time devoted to accommodation is a potential area of concern, in part, because of the uncertainty of accommodation requirements (Johnson 1980). These can be especially important in the small business sector (Premus and Carnes 1982).

Most surveys of the cost implications of reasonable accommodation conclude that the costs are usually not substantial, although administrative and time costs devoted to the issue may be high, especially for smaller businesses.[13] The latter may increase if accommodation draws more disabled persons into the workforce as barriers are reduced, and if employers are pushed towards 'undue hardship' rather than simply 'reasonable accommodation'. However, these costs also may decline if accommodation becomes a normal business practice, if support networks become better known, and if new facilities and equipment are designed with such requirements in mind.

Shifting Cost to Injured Workers

The costs of workplace accommodations that initially fall on employers, and hence on owners or shareholders, can be shifted 'forward' to customers and 'backward' to workers, including injured workers. If they cannot be shifted, then firms may go out of business, especially if the regulatory cost is unusually high. Shifting costs may be entirely appropriate if it is deemed socially desirable that the cost of workplace accommodation should become a normal cost of producing the product or service.

In the case of forward cost-shifting to customers, the resulting higher price may mean that less of the product or service is purchased— especially under global competition if the product or service can be purchased from countries or jurisdictions that do not impose costly

13 Davenport (1989), Gunderson (1992), Johnson (1980), O'Neil (1976), and Premus and Carnes (1982).

regulations. Again, this is appropriate if it is deemed socially desirable that consumers should pay for the cost of any workplace accommodation embodied in the products they consume. Such market responses should not always negate the desirability of regulations that impose costs, although they do make the consequences of such regulations more explicit.

Possible shifting of costs backwards to workers, especially to the injured workers themselves, is likely to be a less intentional and more socially unacceptable market response. After all, if the intent is to provide assistance to disabled workers through workplace accommodation, that intent is thwarted if the disabled workers pay for the accommodation. The mechanism whereby they would pay for the accommodation, of course, is not direct; they would pay through their acceptance of a lower wage in return for the workplace characteristic they value, in this case, the workplace accommodation of disability.

There is an extensive economics literature on the extent to which compensating wage premiums are paid for undesirable work characteristics, such as risk or longer working hours, or conversely, the extent to which lower wages are accepted for desirable work characteristics, such as job security or fringe benefits like pensions.[14] Hyatt (1992) is the only study, however, that estimates the extent to which at least some of the cost of workplace accommodation is shifted back to workers in the form of lower wages.

Hyatt estimated an earnings equation for permanently injured workers based on data both before and after their injury. A probit equation was also estimated predicting the probability of their returning to work after the injury, and these results were used to adjust the earnings equations for the possible nonrandom attrition bias: those who return to work may be a select subsample in terms of unobservable characteristics that are not controlled for in the estimating equation but that affect wages. The panel nature of the data enabled the estimation of a 'random effects' model since the same individual was observed in the pre- and post-injury state. This helped to control for the effect of conventionally unobservable factors that are 'fixed' for the same individual over the pre- and post-injury periods.

The data was based on the Ontario Workers' Compensation Board's Economic Loss Survey for the period 1979 to 1988. Two accommodation measures were used, as identified by the injured worker. The first was whether or not a workplace accommodation was introduced in the form of reduced hours, a flexible work schedule, special training, mod-

---

14 For reviews of the theory and evidence on compensating wage differentials see Brown (1980), Gunderson, Hyatt and Pesando (1992), Rosen (1986), and Smith (1979).

ified equipment or work station, light duties, or other arrangements. The second is whether or not physical demands, such as heavy lifting, bending, squatting, walking, standing, carrying, climbing, reaching, sitting, repetitious handling, or other physical activities were reduced. For both accommodation measures, an index was constructed by simply summing the number of workplace accommodations and the reductions in physical demands respectively.

The data also enabled an analysis of whether the injured worker returned to the time-of-accident employer or to another employer. This is important because it is unlikely that the accident employer could shift the cost of accommodation back to the worker through the payment of lower wages for a variety of reasons. Such an action could be interpreted as overt discrimination—or certainly a 'mean spirited' act—since the employer would effectively be reducing the worker's wage after the accident. It is also difficult for the accident employer to assign the worker to a lower paying job, because the employee's duties at the firm at the time of the accident are obvious. If a lower paying job was assigned, the employer would at least be expected to 'red-circle' the job and pay the same wage as was paid for the time-of-accident job. The accident employer may also willingly bear the cost of accommodation to re-employ the worker and retain firm-specific human capital. The accident employer may also not reduce the wage in return for accommodation in order not to increase liability for long-term disability payments. In contrast, another employer who would essentially be making a new hire, would not be under these constraints, and, hence may hire the worker requiring the accommodation only if lower wages could be paid.

The empirical results from Hyatt's analysis are summarized in Table 1. The top panel indicates that workers who return to their accident employer do not experience any wage reduction associated with either workplace accommodations or with reduced physical demands that they may experience. In fact, their wages are slightly higher, although this differential is less than 1 percent higher than pre-injury wages. In contrast, workers who return to work for employers other than the accident employer receive wages that are 18.3 percent lower for each workplace accommodation they receive, and 4.2 percent lower for each reduced physical demand. For workers who return to other employers, the average number of workplace accommodations is 0.4 and the average number of reduced physical demands is 5.3 (middle panel). This implies that the average wage reduction they accept for the average number of accommodations is 7.3 percent, and for the average number of reduced physical demands it is 22.2 percent, for a total wage reduction of 29.5 percent for both types of accommodation.

Table 1

Wage Reduction (%) Associated with Accommodation

Type of accommodation	Accident employer	Other employer
Wage reduction per accommodation		
Workplace accommodation	0.2	-18.3
Reduced physical demands	0.6	-4.2
Average number of accommodations		
Workplace accommodation	0.5	0.4
Reduced physical demands	2.2	5.3
Total wage reduction for all accommodations		
Workplace accommodation	0.1	-7.3
Reduced physical demands	1.3	-22.2
Both accommodations	1.4	-29.5

Source: Hyatt (1992).

In summary, workers who return to their accident employer do not receive any wage reduction associated with the accommodations they receive. In contrast, workers who return to another employer receive a compensating wage reduction of 30 percent, three-quarters of which is associated with reduced physical demands and one-quarter with specific workplace accommodations. At least some of the cost of workplace accommodation and reduced physical demands are shifted back to workers, but only to those workers who return to a different employer. For the reasons discussed above, accident employers do not shift such costs back to their injured workers. This clearly highlights the importance of re-employment and accommodation provisions imposed on the accident employer in minimizing wage loss for injured workers.

Concluding Observations

Clearly, the requirements of re-employment and accommodation, key ingredients of recent reforms to workers' compensation in Ontario, are intricately related to other aspects of those reforms, especially vocational rehabilitation and compensation for wage loss. They are also part and parcel of broader social issues pertaining to human rights of disabled persons in general and to accommodation requirements for reasons other than disability.

Little is known about the costs of reasonable accommodation and reemployment and these costs are shared between employers, workers and consumers. Clearly this is an area requiring further research. The evidence that does exist suggests that, in most instances, the direct costs are modest, and that those returning to a different employer share the costs through lower wages. On the other hand, those returning to the time-of-accident employer do not seem to experience wage reductions. This result highlights an important benefit of encouraging reemployment with the time-of-accident employer. Data being gathered in Canadian jurisdictions which have enacted reemployment and accommodation initiatives, namely New Brunswick, Québec and Ontario, will provide opportunities to reexamine these cost issues.

Ontario legislation has been at the forefront of reform in this area, both with respect to workers' compensation legislation and human rights legislation pertaining to disabled persons. Reasonable accommodation requirements are key aspects of these reforms. As such, these reforms merit considerable attention, especially given the growing importance of this area.

References

Abt Associates. 1989. *Status report: Persons with disabilities*. Toronto: Ontario Ministry of Citizenship.

Adell, B. 1991. The rights of disabled workers at arbitration and under human rights legislation. In *Labour arbitration yearbook*, vol. 1, edited by W. Kaplan, J. Sack and M. Gunderson, pp.167–86. Toronto: Butterworths.

Allingham, R. and S. Sangster. 1990. Rehabilitation strategies for injured workers in Ontario: A unified approach. *Labor Law Journal* 41:534–40.

Annable, Gary. 1989. *Supported employment in Canada, 1988*. Winnipeg: Canadian Council on Rehabilitation and Work.

Baker, D. and G. Sones. 1990. Employer obligations to reinstate injured workers. *Journal of Law and Social Policy* 6:30–56.

Berkeley Planning Associates. 1982. *A study of the accommodations provided to handicapped employees for federal contractors*. Washington, DC: US Department of Labor, Employment Standards Administration.

Berkowitz, M. 1990. *Returning injured workers to employment: An international perspective*. Geneva: International Labour Office.

Brown, C. 1980. Equalizing differences in the labor market. *Quarterly Journal of Economics* 94:113–34.

Burton, John F. Jr. 1983. Compensation for permanent partial disabilities. In *Safety and the work force: Incentives and disincentives in workers' compensation*, edited by John S. Worrall, pp. 18–60. Ithaca, NY: ILR Press.

Collignon, F. 1989. The role of reasonable accommodation in employing disabled persons in private industry. In *Disability and the labor market: Economic problems, policies, and programs*, edited by Monroe Berkowitz and M. Anne Hill, pp.196–241. Ithaca, NY: ILR Press.

Davenport, C. 1989. Disabled people, able workers. *Human Resources Professional* 5(June):8–10ff.

Employment and Immigration Canada. 1989. *The job accommodation network in Canada*. Ottawa: Supply and Services Canada.

Fasman, Z. 1992. *What business must know about the* ADA. Washington, DC: US Chamber of Commerce.

Ginsburg, M. and C. Bickley. 1992. Accommodating the disabled: Emerging issues under human rights legislation. *Canadian Labour Law Journal* 1:72–99.

Gunderson, M. 1992. Implications of the duty to accommodate for industrial relations practices. *Canadian Labour Law Journal* 1:294–310.

Gunderson, M., D. Hyatt, and J.E. Pesando. 1992. Wage-pension trade-offs in collective agreements. *Industrial and Labor Relations* Review 46:146–60.

Hudson, P., S.E. Schwartz, K.A. Sealander, P. Campbell, and J.W. Hansel. 1988. Successfully employed adults with handicaps. *Career Developments for Exceptional Individuals* 11:7–14.

Hyatt, D. 1992. Issues in the compensation of injured workers: Returns to risk, work incentives and accommodation. Ph.D thesis, Centre for Industrial Relations, University of Toronto.

———. 1993. Work disincentives of workers' compensation permanent disability benefits: Evidence for Canada. Mimeographed.

Johnson, L. 1980. *Reasonable accommodation: Research and remedies.* Washington, DC: US Department of Education.

Konig, A. and R. Schalock. 1991. Supported employment: Equal opportunities for severely disabled men and women. *International Labour Review* 130:21–36.

Krahn, P. 1988. Job accommodation network in Canada. *Ability and Enterprise in Canada* 3:1–8.

Lepofsky, D. 1992. The duty to accommodate: A purposive approach. *Canadian Labour Law Journal* 1:1–22.

Lynk, M. and R. Ellis. 1992. Unions and the duty to accommodate. *Canadian Labour Law Journal* 1:238–82.

Molloy, A.M. 1992. Disability and the duty to accommodate. *Canadian Labour Law Journal* 1:23–45.

Nathanson, R. 1977. The disabled employee: Separating myth from fact. *Harvard Business Review* 55 (May–June):6–8.

O'Neil, D. 1976. *Discrimination against handicapped persons.* Arlington, VA: Public Research Institute.

Ontario Advisory Council for Disabled Persons. 1990. *Workable: Fulfilling the potential of persons with disabilites.* Toronto: The Council.

Ontario Human Rights Commission. 1989. *Guidelines for assessing accommodation requirements for persons with disabilities under the Human Rights Code.* Toronto: Ontario Ministry of Citizenship.

Ontario Ministry of Labour. 1985. *Women with disabilities.* Toronto: Handicapped Employment Program.

Premus, R. and D. Carnes. 1982. *Regulation and small business participation in the federal contract market.* Dayton, OH: Wright State University, School of Business Administration.

Rosen, S. 1986. The theory of equalizing differences. In *Handbook of labor economics,* vol. 1, edited by O. Ashenfelter and R. Layard, pp.641–92. New York: Elsevier.

Smith, R.S. 1979. Compensating wage differentials and public policy: A review. *Industrial and Labor Relations Review* 32:339–52.

Taras, D. 1992. The duty to accommodate disabled employees. *Relations Industrielles* 47:709–28.

US Department of Labor. 1984. *The performance of physically impaired workers in manufacturing*. Washington, DC: US Government Printing Office.

Weiler, Paul. 1986. *Permanent partial disability: Alternative models for compensation*. Toronto: Ontario Ministry of Labour.

Winkler, W. and P. Thorup. 1992. The duty of accommodation and its implications for the employer. *Canadian Labour Law Journal* 1:209–237.

Measuring the Impact of Vocational Rehabilitation on the Probability of Post-Injury Return to Work

Richard Allingham and Douglas Hyatt

Workers' compensation boards, in virtually all North American jurisdictions, have established funds or legislation to provide injured workers with vocational rehabilitation (VR) services. VR services are typically directed toward permanently injured workers—workers who are left with a residual physical disability after reaching maximum medical rehabilitation.[1] The private, social, and compensation costs of permanently disabling work injuries can be extremely high. The goal of vocational rehabilitation, in the context of work-injury programs, is to minimize these costs. Broadly speaking, the goal is thought to be achieved by returning the injured worker as soon as possible following the injury to an occupation and lifetime earnings profile that most closely approximates what the worker would have experienced in the absence of the injury.

Thus, the typical hierarchy of VR objectives is to return the worker to: (1) the pre-injury job with the pre-injury employer, (2) the pre-injury job with a different employer, or finally, (3) an occupation otherwise suitable to the worker's post-injury abilities. The success of vocational rehabilitation programs should therefore be assessed, at least in part, by how they meet this hierarchy of objectives.

A large body of literature has documented the relationship between one's employment and one's sense of self, which can be adversely affected by a serious workplace injury. Vocational rehabilitation seeks to re-establish that relationship following a permanently disabling injury. A return to work can represent a victory over the injury.

Note: Douglas Hyatt is grateful to the University of Wisconsin-Milwaukee for financial support for this research. The opinions expressed in this paper are those of the authors and do not necessarily reflect the positions or policies of the Workers' Compensation Board of Ontario.

1 Maximum medical rehabilitation is the point beyond which the medical condition of the worker is not likely to improve significantly.

From a cost-burden perspective, despite comprising a relatively small proportion of all workplace injuries, workers who experience permanent disabilities account for a relatively large proportion of compensation costs. As a rule of thumb, Burton (1983, 18) suggests that, '[a]lthough permanent partial disabilities account for less than 25 percent of all cases paying cash benefits, they account for more than 60 percent of all dollars expended on cash benefits.' In many instances, these benefits include payments to workers to compensate for lost wages following the injury. In times of growing workers' compensation costs, which fall on employers as a cost of labour and, hence, directly affect competitiveness, it becomes increasingly economical to return injured workers to productive employment as soon as possible and at the highest wage possible, thereby reducing benefit and other related social costs.

Berkowitz (1990, 21) defines vocational rehabilitation as, '. . . the array of services designed to facilitate and ease the return to work.' The types of services typically available to permanently injured workers include, 'vocational training, general skills upgrading, refresher courses, employment counselling (including training in job search skills and identification of employment opportunities), participation in an on-the-job training program, help in looking for employment, and assistance for an employer in adapting the work or the workplace to accommodate the needs of the worker' (Ontario Workers' Compensation Board 1992).

The type, duration, and quality of specific VR programs play a critical role in facilitating an injured worker's return to work (Berkowitz (1990). However, other factors contribute to the success of VR, including the nature and timing of medical rehabilitation programs, particularly in the case of back or soft-tissue injuries; the timing of VR interventions in relation to the date of injury; how candidates are selected to participate in VR; the willingness of workers and employers to cooperate in the rehabilitation process; prevailing conditions in the labour market; and the incentive structures created by the interaction between the workers' compensation benefit system and VR.

Despite the potential importance of VR in improving both the post-injury lives of workers and the balance sheets of workers' compensation insurers, there has been little research on the impact of vocational rehabilitation on the labour market. Part of the reason for this is a lack of consistently collected data on injured workers. The provider of workers' compensation insurance (and benefits) is often not the provider of vocational rehabilitation, and instances where hard data on the worker, the worker's injury, rehabilitation assistance, benefit payments, and post-injury labour-market experiences are found together are rare.

An appropriate data set for examining vocational rehabilitation outcomes, according to Berkowitz (1990), would include information on the education, training, and work experience of the injured worker; the part of the body injured; the nature of the injury; medical interventions received; and a measure of the worker's residual functioning capacity. The data set used in this study is complete in most of these dimensions, and includes information on when the worker participated in vocational rehabilitation programs, an array of demographic characteristics of the worker, as well as detailed information on the post-injury work experiences of the injured worker and a permanent impairment rating. This post-injury labour-market information includes the occupations, wages, and duration of employment and unemployment spells for up to six post-injury employment situations.

This study of the contribution of vocational rehabilitation to facilitating post-injury return to work examines the factors that influence the probability of return to work conditional upon participating in a VR program, as well as factors that influence participation in a vocational rehabilitation program when participation is assumed to be endogenous. Following a brief review of some recent studies of the impact of VR on post-injury return to work, the pre- and post-Bill 162 approaches to vocational rehabilitation by the Ontario Workers' Compensation Board are compared. The empirical model and estimation strategy are then outlined and the data set described. Presentation of the estimation results precedes summary comments.

Previous Research

As suggested in the introductory remarks, despite the importance of vocational rehabilitation in the strategies of workers' compensation boards in assisting the return of injured workers to the workplace, there has been little research on the effectiveness of VR, at least as provided under the workers' compensation system. To a very large extent, the paucity of research has been due to a lack of an appropriate data set.

The definition of what constitutes an 'outcome' of vocational rehabilitation is controversial. Rather than contribute to this debate, this section reviews some of the *recent* studies which have looked at the probability of post-VR employment. The review is not intended to be exhaustive. Rather, it is intended merely to provide some context for the empirical work to follow.

Gardner (1988) estimated the impact of a number of specific VR programs on the probability of return to work, conditional upon having completed a VR program. Probit models were estimated separately for male and female injured workers who completed VR services between

March and May of 1985 under the Florida workers' compensation system. The VR programs considered in the analysis included school *and* training, school, training, job modification, evaluation, counselling, and placement (the reference category).[2]

For men, Gardner found that younger and English-speaking injured workers experienced a significantly higher probability of returning to work following completion of their VR program than older and non-English speaking workers. Men who had some vocational training prior to their injury, who were moderately disabled, and who had worked since their injury were significantly more likely to return to work than their high school educated, completely disabled, never post-injury employed counterparts. Those receiving 'job modification' VR interventions were significantly more likely, and those receiving an 'evaluation' intervention significantly less likely, to return to work following the intervention, relative to those receiving job placement assistance. Older women and women with children were significantly less likely to return to work following VR. Those with vocational training were more likely to return to work than those with a high school diploma. 'Evaluation' VR interventions with this population were significantly less likely to result in return-to-work than 'job placement' interventions.

A limitation of this study is that return-to-work information was not collected for those who did not complete a VR program; thus, Gardner was unable to estimate the influence of vocational rehabilitation on the probability of return to work for those who participated in a VR program, compared to those who did not receive VR services.

Gardner (1986) also examined the impact of vocational rehabilitation on labour-market outcomes under the New York workers' compensation scheme, based on VR cases that were closed between 1981 and 1983. He found that workers who received privately provided VR were more likely to return to work than those who received publicly provided VR services. He also found that early intervention increased the probability of return to work.[3]

Skaburskis and Collignon (1991) used tabular and regression analysis to examine the impact of several vocational rehabilitation programs

2 Also included in the list of regressors were the log of the worker's age, an indicator of the worker's ability to speak English, an indicator of the presence of a working spouse, the presence of a child in the family, education, categorical measures of the severity of disability, a dummy variable indicating whether the worker had worked since his or her injury, the log of the pre-injury wage, years of work experience, a dummy variable indicating whether or not the worker could return to work with the time-of-accident employer, the log of the duration from date of accident to date of VR referral, and the log of the monthly workers' compensation benefit.

3 The Gardner studies considered a broader range of vocational rehabilitation outcomes than just the return to work. The other outcomes he examined included successful completion of the program, the length of the program, and earnings recovery.

on a 'successful' closure and post-VR earnings using the data from the Berkeley Planning Associates (1973, 1975) studies. This vocational rehabilitation was not provided as part of a work-injury program. A 'successful' closure was recorded when a worker was placed in a job, including homemaking, and he or she remained at work for at least one month. They found that more severely disabled individuals were more likely to experience success than the less severely disabled, in part because the more severely disabled were more likely to receive substantive VR interventions. Women were found to be more likely to experience success than men, controlling for severity of the disability. Some of this result may be due to the inclusion of return to housework as a successful closure.

Vocational Rehabilitation in Ontario: The Old and the New

Administrative models of vocational rehabilitation have widely varying shapes and forms. Berkowitz (1990) distinguished VR models on the basis of various criteria, including the specified objectives of VR; the selection criterion, that is, whether or not selection is based on duration of injury or on a screening of all cases at a particular time; whether or not participation in the rehabilitation program is voluntary or mandatory on the part of both workers and employers; the incentives created to encourage injured workers and firms to participate and to effect a return to work; and, a separate aspect of the previous point, the interrelationship between benefit payments and VR.

Berkowitz (1990, 27) suggested a spectrum of VR models. At one end is the 'insurance model' which he described as

> the conscious use of the mechanisms of rehabilitation to affect the cost of the beneficiary program (i.e., the cost of workers' compensation benefit payments). Also, part and parcel of this belief is the notion that such activities can and do redound to the benefit of the injured worker. There is implicit in these formulations the idea of a harmony of interest between the insurer and the worker. The creed is that rehabilitation is good business and that it is good for the worker.

At the other end of the spectrum is the 'traditional rehabilitation model' (Berkowitz 1990, 28–29), characterized as a system in which

> clients seek admission and are evaluated for suitability. The rehabilitation officer may not even be aware of the client's work injury pro-

gram status and may care little about the details of the benefits program. . . .

Reference to a rehabilitation officer in the singular may be inappropriate. . . . There may be no one such person who acts in the capacity of a case manager. Several persons may be involved in the case. A psychologist might be concerned with the evaluation of human behavior and perhaps therapy, a social worker may be focused on resource issues and a labour market official might be concerned with placement. If the focus is not on quick return to the former job, training and retraining become important with the consequent involvement of vocational training officials.

The injuries which resulted in the injured worker and vocational rehabilitation data analyzed in this chapter occurred primarily in the middle 1980s. Thus, the vocational rehabilitation program which operated in these years is first described. Then details of the changes which have occurred, both by policy and legislation, since 1986 are provided. The old and new systems are characterized using the criteria and definitions put forward by Berkowitz (1990).

Brief History to 1986

Rehabilitation services were first offered in Ontario in 1924 to severely disabled workers only, and an expenditures ceiling was applied. Services consisted primarily of negotiating with employers for re-employment and retraining. In 1938, a separate VR department was established which provided personal, occupational, and social counselling. The ceiling on expenditures was lifted in 1974, and support for both academic and vocational training added. By the mid-1980s, with staff located across the province, the WCB provided many vocational services, including vocational evaluation, specialized counselling by disability and occupational grouping, worksite analyses, and job-search and placement assistance (WCB 1987a).

Whereas most injured workers who lose time from work return to work within a few weeks without permanent impairment, a small percentage do not. Vocational rehabilitation services are typically provided to injured workers for whom the disabling consequences of their injuries are relatively more 'serious' i.e., they result in permanent physical impairment or make it impossible for the workers to return to the work they were doing before the injury. Two statistics which indicate the relative size of the group of workers who are more seriously disabled are:

For 1986, the percentage of lost-time injuries newly referred to receive vocational rehabilitation services was 4.3 percent. (WCB 1987b, 4)

For 1986, the percentage of original lost-time injuries receiving an award for permanent impairment was about 7.7 percent. (Allingham, Hale and Ross 1987, 107)

These two statistics show that the more seriously disabled injured workers constitute a small proportion overall, although the two groups are not coincident. The second percentage (permanently impaired cases) is higher than the first because, for some cases of permanent impairment, a return to work is possible without VR intervention.

The cases analyzed in this chapter are all from the permanently impaired population of Ontario injured workers. It may be inferred from Table 1 that the selection of cases for VR services focuses on those who are more seriously disabled in their return to work potential. For example, the percentage of those not receiving VR services who returned to work was about 91 percent, while for those who received VR services, it was only 39 percent.

The following data summarize vocational rehabilitation services provided in 1986 (WCB 1987b):

Lost-time injuries (1986)	196,000
Active VR cases	10,731
Total closures of VR services	10,101
Total employed closures	5,151
VR programs	
Training on the job	978
Formal education	1,248
Skill development	892
Assessments	4,789
Average time to VR referral	17 months
Average length of VR service	11 months

Using Berkowitz' criteria and definitions, the mid 1980s VR program at the WCB may be characterized as close to the insurance model under which the insurer for benefits and provider of rehabilitation services are one and the same. However, a conscious and concerted communications program may not have been carried out to staff and employers to make all of the parties fully aware of the direct relationship between successful VR and reduced compensation costs. The goal of VR was stated as the restoration of earnings capacity by providing effective services to facilitate an early return to work including arrangements, wherever possible, for productive employment. It was further recognized that effective VR services result in benefits to society as a whole (WCB 1987a).

Selection criteria were based on achievement of maximum medical rehabilitation and evidence of the ability to carry out work at some level, but not on availability of suitable work with the pre-accident employer. Also, cases referred for VR services were judged capable of benefitting from such services. Participation by the worker was effectively mandatory, since 'non-cooperation' could result in the reduction of benefits. For employers, no mandatory requirements existed.

Incentives for the injured worker to return to work and/or participate in VR programs were affected by fairly high wage-replacement ratios: 75 percent of gross wages for injuries before 1 April 1985, 90 percent net (of taxes) wages thereafter. The primary incentives for some employers were the possibility of reducing overall workers' compensation costs—an important consideration for experience-rated employers—and the cost sharing of some training-on-the-job programs.

Benefits entitlement staff and VR staff were in reasonably close contact in referral and case management. However, VR personnel had some control over benefits entitlement in that, as noted above, participation by the injured worker was almost mandatory. However, VR plans were developed with a substantial amount of consultation with the worker.

Developments Since 1986 Leading to Bill 162

In 1986, the Ontario Ministry of Labour commissioned a task force on the vocational rehabilitation services of the WCB. A series of recommendations were made in the task force report of 1987 which led to development of a new Vocational Rehabilitation Strategy (VRS). The VRS adopted many of the principles enunciated in the task force report including partnership in the development of VR goal-oriented plans; early intervention; accessible, timely and intensive services; and the separation of entitlement from decisionmaking. Parallel legislation was also being developed. Various sections of Bill 162, which came into effect 2 January 1990, provide legislative support to the VRS:

Early intervention:

45 day contact for workers who have not returned to their work to identify the need for vocational rehabilitation services.

Offer of vocational rehabilitation assessment at six months for all workers who have not returned to work.

Support for the principle of partnership:

Design of vocational rehabilitation programs in consultation with the worker and, if possible, with the employer and the worker's physician.

Obligation to re-employ:

Provisions which, in most cases, require larger employers to re-employ an injured worker who had been continuously employed by that employer for at least one year prior to the work-related injury.

Confirmation of the hierarchy of objectives as outlined in the Vocational Rehabilitation Strategy.

It can be seen that VRS and Bill 162 strengthened the old VR program and provided powerful incentives for its use: together they re-emphasized the goal of restoring the injured worker's pre-injury earnings profile and the notion that employers' workers' compensation costs could be reduced by effective VR. Selection criteria are now clearly focused on very specific and early intervention (often before maximum medical rehabilitation); they relate to those who cannot return to their pre-injury employer and to those who can benefit from VR. For workers, participation is still 'mandatory' even though there has been some dissociation of benefits' payments from VR case management. Wage-replacement rates remain at 90 percent of net pre-accident wages. For most large employers, participation through worker reinstatement rights is now mandatory. The legislation also specifies the parties to the development of VR plans. With today's emphasis on cost control, and more targeted communications' initiatives to stakeholders by the WCB emphasizing the benefits of effective VR, it is clear that the Ontario system has moved even closer to the 'insurance' model described by Berkowitz.

The Models

The goal of workers' compensation programs in general, and of vocational rehabilitation in particular, is to mitigate the disabling consequences of a workplace injury. The effect of vocational rehabilitation can be realized with respect to both labour-market and nonlabour-market activities. Labour-market outcomes that could be influenced by VR include the probability of return to work, post-injury wage loss, stability of post-injury employment and maintenance of post-injury occupational status.

This analysis focuses on one potential labour market outcome of vocational rehabilitation—enhancing the probability of return to work following a permanently disabling injury. That is, it is hypothesized that vocational rehabilitation reduces the expected negative impact of the worker's residual disability on the post-injury return to work.

The impact of vocational rehabilitation on the post-injury return to work of permanently injured workers is considered within the framework of a discrete dependent variable model. The probability that an individual returns to work (Prob[P=1]) is related to an indicator of whether or not the worker participated in a VR program following the injury (VR), a measure of the worker's residual disability (RD), and a vector of other variables which may influence the return to work (X). This relationship can be summarized as:

$$Prob[P = 1] = F(VR, RD, X) + \varepsilon$$

$P = 1$, if the worker does return to work,

$P = 0$, if the worker does not return to work.

The variable ε is a random error term. Assuming that the function is linear in the parameters of the arguments, and that the error term is distributed with a Type I Extreme Value distribution, a closed form for the probability that an injured worker returns to work following an injury is given by the logit function:

$$Prob[P = 1] = \exp(\alpha VR + \tau RD + \beta'X) / [1 + \exp(\alpha VR + \tau RD + \beta'X)]$$

where α, τ and β are parameters to be estimated.

Another way of saying this is that vocational rehabilitation reduces the negative consequences for return to work of a disabling injury for all degrees of permanent disability. Thus, given two workers identical in their characteristics and in the degree of their residual disability, the impact of the residual disability should be less for the one who participated in a VR program. In other words, the derivative, $\delta P/\delta RD$, which is expected to be negatively signed, should be smaller in absolute terms for those who experienced a VR intervention.

This suggests that at a minimum, the vocational rehabilitation variable should be interacted with the residual disability variable. In order to accommodate this interaction, the return-to-work model is estimated using the full sample, including a VR/residual disability interaction variable. An alternative specification, in which the model is estimated separately on the subsamples of those who received VR and those who did not, permits interaction of vocational rehabilitation with all of the independent variables.

It is unlikely that permanently injured workers are randomly assigned into a vocational rehabilitation program. In fact, if a worker is either able to return to work or suffers no residual disability following an injury then the need for vocational rehabilitation is essentially eliminated.

This suggests two things. First, selection to participate in a VR program may simply indicate that the worker is more seriously disabled in the sense that he or she has not been successful in returning to work and, second, participation in a VR program will depend on the perceived (by the worker and/or the WCB) ability of the worker to return to work following VR. A typical criterion for selection is an assessment that the worker is likely to benefit from a VR intervention.

The point is that participation in a VR program may be endogenously determined, and many of the same factors that influence the return to work will also influence VR participation. Referral to VR will be based on the extent of the residual disability and the nature of the injury experienced by the worker. If selection criteria include the likelihood that the worker will benefit from VR in the sense of returning the worker to the labour force, then selection may be influenced by the worker's age, level of education, and vocational training received prior to the injury, and other human capital characteristics. If the costs of permanent disability fall more directly on employers, as may be the case with experience-rated employers, then these employers may encourage the individual to participate in a VR program with the expectation that a successful VR episode will result in enhanced labour-market earnings for the worker, and lower benefit costs for the employer.

In order to address the endogeneity of participation in a vocational rehabilitation program, a logit function of the probability of participation in a VR program is estimated, based on the worker's residual disability, the pre-injury annual wage, demographic and human capital characteristics of the worker, the labour market in which the worker resides, the nature of the injury, the part of body injured and whether or not the employer was enroled in one of Ontario's experience-rating plans, or was self-insured. Fitted values from this model are included as instruments in a return-to-work logit equation estimated on the full sample of permanently injured workers.

The Data and Variables

The data are drawn from the Ontario Workers' Compensation Board. Components of the working data set were extracted from a number of the Board's administrative files, and merged with a recently completed survey of permanently impaired workers in Ontario.

The Survey of Ontario Workers with Permanent Impairments (SOW) collected demographic, human capital, and pre- and post-injury labour-market data on permanently impaired workers injured before Bill 162 came into effect. Workers were interviewed as they visited the WCB for the purpose of establishing their clinical permanent disability rating. This disability rating was multiplied by the worker's pre-injury earnings to determine the lifetime permanent disability pension under the pre-Bill 162 regime. The interviews took place between July 1989 and August 1990. The demographic information includes age at the time of interview, gender, ability to speak English, and marital status. The human-capital variables consist of education and pre-injury vocational training. The labour-market information includes earnings, occupation and experience, and was recorded for the time-of-injury job and for up to six post-injury jobs.

The SOW collected very limited data on the injured worker's experiences with vocational rehabilitation. Thus, data from the WCB's vocational rehabilitation administrative files were merged with the economic-loss survey data. The information available from the VR database included the dates of VR interventions the workers experienced since the time of their injury. Information on the specific type of intervention received by the worker (education, or vocational training, for example,) was not available from the VR database.

Information on the nature of the worker's injury, the part of body injured and the worker's permanent disability rating (a measure of the worker's residual physical impairment), and VR data were extracted from the WCB's systems and merged with the survey data.

The sample consisted of 6,613 permanently injured workers, of whom 3,478 participated in a VR program and 3,135 did not. Of the 6,613 individuals in the full sample, 63.6 percent (4,206) returned to work. Of those who did not participate in a VR program, 90.6 percent (2,839) returned to work. Only 39.3 percent (1,367) of those participating in a VR program returned to work.

The binary-coded dependent variable takes a value of 1 if the worker returned to work following his or her permanently disabling injury, and 0 if the worker did not. There are two key independent variables. The first is a dummy variable indicating whether or not the worker participated in a vocational rehabilitation program following injury. The second is the worker's permanent disability rating, which provides a measure of the worker's permanent residual disability. The permanent disability rating takes a value between 0 and 100 percent and was assigned by a workers' compensation board doctor after the worker reached maximum medical rehabilitation. For example, a permanent disability rating of 40 percent would indicate that the injury had reduced the worker's physical abilities, relative to those of a non-injured worker, by 40 percent.

A number of other control variables assumed to influence injured workers' return to work were included in the regressions. The time-of-injury annual wage was included as a measure of the workers' potential wage in the labour market following an injury. A positive association between the pre-injury wage and return to work was expected.

The remaining independent variables were classified into seven categories: demographics, education, location, nature of injury, part of body injured, experience rating of the time-of-accident employer, and the time-of-injury occupation. The demographic variables included (with hypothesized relationship to return to work, where they are not ambiguous in brackets): age at the time of injury (-), a dummy variable indicating whether or not the worker is married; a dummy variable coded as 1 if the worker is male, and 0 if the worker is female; a marital-status/gender-interaction term (indicating that the survey respondent is a married male); a dummy variable indicating whether the worker can speak English (+); and a dummy denoting union membership at the time of injury (+).

The education variables included two mutually exclusive dummy variables one indicating that the worker has a high school diploma and another that the worker has an education beyond a high school diploma. The reference category was education below a high school diploma. Return to work was expected to be an increasing function of education.

The location dummy variables indicated the WCB's regional office at which the worker's claim was administered. The reference regional office was Toronto. In most instances, the worker's claim is administered at the regional office closest to the worker's place of time-of-injury employment. Thus, these variables may control for regional labour market factors which could influence the worker's return to work. They may also pick up differences across regions in the availability and quality of vocational rehabilitation services.

A number of dummy variables were constructed to indicate the nature of the worker's injury and the part of body injured. The reference nature-of-injury category included bruises, contusions, cuts, scratches, and inflammations. The reference part-of-body-injured category was hand, including fingers.

Five dummy variables were constructed to identify the experience-rating program to which the worker's time-of-accident employer belonged.[4] The reference category was 'not experience rated.'

Finally, 14 dummy variables indicating the worker's time-of-injury occupation were constructed. The reference category included administrative, professional, sales, and service occupations.

Means and standard deviations for all of the variables, broken down by employment status and whether or not the worker experienced a VR intervention, are presented in Table 1.

Estimation Results

Table 2 presents the logit coefficients for the return-to-work model estimated on the full sample and on the subsamples of those workers who did and did not experience a VR intervention.

The full-sample results presented in column 1 of Table 2 indicate that participation in a VR program is associated with a significantly lower probability of return to work. Evaluated at the mean probability of returning to work (0.636) and the mean permanent disability rating (0.12), participation in a VR program reduces the probability of return to work by 68 percent. This result suggests that participation in a VR program is simply a signal that the individual has been chronically unable to return to work since the injury occurred as a result of various possible barriers.

The change in the probability of a return to work given a one percentage point change in the permanent disability rating is -1.4 percent for individuals who did not participate in a VR program, when evaluated at the mean of the dependent variable. For those who did participate in VR, the change in the probability of return to work given a one percentage point increase in the permanent disability rating falls, in absolute terms, to -0.09 percent. Thus, it appears that vocational rehabilitation is having the intended effect—it is reducing the negative impact of residual disabilities on the return to work of injured workers.

4 The experience-rating programs are designed to tailor a firm's workers' compensation insurance premiums to reflect more closely the firm's claims-cost experience. Firms experiencing accident costs below the industry average will be charged a lower rate for workers' compensation insurance than firms with above average costs. This creates an incentive for firms to lower the costs of workers' compensation claims. During the period relevant to this study the Ontario WCB operated three experience-rating programs—NEER (New Experimental Experience Rating program), CAD-7 (Council Amended Draft 7) and the Voluntary plan, which differ in the size of the financial incentives they create, and the industries they cover. Some employers in Ontario are self-insured implying that they are fully experience rated. Details on Ontario's experience rating programs can be found in Hyatt and Kralj (1995).

Table 1

Variable Means and Standard Deviations (standard deviation in parentheses)

Variable	Employed after injury VR	Employed after injury No VR	Not employed after injury VR	Not employed after injury No VR
Permanent disability rating	0.12 (0.08)	0.09 (0.07)	0.15 (0.10)	0.15 (0.10)
Pre-injury annual wage	18,160 (7,460)	19,430 (8,570)	17,339 (8,012)	17,143 (8,688)
Demographics				
Age	37.1 (9.68)	40.56 (11.66)	42.57 (11.43)	49.20 (11.70)
Married	0.73 (0.44)	0.77 (0.42)	0.78 (0.42)	0.79 (0.41)
Male	0.67 (0.47)	0.80 (0.40)	0.66 (0.47)	0.64 (0.48)
Married * male	0.51 (0.50)	0.63 (0.48)	0.53 (0.50)	0.51 (0.50)
Non-English speaking	0.04 (0.21)	0.08 (0.28)	0.14 (0.35)	0.26 (0.44)
Union member at time of injury	0.59 (0.49)	0.61 (0.49)	0.53 (0.50)	0.47 (0.50)
Education [Less than high school diploma]				
High school diploma	0.24 (0.43)	0.26 (0.44)	0.17 (0.37)	0.16 (0.37)
> high school diploma	0.16 (0.37)	0.16 (0.37)	0.08 (0.28)	0.10 (0.30)
Pre-injury vocational training	0.41 (0.49)	0.42 (0.49)	0.34 (0.47)	0.27 (0.44)
Location [Toronto]				
Thunder Bay	0.06 (0.23)	0.07 (0.25)	0.05 (0.22)	0.03 (0.18)
Ottawa	0.14 (0.35)	0.12 (0.33)	0.11 (0.31)	0.13 (0.34)
Sudbury	0.09 (0.28)	0.10 (0.31)	0.11 (0.31)	0.15 (0.35)
Windsor	0.07 (0.26)	0.05 (0.22)	0.06 (0.24)	0.02 (0.13)
Hamilton	0.13 (0.33)	0.12 (0.32)	0.11 (0.31)	0.15 (0.36)
London	0.12 (0.32)	0.07 (0.25)	0.12 (0.32)	0.04 (0.19)
Nature of injury [Bruises, contusions, cuts, scratches, inflammations]				
Dislocation/fracture	0.06 (0.25)	0.13 (0.33)	0.06 (0.24)	0.07 (0.26)
Sprain	0.65 (0.48)	0.43 (0.50)	0.64 (0.48)	0.60 (0.49)
Unspecified	0.08 (0.27)	0.07 (0.26)	0.08 (0.27)	0.08 (0.27)
Part of body injured [Hand, fingers]				
Head/neck	0.03 (0.16)	0.03 (0.16)	0.03 (0.17)	0.04 (0.19)
Wrist	0.04 (0.19)	0.03 (0.18)	0.03 (0.18)	0.03 (0.17)
Back	0.41 (0.49)	0.23 (0.42)	0.44 (0.50)	0.42 (0.49)
Shoulder	0.09 (0.28)	0.06 (0.24)	0.08 (0.27)	0.08 (0.27)
Knee	0.05 (0.22)	0.08 (0.28)	0.05 (0.22)	0.04 (0.19)
Arm	0.07 (0.26)	0.07 (0.26)	0.05 (0.22)	0.03 (0.18)
Trunk	0.02 (0.14)	0.02 (0.14)	0.03 (0.16)	0.03 (0.17)
Lower extremity	0.04 (0.20)	0.06 (0.24)	0.05 (0.21)	0.05 (0.22)
Foot/toe	0.02 (0.13)	0.03 (0.18)	0.02 (0.15)	0.01 (0.12)
Multiple parts	0.10 (0.30)	0.08 (0.27)	0.13 (0.33)	0.15 (0.36)
Unspecified	0.06 (0.25)	0.06 (0.24)	0.05 (0.22)	0.08 (0.27)
Time-of-injury employer experience rating [Not experience rated]				
NEER	0.19 (0.39)	0.14 (0.34)	0.17 (0.37)	0.19 (0.39)
CAD-7	0.12 (0.33)	0.09 (0.29)	0.13 (0.34)	0.14 (0.34)
Voluntary	0.40 (0.49)	0.41 (0.49)	0.39 (0.49)	0.29 (0.46)
Self-insured	0.08 (0.28)	0.12 (0.32)	0.07 (0.26)	0.07 (0.26)
Unspecified	0.00 (0.00)	0.02 (0.14)	0.00 (0.00)	0.04 (0.19)

(continued)

Table 1 (continued)

Variable	Employed after injury		Not employed after injury	
	VR	No VR	VR	No VR
Occupation (at time of injury) [Administrative, professional, sales, service]				
Clerical	0.05 (0.21)	0.05 (0.22)	0.04 (0.20)	0.05 (0.22)
Medicine	0.07 (0.26)	0.02 (0.15)	0.04 (0.20)	0.04 (0.19)
Farming	0.02 (0.12)	0.01 (0.12)	0.01 (0.12)	0.03 (0.16)
Forestry	0.01 (0.12)	0.01 (0.11)	0.02 (0.14)	0.01 (0.12)
Mining	0.01 (0.11)	0.03 (0.18)	0.02 (0.13)	0.02 (0.14)
Processing	0.08 (0.27)	0.07 (0.26)	0.07 (0.25)	0.08 (0.27)
Machining	0.06 (0.25)	0.09 (0.29)	0.08 (0.26)	0.06 (0.23)
Fabricating	0.19 (0.39)	0.20 (0.40)	0.17 (0.37)	0.15 (0.36)
Construction	0.15 (0.36)	0.14 (0.35)	0.16 (0.36)	0.18 (0.38)
Transportation	0.09 (0.29)	0.07 (0.25)	0.08 (0.27)	0.04 (0.21)
Materials handling	0.05 (0.21)	0.06 (0.24)	0.06 (0.24)	0.06 (0.23)
Equipment operating	0.01 (0.10)	0.01 (0.10)	0.01 (0.09)	0.01 (0.08)
Other	0.04 (0.20)	0.05 (0.22)	0.05 (0.21)	0.05 (0.23)
Unspecified	0.04 (0.18)	0.03 (0.18)	0.04 (0.19)	0.03 (0.16)
Number of observations	1367	2839	2111	296

Table 2

Return to Work Logit Estimates (t-statistics in parentheses)

Variable	Full sample	No VR	VR
Participated in VR program *(VR)*	-3.205 (-21.63)		
Permanent disability rating *(PDR)*	-6.212 (-8.01)	-5.415 (-6.49)	-4.184 (-7.78)
VR ***PDR*	2.115 (2.34)		
Pre-injury annual wage	0.019 (3.86)	0.024 (2.29)	0.020 (3.43)
Demographics			
Age	0.135 (6.06)	0.146 (3.16)	0.139 (5.05)
Age squared	-0.002 (-8.23)	-0.002 (-4.45)	-0.002 (-6.60)
Married	-0.095 (-0.74)	-0.124 (-0.44)	-0.047 (-0.32)
Male	0.059 (0.40)	0.116 (0.35)	0.064 (0.39)
Married * male	0.303 (1.87)	0.562 (1.58)	0.187 (1.03)
Non-English speaking	-0.729 (-6.32)	-0.648 (-3.50)	-0.791 (-4.97)
Union member at time of injury	0.312 (4.44)	0.627 (4.25)	0.214 (2.64)
Education [Less than high school diploma]			
High school diploma	0.324 (3.74)	0.129 (0.66)	0.372 (3.82)
> high school diploma	0.513 (4.68)	0.062 (0.26)	0.587 (4.83)
Pre-injury vocational training	0.245 (3.44)	0.403 (2.54)	0.190 (2.35)
Location [Toronto]			
Thunder Bay	0.221 (1.42)	0.318 (0.86)	0.217 (1.21)
Ottawa	0.193 (1.79)	-0.226 (-1.02)	0.299 (2.45)
Sudbury	-0.317 (-2.58)	-0.815 (-3.55)	-0.162 (-1.13)
Windsor	0.068 (0.47)	0.427 (0.84)	0.046 (0.29)
Hamilton	0.088 (0.82)	-0.387 (-1.83)	0.218 (1.75)
London	0.040 (0.35)	0.173 (0.49)	0.028 (0.22)

(continued)

Table 2 (continued)

Variable	Full sample	No VR	VR
Nature of injury [Bruises, contusions, cuts, scratches, inflammations]			
Dislocation/fracture	0.240 (1.53)	0.330 (1.03)	0.292 (1.52)
Sprain	-0.113 (-1.12)	-0.351 (-1.60)	-0.008 (-0.07)
Unspecified	0.057 (0.41)	0.088 (0.31)	0.087 (0.54)
Part of body injured [Hand, fingers]			
Head/neck	-0.580 (-2.47)	-1.636 (-3.44)	-0.148 (-0.53)
Wrist	-0.628 (-2.83)	-1.500 (-3.05)	-0.277 (-1.06)
Back	-0.561 (-3.58)	-1.552 (-4.20)	-0.165 (-0.87)
Shoulder	-0.389 (-2.09)	-1.524 (-3.63)	0.047 (0.22)
Knee	-0.399 (-2.03)	-0.746 (-1.61)	-0.191 (-0.81)
Arm	-0.058 (-0.30)	-0.916 (-1.94)	0.301 (1.33)
Trunk	-0.441 (-1.79)	-1.225 (-2.37)	-0.113 (-0.38)
Lower extremity	-0.598 (-2.91)	-1.425 (-3.22)	-0.291 (-1.16)
Foot/toe	-0.800 (-3.19)	-0.795 (-1.29)	-0.675 (-2.15)
Multiple parts	-0.670 (-4.02)	-1.686 (-4.60)	-0.244 (-1.20)
Unspecified	-0.410 (-2.19)	-1.490 (-3.79)	0.059 (0.26)
Occupation (at time of injury) [Administrative, professional, sales, service]			
Clerical	0.267 (1.51)	0.251 (0.75)	0.283 (1.38)
Medicine	0.280 (1.56)	0.026 (0.07)	0.319 (1.62)
Farming	0.154 (0.55)	-0.279 (-0.56)	0.347 (1.07)
Forestry	-0.480 (-1.62)	-0.828 (-1.34)	-0.403 (-1.20)
Mining	-0.170 (-0.64)	0.332 (0.65)	-0.425 (-1.24)
Processing	0.176 (1.18)	0.028 (0.09)	0.232 (1.34)
Machining	-0.222 (-1.42)	-0.127 (-0.39)	-0.258 (-1.40)
Fabricating	0.112 (0.93)	0.118 (0.48)	0.100 (0.71)
Construction	-0.067 (-0.51)	-0.483 (-1.89)	0.053 (0.35)
Transportation	0.307 (2.03)	0.399 (1.11)	0.261 (1.53)
Materials handling	-0.073 (-0.45)	0.082 (0.26)	-0.162 (-0.84)
Equipment operating	0.131 (0.36)	-0.050 (-0.06)	0.147 (0.36)
Other	0.100 (0.56)	-0.163 (-0.47)	0.144 (0.68)
Unspecified	0.024 (0.12)	0.391 (0.85)	-0.079 (-0.35)
Constant	1.321	1.790	-2.355
-2 x log likelihood ratio	2933.1	451.8	517.5
Number of observations	6613	3135	3478

When the sample is split into those who did not have VR (column 2) and those who did (column 3), thereby effectively allowing VR to interact with all of the variables in the model, the results based on the full sample are confirmed. The coefficient for the permanent disability rating in the model estimated for the 'No VR' subsample is larger (in absolute terms) than the coefficient on the same variable using the 'VR' sample.

The size of the pre-injury annual wage was positive and statistically significant in all three of the regressions reported in Table 2. Age appears to have a nonlinear relationship with respect to the return to work. Male workers were more likely to return to work than female workers, while married males were more likely to return to work than both females and nonmarried males. Non-English speaking workers were found to be significantly less likely to return to work in all three of the regressions.

Workers who were union members at the time of their injury were always found to be significantly more likely to return to work. This result may reflect the ability of unions to help protect the jobs of injured workers, and to facilitate their return to the workplace.

Those who had a high school education or beyond were more likely to return to work than those with less than a high school diploma in the full sample and 'VR' regressions. However, neither of the education variables was significant in the 'No VR' regression. Thus, those who were more 'labour market advantaged,' at least in terms of education, prior to a VR intervention, will be more likely to find employment following the intervention. Pre-injury vocational training was a positive and significant predictor of return to work in both the 'No VR' and 'VR' samples.

Workers who were injured in the Sudbury region, and who did not receive VR were less likely to return to work than workers injured in the Toronto region. Workers who lived in Ottawa and received VR following their injury were significantly more likely to return to work following their injury relative to workers injured in the Toronto region.

Those workers who experienced dislocations/fractures, sprains, or unspecified injuries were no more or less likely to return to work than those experiencing any of the reference injuries (bruises, contusions, cuts, scratches and inflammations), regardless of whether or not they participated in a VR program. Those who experienced injuries to the head/neck, wrist, back, shoulder, trunk, lower extremities, multiple, or unspecified body parts, and who did not receive a VR intervention, were significantly less likely to return to work than those who injured the reference part of body (hand/fingers). Of those workers who received VR, only those who experienced injuries to feet and toes were significantly less likely to return to work, relative to those who had injured their hands and fingers.

As indicated earlier, it is necessary to take account of the endogeneity of a vocational rehabilitation intervention. The first column of results in Table 3 shows the parameter estimates for a logit model of the probability that an individual was selected to participate in a vocational rehabilitation program following his or her injury. The probability of program participation is a nonlinear function of residual disability (as measured by the permanent disability rating). The probability of participating in VR increases up to permanent disability ratings of 53 percent, and declines for higher ratings. The pre-injury annual wage is negatively associated with VR program participation. Older, married, and male workers are less likely to participate in VR, as are those workers with education levels of a high school diploma and beyond.

Those workers who were injured in the Windsor and London regions were significantly more likely than those living in Toronto to participate in a VR program. Those experiencing dislocations and fractures were less likely, and those experiencing sprains more likely, than those with reference injuries to participate in VR. All of the part-of-body dummy variables were positive and significant, relative to the reference part-of-body category (hand/finger).

Workers who had been employed by firms participating in the CAD-7 experience-rating program at the time of the accident were more likely to participate in VR than those who had been working for nonexperience-rated employers. Those working for self-insured employers at the time of their injury were significantly less likely to participate in VR, relative to the not experience-rated reference category.[5]

Finally, workers in the medical, forestry, and transportation occupations are more likely to experience a VR intervention than those in administrative, professional, sales, and service occupations (the reference occupational category).

Table 3

VR Participation and Return to Work Logit Estimates
(t-statistics in parentheses)

Variable	Participate in VR	Return to work
Participated in VR program (fitted)		-3.777 (-8.07)
Permanent disability rating	9.196 (12.82)	-3.861 (-2.94)
Permanent disability rating squared	-8.689 (-7.22)	
VR *PDR		2.308 (1.32)
Pre-injury annual wage	-0.020 (-4.89)	0.011 (2.33)
Demographics		
Age	0.026 (1.43)	0.096 (4.96)
Age squared	-0.001 (-2.47)	-0.002 (-6.89)
Married	-0.060 (-0.51)	-0.076 (-0.66)
Male	-0.421 (-3.31)	-0.097 (-0.71)
Married * male	-0.100 (-0.71)	0.196 (1.36)
Non-English speaking	-0.173 (-1.78)	-0.529 (-5.42)
Union member at time of injury	-0.097 (-1.58)	0.199 (3.16)

(continued)

5 The experience-rating variables were included to help identify the system of equations. Thus, the experience-rating variables were not included among the regressors in the return-to-work logit in Table 3. This is unsatisfactory since one might well expect that experience rating may also influence employers to assist injured worker's return to employment. In related research, we are endeavouring to find less arbitrary identifying restrictions.

Table 3 (continued)

Variable	Participate in VR	Return to work
Education [Less than high school diploma]		
High school diploma	-0.366 (-5.18)	0.132 (1.60)
> high school diploma	-0.494 (-5.63)	0.245 (2.26)
Pre-injury vocational training	-0.074 (-1.25)	0.162 (2.60)
Location [Toronto]		
Thunder Bay	-0.013 (-0.11)	0.154 (1.15)
Ottawa	0.065 (0.73)	0.168 (1.78)
Sudbury	0.173 (1.69)	-0.209 (-1.98)
Windsor	0.634 (5.02)	0.189 (1.35)
Hamilton	0.159 (1.77)	0.100 (1.06)
London	0.774 (7.36)	0.196 (1.62)
Nature of injury [Bruises, contusions, cuts, scratches, inflammations]		
Dislocation/fracture	-0.336 (-2.83)	0.153 (1.14)
Sprain	0.290 (3.50)	0.014 (0.15)
Unspecified	-0.065 (-0.57)	0.065 (0.54)
Part of body injured [Hand, fingers]		
Head/neck	1.060 (5.65)	-0.185 (-0.81)
Wrist	1.304 (7.51)	-0.207 (-0.93)
Back	1.265 (10.26)	-0.114 (-0.61)
Shoulder	1.353 (9.26)	-0.005 (-0.03)
Knee	0.827 (5.65)	-0.182 (-1.00)
Arm	1.074 (7.50)	0.107 (0.56)
Trunk	1.121 (5.56)	-0.049 (-0.21)
Lower extremity	1.027 (6.63)	-0.257 (-1.30)
Foot/toe	1.120 (5.85)	-0.334 (-1.41)
Multiple parts	1.253 (9.66)	-0.203 (-1.07)
Unspecified	1.536 (10.03)	-0.019 (-0.09)
Time-of-injury employer experience rating [Not experience rated]		
NEER	0.165 (1.73)	
CAD-7	0.571 (4.51)	
Voluntary	0.051 (0.65)	
Self-insured	-0.257 (-2.29)	
Unspecified	-14.21 (-0.10)	
Occupation (at time of injury) [Administrative, professional, sales, service]		
Clerical	-0.247 (-1.71)	0.139 (0.90)
Medicine	0.371 (2.16)	0.390 (2.33)
Farming	-0.118 (-0.51)	0.058 (0.24)
Forestry	0.864 (3.41)	-0.112 (-0.43)
Mining	-0.247 (-1.15)	-0.155 (-0.69)
Processing	0.116 (0.90)	0.191 (1.45)
Machining	0.146 (1.11)	-0.085 (-0.64)
Fabricating	0.068 (0.66)	0.120 (1.15)
Construction	0.138 (1.09)	0.053 (0.44)
Transportation	0.325 (2.55)	0.317 (2.34)
Materials handling	-0.161 (-1.18)	-0.066 (-0.48)
Equipment operating	0.427 (1.40)	0.259 (0.80)
Other	0.019 (0.13)	0.070 (0.46)
Unspecified	0.223 (1.35)	0.081 (0.47)
Constant	-1.368	1.536
-2 x log likelihood ratio	1337.5	1303.8
Number of observations	6613	6613

The fitted probability of participating in a VR program was obtained for all workers in the sample based on the parameter estimates from the VR participation logit. This fitted probability was included on its own and interacted with the permanent disability rating variable in a return-to-work logit model estimated using the full sample. The estimation results for the return-to-work model using the VR-program-participation instrument are presented in the second column of Table 3.

The sign on the fitted program participation variable remains negative and statistically significant, as does the coefficient on the permanent disability rate variable. The coefficient on the VR-program/permanent-disability-rating interaction term is positive, but insignificant at the 5 percent level in a two-tailed test (it is significant at the 10 percent level in a one-tailed test). Evaluated at the mean of the dependent variable and the mean permanent disability rating, participation in a VR program is associated with an 81 percent reduction in the probability of returning to work. The change in the probability of return to work given a one percentage point increase in the permanent disability rating is -0.9 percent for those workers who did not receive VR, and -0.4 percent for those who did experience a VR intervention. Failure to account for the endogeneity of VR participation in the models presented in Table 2 appears to have resulted in overestimates of the effect of the residual disability on the return to work. In addition, the negative association between post-injury employment and participation in a VR program was understated in the Table 2 models which were estimated based on the assumption that VR was an exogenous variable.

The other variables in the return-to-work equation in column 2 of Table 3, in which participation in VR was assumed to be endogenous, generally have the same sign and significance patterns as the full sample results in column 1 of Table 2. However, the coefficients for the non-English, union, and education variables are considerably smaller when the endogeneity of VR is controlled for than when it is not. In addition, the high school diploma dummy variable is not statistically significant, as it is in the results presented in column 1 of Table 2.

Summary and Concluding Remarks

The impact of vocational rehabilitation on the probability of post-injury return to work of permanently injured workers was estimated under alternative specifications of a basic logit model. The results generally support the notion that vocational rehabilitation mitigates the disabling consequences of workplace injuries with respect to returning the injured worker to employment. The support for this hypothesis is less robust when the potential endogeneity of vocational rehabilitation is addressed by the estimation strategy.

This chapter examined only one labour-market-outcome measure of the impact of vocational rehabilitation—return to work. The agenda for future research includes analyses of the impact of vocational rehabilitation on post-injury earnings and post-injury employment 'stability' (i.e., turnover, and duration of employment in post-injury jobs).

In addition, the Ontario Workers' Compensation Board has recently compiled a database indicating the types of medical rehabilitation interventions received by the Survey of Ontario Workers with Permanent Impairments participants. Also included in this data set is the amount of money spent on the interventions and the service dates. This permits the data set used in this study to be expanded to include not only the types of medical interventions, but also some measure of the accessibility, timeliness, and intensity of the intervention. Since the primary programs of workers' compensation for injured workers include medical rehabilitation, vocational rehabilitation, and financial compensation, the augmented data set will provide in large measure, at least in theory, much of the information needed to evaluate the effect of the workers' compensation system as a whole on the post-injury, labour-market experiences of permanently injured workers in pre-Bill 162 Ontario.

References

Allingham, R. and S. Sangster. 1990. Rehabilitation strategies for injured workers in Ontario: A unified approach. *Labor Law Journal* 41:534–40.

Allingham, R., K. Hale and M. Ross. 1987. *Workers' Compensation Board cost study: Main report.* Toronto: KPMG Peat Marwick.

Bellante, D. 1974. A multivariate analysis of a vocational rehabilitation program. *Journal of Human Resources* 7:226–41.

Berkeley Planning Associates. 1975. *An evaluation of the costs and effectiveness of vocational rehabilitation service strategies for individuals most severely handicapped.* Report to the US Department of Health, Education and Welfare. Washington, DC: US Government Printing Office.

———. 1978. *Implementing the Rehabilitation Act of 1983: The VR program response,* 2 vols. Report to the US Department of Health, Education and Welfare. Washington, DC: US Government Printing Office.

Berkowitz, Monroe. 1990. *Returning injured workers to employment: An international perspective.* Geneva: International Labour Office.

Burkhauser, R. 1989. Disability policy in the United States, Sweden, and the Netherlands. In *Disability and the labor market: Economic problems, policies, and programs,* edited by Monroe Berkowitz and M. Anne Hill, pp.262–84. Ithaca, NY: ILR Press.

Burton, John F. 1983. Compensation for permanent partial disabilities. In *Safety and the work force: Incentives and disincentives in workers' compensation,* edited by John D. Worrall, pp.18–60. Ithaca, NY: ILR Press.

Conley, R. 1965. *The economics of vocational rehabilitation*. Baltimore, MD: Johns Hopkins University Press.

Dean, D. and R. Dolan. 1991. Assessing the role of vocational rehabilitation in disability policy. *Journal of Policy Analysis and Management* 10:568–87.

Greenblum, J. 1977. Effect of vocational rehabilitation on employment and earnings of the disabled: State variations. *Social Security Bulletin* 40, 12:3–16.

Hyatt, Douglas E. and Boris Kralj. 1995. The impact of workers' compensation experience rating on employer appeals activity. *Industrial Relations* 34:95–106.

Ontario Workers' Compensation Board. 1987a. *An overview of vocational rehabilitation services*. Rev. ed. Toronto: The Board.

———. 1987b. *Vocational rehabilitation services: Operational statistics 1982–1986*. Toronto: The Board.

———. 1992. *Vocational rehabilitation handbook*. Toronto: The Board.

Skaburskis, A. and F. Collignon. 1991. Cost-effectiveness analysis of vocational rehabilitation services. *Canadian Journal of Program Evaluation* 6:1–23.

Worrall, J. and R. Butler. 1986. Some lessons from the workers' compensation program. In *Disability and the labor market: Economic problems, policies, and programs*, edited by Monroe Berkowitz and M. Anne Hill, pp.95–123. Ithaca, NY: ILR Press.

The Economic Determinants of the Occupational Risk of Injury

Jean-Michel Cousineau, Robert Lacroix and Anne-Marie Girard

At the beginning of the 1970s, the economic literature on workplace health and safety focused on the role of employers as safety providers and decisionmakers. It was assumed that safety investments were the principal determinants of accident rates at the level of the firm, and that accident rates were negatively related to safety expenditures. It was also assumed that employers were the sole or primary buyers of such equipment or measures. As a result, the incidence of accidents was hypothesized to be determined by employers' safety decisions, which were based on a calculus that minimized the sum of accidents and prevention costs (Calabresi 1970, Oi 1974, Smith 1973, Chelius 1974, and Steele 1974). Further theoretical development (Viscusi 1979) introduced interactive effects between workers and employers by showing that workers consider the employer's behaviour when making their own decisions affecting workplace safety.

The econometric literature (Smith 1973, Chelius 1974, Steele 1974, Viscusi 1979, and Lanoie 1987) referred to this basic theoretical framework when investigating the empirical determinants of occupational injuries. Variables such as the capital-labour ratio, hours of work, socioeconomic characteristics of workers, and specific regulatory measures were used to predict a risk variable based on industrial accident rates, i.e., using data aggregated by industrial sector.[1] This study, how-

Note: The authors thank professors Charles Beach, Richard P. Chaykowski, Claude Montmarquette, François Vaillancourt and participants at the Challenges to Workers' Compensation in Canada conference for useful comments on a previous version of this chapter, as well as Sophie Mahseredjian and Nicholas Gravel for their contribution to this project. The research was funded by the Fonds pour la Formation de Chercheurs et l'aide a la recherche, the Conseil de recherche en sciences humaines du Canada, and the Institut de recherche en santé et en sécurité du travail.

1 Most of the literature on the effects of workers' compensation benefits and occupational safety and health regulations on the incidence of work-related accidents is based on industry-level data (see Butler and Worral 1983, Butler 1983 and Ruser 1985 for the effect of benefits and Viscusi 1979 and Viscusi 1983 for the effect of safety and health regulations). For Canadian evidence, see Lanoie (1992a and 1992b).

ever, examines occupational accident rates. Generally speaking, data aggregated by occupational classification are not readily available; the data on work accidents by occupational classification used here were obtained from the Commission de la santé et de la sécurité du travail du Québec (CSST).

There are at least four good reasons for studying work-related accidents using data aggregated by occupation. First, the use of industrial accident rates implicitly assumes that risks are homogeneous across occupations within an industry. This is quite unrealistic given that industries typically include workers representing a wide range of occupations—for example, secretaries, salesmen, repairmen, maintenance employees, and production workers—each of which faces quite different risks.[2] If risks belong first and primarily to an occupation, then the accident rate for a given occupation is more likely to affect the occupational choices of workers in the labour market than the accident rate associated with a given industry.

Second, relationships between some socioeconomic variables, such as the level of education and training of workers in the reference group (industry or occupation), and the accident rate are more direct at the occupational level.

Third, use of occupational data makes it possible to control more directly for technological characteristics as well as features of the physical environment (e.g., heat, humidity, and noise conditions) associated with particular jobs. Previous research examining industry-level accident rates could only indirectly control for these characteristics with variables such as the capital-labour ratio.

Finally, using occupational data provides a better understanding of the relationship between the accident rate and the technological or physical characteristics of particular jobs. Knowledge of the effects of both changing technologies and the occupational composition of the labour force on the accident rate, could be useful in predicting long-term trends in accident rates.

The first section of the chapter briefly recalls the employer/employee-based theoretical framework. The following two sections present the data, the variables, and the model. The fourth reports and comments on the estimated results, and the main findings are summarized in the conclusion.

The Theoretical Framework and Some Empirical Implications

If it is assumed that employers are solely responsible for accident prevention costs and investment in safety equipment and that a definite

---

2 For a critical review of the literature and some similar comments, see Digby and Riddell (1986) and Haydon et al. (1977).

trade-off exists between the level of investment in safety and the risk of accidents, it follows that the factors that determine safety investment will also determine risks in the workplace.

In his or her decision to purchase safety equipment or other safety-enhancing measures,[3] the cost-minimizing or profit-maximizing employer will have to balance the savings in accident costs resulting from the adoption of such measures with the costs of these accident prevention measures.[4] The optimal amount of safety equipment is reached when marginal savings are equal to marginal costs. Thus, whatever affects marginal costs and savings will also affect investment in safety equipment and, hence, the risk of workplace accidents.

Generally speaking, the marginal costs of safety equipment or other prevention measures depend upon technological characteristics. Accident costs include both direct and indirect costs. Direct costs are workers' compensation benefits (wage-replacement or lump-sum payments) and medical expenses. Indirect costs include the costs of interrupted production due to the accident, administrative costs, the costs of material and equipment repair or replacement, the cost of replacing injured workers, and the productivity losses that might result from this.[5]

An empirical framework that investigates three specific hypotheses is presented: the incidence of work-related accidents is (1) negatively related to the direct costs of accidents, (2) positively related to prevention costs, and (3) negatively related to indirect accident costs. The validity of the first hypothesis, however, is conditional upon whether or not and to what extent employers are experience rated. Inadequate experience rating means that direct costs are insensitive to safety decisions made by the firm, making the relationship between the accident rate and direct accident costs inoperative.[6]

The Data Sets and Variables

To test the preceding hypotheses, three large data sets were pooled. First, a sample of administrative records from the CSST was drawn to construct the dependent variable—the risk of accident (*RISK*)—as well as a measure of the average 'direct' cost of compensation (*DCOST*). Second, data on relevant socioeconomic characteristics pertaining to each

3 These measures could include a slowdown in the pace of production or a costly reorganization of work.
4 As noted by Viscusi (1979), the effect of additional safety investment may be partially offset by a reduction in the preventive behaviour of workers, who feel better protected.
5 For a recent survey and estimation of indirect costs, see Brody et al. (1990).
6 In an experience-rated system, insurance premiums increase with the accident record. Poor records mean higher premiums while safer records may result in significant discounts.

occupational group were obtained from the 1981 Census of Canada. Finally, the *Canadian Classification and Dictionary of Occupations* (*CCDO*) was used to identify various technological and physical characteristics of occupations. Variables derived from these three sources are listed in Table 1.

As mentioned earlier, the micro-administrative files of the CSST, which identify the occupation of the injured worker, were used to build a database. To construct a 'risk' measure, defined as the proportion of workers by occupation who had suffered a work-related accident or an injury over a certain period of time, a one in ten sample was drawn from the original CSST database. This sample of 99,600 observations (compensated claims) was then aggregated by occupation at the four-digit level.[7] These data supplied information on the total number of injuries occurring between January 1981 and May 1985 for 261 occupational groups. Occupational accident rates were constructed by dividing the total number of accidents for each occupation by

Table 1

Variable Names and Definitions

Variable	Variable Definition
ln *INC*	Natural logarithm of average annual labour income for occupation.
EDUC	Average level of education for occupation.
EXP	Average level of work experience for occupation: age—years of education—6.
*EXP*²	Average work experience squared.
GEDVST	Years of general education and specific vocational training required by the occupation.
DISPER	Income dispersion for occupation: the difference between the third and fourth quartiles of the labour income distribution.
FULL	Proportion of full-time/full-year workers in occupation.
RISK	Risk of work injury in occupation: (total number of accidents/employment) x 100.
HUMID	1,0—occupation is subject to conditions of extreme humidity.
NOISE	1,0—occupation is subject to conditions of extreme noise.
HEAT	1,0—occupation is subject to conditions of extreme heat.
STRENGTH	1,0—occupation requires lifting of 50 or more kilograms.
MAR	Proportion of married workers in occupation.
SING	Proportion of single workers in occupation.
DCOST	'Direct' costs of work accidents, by occupation: average workers' compensation costs per claim by occupation.

7 The original file contained 1.5 million claims of which 66.4 percent were compensated between January 1981 and May 1985. No information was available on the number of employees, wage rates, or other relevant variables at the level of the individual firm.

employment in that occupational group.[8] This ratio (accidents/employment) was multiplied by 100 to produce the *RISK* variable.[9]

Data from a multi-year period rather than data limited to a single year was used in order to capture, as much as possible, structural differences in the incidence of work-related accidents between occupations.

Socioeconomic variables were taken from the 1981 Census of Canada data for the Province of Québec, which collected information on the occupation, level of education, marital status, age, employment status (full time, part time, full year, part year) and annual income for one out of every five Canadians. From these data the following measures were constructed: the average number of years of education (*EDUC*), average annual labour income (*INC*), the proportion of workers who are married or single (*MAR* and *SING*—widows and divorced persons are the unit of comparison), average job experience (age minus years of education minus six: *EXP*, *EXP*^{2}), the proportion of workers who are full-time and full-year employees (*FULL*), and income dispersion (the difference between the third and first quartiles of the labour income distribution, *DISPER*) by occupation. These variables were constructed for each of the 261 four-digit occupations included in the data set.

Information on the technological and physical characteristics of sample occupations was taken from the *CCDO*, which was first published in 1971 and is now revised regularly. No significant changes in these characteristics were noted during the observation period for the sample of occupations.

The *CCDO* provides information on the General Educational Development (*GED*) and Specific Vocational Training (*SVT*) required for each occupation, and various other working conditions or job requirements. *GED* data are coded according to the level of education required for the occupation, i.e., primary school, secondary school, etc. Codes for *SVT* data correspond to the specific durations of vocational training required for each occupation (e.g., *SVT* = 0 = simple demonstration, i.e., between 0 and 1 month, *SVT* = 1 = between 1 and 6 months of training, etc.) To obtain a measure of total years of education and training required for each occupation, both *CCDO* measures (*GED* and *SVT*) were transformed into years (and fractions of years) and summed.

The *HEAT, NOISE, STRENGTH,* and *HUMID* variables were also taken from the *CCDO*. They are defined as dummy variables that identify whether the occupation has to be performed under conditions of

8 Since injuries occurred over a period of 4.42 years, the ratio was normalized by multiplying it by the reciprocal of 4.42.
9 Average total employment for Québec, estimated using data from the *Labour Force Survey*, was 2,692,000 for 1980 and 2,675,000 for the 1981-85 period. No other data exist that report employment at the four-digit occupational level by year for the Province of Québec.

extreme heat, noise, strength, or humidity conditions (= 1 when such is the case, 0 otherwise).[10] Since this information was only available at the seven-digit level in the *CCDO*, to construct these variables for four-digit occupations, it was aggregated on the basis of the frequency of such attributes at the suboccupation level.

Finally, the average 'direct' cost of an accident by occupation (*DCOST*) was estimated with the same micro-data sample that was used to construct *RISK*. This data set (called *STAT*-35) contains information on workers' compensation costs for each claim that was paid by the CSST. It includes medical expenses as well as wage replacement benefits and/or other costs paid by the CSST. *DCOST* is the average of such costs per compensated claim by occupation.

The Model

The model includes two equations that are estimated simultaneously: a wage (ln *INC*) and an accident rate (*RISK*) equation. Since the wage variable enters the risk equation to control for variation in the demand for safety—health and safety are expected to be income-dependent goods—it was necessary to control for risk effects that also affect wages.[11]

The Wage Equation

The wage equation (equation 1 below) controls for variation in wages across occupations due to differences in human capital requirements as well as variation due to occupational differences in hedonic characteristics.

Human capital theory distinguishes between general and specific training. General training refers to the knowledge and skills acquired by workers that are useful in many firms, while specific training refers to acquired knowledge and skills that are only useful to the specific firm in which the worker is employed.

The costs of general education are expected to be borne entirely by the worker. Such costs include opportunity costs (i.e., loss of income during the acquisition of knowledge and skills) and direct or out-of-pocket costs, such as the cost of tuition and books). These costs are compensated by higher wages, following graduation, paid out over the individual's working life. If everything else is equal, labour income (ln *INC*) is expected to be positively related to educational level (*EDUC*)

10 The strength variable is equal to 1 when the occupation requires the lifting of 50 kilograms or more, otherwise it = 0.

11 Chelius (1974), McLean et al. (1978), Garen (1988) also employ simultaneous estimation methods.

and to the general educational development required by the occupation (*GED* in the *GEDSVT* variable).

Specific training costs are shared by both the employer and the employee, giving both an interest in maintaining the employment relationship, at least to the point where the parties actuarially recover these costs. The employer recovers his or her costs in the form of higher labour productivity, while the employee receives higher wages once the training is completed. Thus, from the point of view of both the employer and the employee, wages should be a positive function of specific vocational training (*SVT* in the *GEDSVT* variable).[12]

Job experience is also a form of occupational training; employees develop their skills with increased experience. However, there are diminishing returns to increased experience, such that the relationship between wages and experience is expected to be positive in the early stages of an employee's career and negative later on. The relationship between experience and earnings is therefore predicted to be concave. A positive coefficient is expected for *EXP*, while the coefficient for EXP^2 should be negative.

The second part of the wage equation is based on the hedonic theory of wages. This theory assumes that workers prefer agreeable jobs to disagreeable ones, and they demand a premium (or compensating differential) for jobs with disagreeable characteristics (Thaler and Rosen 1975). Employers with disagreeable working conditions must pay higher wages in order to attract an adequate workforce. Otherwise, workers would offer their services to employers with less disadvantageous working conditions.

One proxy for disagreeable working conditions included in equation (2) is *RISK*. This variable, which is the average annual percentage of workers, by occupation, who had suffered a compensated work injury during the reference period (January 1981 to May 1985), discriminates between occupations that are more and less risky. If the risk of injury represents a disagreeable characteristic, then the more hazardous the occupation (i.e., the higher the value of *RISK*) the higher will be its wage or labour income (ln *INC*).

HEAT, NOISE, STRENGTH, and *HUMID* are other proxies for disagreeable working conditions that potentially affect the income variable. However, since these measures also potentially affect the risk of injury (see equation 1), their net effect on labour income may only be indirect. Indeed, conditions of 'extreme' heat, noise, strength, and humidity are working conditions that hinder work (*CCDO*) and that may be

---

12 *GED* and *SVT* were aggregated together to avoid multicollinearity problems between these two highly correlated variables.

responsible for occupational injuries. If so, then the chain of causality may run from these working conditions to *RISK*, and *only* then from *RISK* to the labour income variable (ln *INC*). While positive effects of these variables would appear in the *RISK* equation, no significant effect would appear in the wage equation. The empirical analysis that follows sheds some light on this issue.

DISPER is a proxy for another disagreeable job characteristic. *DISPER* measures the difference in labour income between the first and third quartiles of the labour income distribution by occupation. The higher the income disparity between high and low wage earners within the same occupation, the more the occupation is assumed to be risky in terms of professional or monetary success (Kumar and Coates 1982). Classic examples, which illustrate the riskiness of financial success for particular occupations, are artistic occupations where many, if not most, artists earn less than a few thousand dollars a year, while a few earn several hundred thousand dollars annually. Our measure of income inequality by occupation (*DISPER*) is expected to capture this effect and thus should have a positive coefficient.

Finally, *FULL* controls for time worked during the year. Everything else being constant, full-time and full-year workers are expected to have a larger annual labour income than part-time or seasonal workers. The coefficient for *FULL* should be positive. Equation (1) summarizes our expectations for wages.

$$\ln INC = b_0 + b_1 EDUC + b_2 EXP - b_3 EXP^2 + b_4 GEDSVT$$
$$+ b_5 DISPER + b_6 FULL + b_7 HEAT + b_8 NOISE \qquad (2)$$
$$+ b_9 STRENGTH + b_{10} HUMID + b_{11} RISK + u_2 .$$

The Accident Rate Equation

The accident rate (*RISK*) equation tests some of the predictions that emerge from the theoretical framework briefly outlined in the first section. This framework assumes that there are physical or technological constraints that fix inherent risk factors and that it is technologically impossible or economically too expensive to eliminate these risks completely, at least for workers in some occupations (e.g., construction workers and policemen). The marginal costs of accident prevention are simply too high. Such technological characteristics may thus partially account for risk differentials between occupations (Oi 1974). The technological characteristics that appear in equation (1) in the form of dichotomous variables (*HEAT, NOISE, STRENGTH,* and *HUMID*) were discussed in the previous section. It is assumed that each represents a potential risk factor that varies between occupations. Positive coefficients are thus expected for each of these variables.

In addition, economic theory also hypothesizes that employers are motivated to reduce accident costs. As accident costs increase, employers will increase accident prevention efforts. It is assumed that *DCOST*, *GEDSVT*, and *EXP*, variables which appear in equation (1), control for some, if not most, of these costs.

As noted, the 'direct' costs of accidents provide employers with an incentive to reduce accident rates to the extent that these costs are fully transmitted to the employer. *DCOST* captures workers' compensation costs paid to injured workers by the CSST (i.e., medical expenses, wage replacement costs, etc.). If the employer is fully experience rated, so that he or she has to pay most, if not all, accident costs, then he or she will have a clear incentive to reduce the accident rates in occupations where the savings are expected to be larger, i.e., where accident costs are higher. Therefore, the coefficient for *DCOST* is expected to be negative if insurance premiums are adequately experience rated. During the observation period, however, insurance premiums for most employers in Québec were only partially experience rated.

GEDSVT and *EXP* measure some of the indirect costs of work injuries. Highly qualified workers (i.e., workers in occupations with a high *GEDSVT* value) should be more difficult and expensive to replace than workers who are less qualified for several reasons. First, the unemployment rate for highly qualified workers is usually lower than it is for less qualified workers. Second, the cost and time required to select, recruit, and train highly qualified workers is usually significantly higher than the associated cost for less qualified workers. The sign of *GEDSVT* in the *RISK* equation is thus expected to be negative.

For similar reasons, work experience (*EXP*) should be negatively related to the risk of work accident. The more experience a worker has in an occupation and with a particular firm—these two measures of work experience are highly correlated—the more difficult it should be for the employer to replace the injured worker with another who has similar knowledge and skills. If an identical worker is not available, then the less experienced substitute will likely be less productive. Replacement costs take the form of lower production and/or more overtime. *RISK* is therefore expected to vary inversely with the experience variable.

As previously mentioned, the demand for health and safety is expected to be income elastic: the higher the level of income of an individual or a group of individuals, the higher their demand for health and safety. If so, then *RISK* will vary inversely with labour income (ln *INC*).

Other variables control for the marital status of workers (*MAR* and *SING*) although no prior hypothesis was made with respect to the relationship between marital status and the risk of injury, and for average annual labour income (ln (*INC*). Equation (2), presented below, summarizes our expectations for the risk variable.

$$RISK = a_0 - a_1 \, GEDSVT - a_2 \, EXP - a_3 \, DCOST + a_4 \, HEAT$$
$$+ a_5 \, NOISE + a_5 \, STRENGTH + a_6 \, HUMID \tag{2}$$
$$- a_7 \, \ln INC \pm a_8 \, MAR \pm a_9 \, SING + u_1$$

The Results

As shown in Table 2, except for *STRENGTH* and *MAR*, the estimation results do not differ substantially between estimation methods—two- or three-stage least squares. However, given the slightly higher *t* values for most of the important variables, comments are limited to columns 3 and 4 of Table 2—the results from three-stage least-squares estimation.

The Wage Equation

Full-time employment (*FULL*) positively influences wages. The education variable (*EDUC*) has a positive and significant coefficient. The income curve is concave with respect to work experience (*EXP, EXP²*). The combined measure of general education and specific vocational training (*GEDSVT*) has a positive effect that is specific to and independent of the level of education reached by workers in each occupation. The index of income dispersion (*DISPER*) also has a positive and significant impact on wages.

The risk of work injury and the noise condition (*NOISE*) positively influence labour earnings. Conversely, other unpleasant characteristics in the wage equation, namely *HEAT, STRENGTH*, and *HUMID* do not affect wages directly. However, as mentioned earlier, they may affect labour income indirectly by affecting the risk of occupational injuries.

The Accident Rate Equation

The results for the accident rate equation also confirm, to a large extent, theoretical expectations.

Income has a negative and significant effect on the rate of work-related accidents—indicating that health and safety in the workplace are normal goods with positive income elasticities. The coefficient for ln(*INC*) indicates that a one percent increase in wages results in a tenth of a percentage point decrease in the rate of occupational injuries.

Table 2
Estimation Results for Wage and Accident Rate Equations

	Two-stage least squares		Three-stage least squares	
Coefficient	Risk equation (RISK) (1)	Wage equation (ln INC) (2)	Risk equation (RISK) (3)	Wage equation (ln INC) (4)
Constant	86.36 (2.85)*	5.20 (12.09)*	98.98 (3.28)*	5.46 (13.64)*
ln INC	- 5.47 (-1.77)*	—	-7.27 (-2.37)*	—
EDUC	—	0.142 (5.93)*	—	0.144 (6.45)*
EXP	-0.300 (-2.42)*	0.160 (5.31)*	-0.588 (-4.97)*	0.133 (5.33)*
EXP^2	—	-0.003 (-4.06)*	—	-0.002 (-3.84)*
GEDSVT	-0.215 (-1.48)	0.0241 (3.13)*	-0.367 (-2.57)*	0.025 (3.33)*
DISPER	—	0.000018 (2.74)*	—	0.000001 (1.82)*
FULL	—	0.0043 (3.08)*	—	0.005 (4.00)*
RISK	—	0.037 (2.93)*	—	0.040 (3.19)*
HUMID	0.0451 (3.42)*	-0.0016 (-1.65)*	0.047 (3.55)*	-0.002 (-1.81)*
NOISE	0.015 (1.55)	0.0012 (2.47)*	0.009 (0.97)	0.001 (2.41)*
HEAT	0.0291 (1.94)*	-0.0006 (-0.751)	0.027 (1.81)*	-0.0007 (-0.87)
STRENGTH	2.37 (2.19)*	-0.054 (-0.812)	2.03 (1.88)*	-0.046 (-0.71)
MAR	-0.179 (-2.63)*	—	-0.004 (-0.06)	—
SING	-0.345 (-4.13)*	—	-0.343 (-4.12)*	—
DCOST	-0.00006 (-0.558)	—	0.00007 (0.81)	—

* 't' statistic is significant at the 5 percent level (one-tailed test).

General educational development and the degree of specific vocational training are also associated with a reduction in the frequency of work-related accidents. Given the higher costs of occupational injuries for more qualified categories of workers, the risk of injury appears to be lower for these occupations. It is estimated that each additional year of general education or professional training reduces the accident rate by a third of a percentage point.

Work experience has a negative and statistically significant effect on the rate of occupational injuries. The cost of replacing experienced workers, as well as the development of measures of prevention for these workers, contributes to a reduction in the risk of accidents in the workplace. The estimated impact corresponds to a reduction of a little more than half a percentage point in the accident rate for each additional year of experience. Work experience appears to have a substantial effect on accident rates when one compares workers with twenty years of experience to workers who have just begun their careers.

The coefficient for the 'married' variable is positive, although not significant, and the coefficient for *SING* is negative and significant. Each percentage point increase in the proportion of single workers reduces the accident rate by a third of a percentage point. The costs of an accident for single workers—the loss of utility—would seem to be higher than that for married workers.[13]

As far as technological characteristics are concerned, all variables except one (*NOISE*) are positively and significantly related to the accident rate. The effects of humidity, heat, and required strength that define the physical characteristics of a given occupation are equal to 4.7, 2.7 and 2.0 percentage points, respectively. In other words, the presence or absence of these conditions can produce significant variation in the risks of occupational injury. Finally, the average direct costs of work-related accidents by occupation (*DCOST*) does not have any significant impact on the rate of occupational injuries.

Conclusion

The study reported in this chapter focused on two large groups of variables that explain the incidence of workplace injuries: the technological characteristics of different occupations and accident costs incurred by workers and employers. As expected, the results tend to support the hypothesis that employers are sensitive to changes in the costs of work-related injury. As these costs increase, the accident rate declines.

This result has at least two policy implications: (1) there is a need for an 'accident' tax to close the gap between optimal and observed wage-risk premiums, the premium paid to compensate for increased risk as measured by the coefficient on the *RISK* variable in the wage equation, and (2) there is a need to improve labour market information to better inform workers of the risk of injury. Such policies would help to efficiently reduce both the incidence and the costs of work accidents. The results also indicate that the technological characteristics of an occupation play a significant role in determining work-related accidents. Furthermore, the use of occupational data seems particularly appropri-

---

13 This is expected because a family generates positive externalities for the injured worker.

ate, both for the study of wage-risk premiums and for the study of the determinants of occupational risk. Most of the explanatory variables have a statistically significant relationship with the two dependent variables, and the estimated effects of these variables are plausible.

Finally, the results indicate that the direct costs of work injury—compensation benefits paid by the CSST—have no influence whatsoever on the risk of occupational injuries. This implies that the methods used to finance these compensation benefits provide employers with little or no incentive to prevent work-related accidents.

References

Brody, B., Y. Létourneau, and A. Poirier. 1990. Real indirect costs of work accidents: Results from our new model. *Journal of Occupational Accidents* 12:99–104.

Butler, Richard J. 1983. Wage and injury rate response to shifting levels of workers' compensation. In *Safety and the work force: Incentives and disincentives in workers' compensation*, edited by John D. Worrall, pp.61–86. Ithaca, NY: ILR Press.

Butler, Richard J. and John D. Worrall. 1983. Workers' compensation benefit and injury claims rates in the seventies. *Review of Economics and Statistics* 65:580–89.

Calabresi, G. 1970. *The cost of accidents: A legal and economic analysis.* New Haven, CN: Yale University Press.

Canadian classification and dictionary of occupations. Ottawa: Supply and Services Canada.

Chelius, James. 1974. The control of industrial accidents: Economic theory and empirical evidence. *Law and Contemporary Problems* 38:700–729.

Digby, C. and W.C. Riddell. 1986. Occupational health and safety in Canada. In *Canadian labour relations*, edited by W.C. Riddell, pp.285–32. Toronto: University of Toronto Press.

Garen, J. 1988. Compensating wage differentials and the endogeneity of job riskiness. *Review of Economics and Statistics* 70:9–16.

Haydon, Leen K. Jr., Hoi Sing Wai, and Stephen H. Strand. 1977. A review of the literature in the economics of occupational safety and health. In *Workers' Compensation Task Force Report*, vol. 6. Washington, DC.

Kumar, P. and M.L. Coates. 1982. Occupational earnings, compensating differentials, and human capital: An empirical study. *Canadian Journal of Economics* 15:442–57.

Lanoie, Paul. 1992a. Safety regulation and the risk of workplace accidents in Québec. *Southern Economic Journal* 58:950–65.

———. 1992b. The impact of occupational safety and health regulation on the risk of workplace accidents, Québec 1983–87. *Journal of Human Resources* 27:643–60.

McLean, R.A., W.R. Wendling, and P.R. Neergaard. 1978. Compensating wage differentials for hazardous work: An empirical analysis. *Quarterly Review of Economics and Business* 18:97–107.

Oi, Walter Y. 1974. On the economics of industrial safety. *Law and Contemporary Problems* 38:669–99.

Ruser, John W. 1985. Workers' compensation insurance, experience rating and occupational injuries. *Rand Journal of Economics* 16:487–503.

Smith, R.S. 1973. An analysis of work injuries in the manufacturing industry. In *Supplemental studies for the National Commission on State Workmen's Compensation Laws*. Washington, DC: Government Printing Office.

Steele, G.R. 1974. Industrial accidents: An economic interpretation. *Applied Economics* 6:143–54.

Thaler, R. and S. Rosen. 1975. The value of saving a life: Evidence from the labor market. In *Household production and consumption*, edited by Nester E. Terleckyj. Washington, DC: National Bureau of Economic Research.

Viscusi, W. Kip. 1979. The impact of occupational safety and health regulation. *Bell Journal of Economics* 10:117–40.

———. 1983. *Risk by choice: Regulating health and safety in the workplace*. Cambridge, MA: Harvard University Press.

The Compensation of Occupational Disease in Ontario

Lynn Elinson

Policy to allow compensation for occupational disease has existed in Ontario since early in the century. Defining and diagnosing occupational disease is problematic, however, and the Workers' Compensation Board continues to work at recognizing true occupational diseases, developing policies to adjudicate claims fairly and establishing mechanisms to compensate disease claims. This chapter provides an account of the history of occupational disease compensation in Ontario and a description of pertinent current legislation. Problems associated with defining and diagnosing occupational disease are discussed and the development of Board disease policy and Board practice in adjudicating occupational disease claims described. A section on the incidence of occupational disease claims is followed by an examination of issues related to disease claims adjudication and of the possibility of determining the relationship between occupational disease and workers' compensation costs. A brief discussion of progress and Board goals related to disease claims adjudication concludes the chapter.

Historical Perspective

Unlike those who framed workers' compensation programs in other jurisdictions, the drafters of the original *Workers' Compensation Act* in Ontario recognized that occupational disease should be compensable. Mr. Justice William Meredith (later Chief Justice Meredith), the founder of the Ontario workers' compensation system, stated in his 1913 final report to the Legislature:

> By my draft bill . . . industrial diseases are put on the same footing as to the right of compensation as accidents. . . . It would, in my opin-

Note: The author would like to thank Carol Luce, Medical and Occupational Disease Policy Branch, Ontario Workers' Compensation Board, for providing tabulations of the data.
    The contents of this paper are the opinions of the author and not those of the Ontario Workers' Compensation Board.

ion, be a blot on the Act if a workman who suffers from an industrial disease contracted in the course of his employment is not to be entitled to compensation. The risk of contracting disease is inherent in the occupation he follows and he is practically powerless to guard against it. A workman may to some extent guard against accidents, and it would seem not only illogical but unreasonable to compensate him in the one case and to deny him the right to compensation in the other. (Meredith 1913)

When the Act came into effect in 1915, only six diseases (which were listed in the Act's 'Schedule 3') were compensable. They were (1) anthrax, from handling wool, hair, bristles, hides, and skins; (2) lead poisoning and its aftereffects, and poisoning from other metals and substances, such as arsenic, mercury, and phosphorous; and (3) ankylostomiasis, a hookworm disease commonly found among miners. For the diseases named in the Act, there is a clear causal relationship between the disease and employment.

Over the next 32 years, diseases, and usually a description of the processes related to them, were periodically added to the list of compensable industrial diseases. Miner's phthisis, and mining, was added in 1917, although it was deleted in 1931. Silicosis and pneumoconiosis were added in 1926; the first silicosis and asbestosis cases were accepted by the Ontario Board in that year. Bursitis and '[a]ny process involving continuous rubbing, pressure or vibration of the parts affected' were added in 1932. The process opposite bursitis was deleted in 1951, but the disease remained.

In 1947, the *Workers' Compensation Act* was expanded further. Amendments to the Act added particular diseases but also recognized 'any other disease peculiar to or characteristic of a particular process, trade, or occupation' as a potentially compensable industrial disease.

As the Board began to receive claims under this new, expanded definition of industrial disease, it began to develop and use policies and guidelines that created rules of entitlement. By 1951, the Board had allowed the first noise-induced hearing-loss claim under guidelines for adjudication. The Board also began to recognize the kind of occupationally related disease that develops over time from cumulative exposure to a workplace factor, (e.g., cumulative trauma disorders, such as carpal tunnel syndrome). Tuberculosis, an infectious disease, was also added to Schedule 3 in 1951, and the wording of the description of the disease and process was revised in 1965.

In 1963, the 'disablement provision' was added to the Act. This provision, which grew out of recognition that diseases caused by cumulative exposure were compensable, expanded the definition of 'accident' to include 'disablement arising out of and in the course of employment.' Although disablement was never defined, the clause, along with the industrial disease provisions mentioned above, provided authorization for disease compensation.

By the 1970s, policymakers had recognized that work-related diseases are an important cause of disability and death and that they present substantial diagnosis and identification problems. Industrial disease came under increasing scrutiny by government commissions. The Ham Commission, for example, reported on the health and safety of mines and made several recommendations related to the compensation of industrial disease among miners in 1976 (Ham 1976); The Royal Commission on Asbestos, chaired by Dr. Stephen Dupré, produced a report in 1984 on asbestosis, mesothelioma, lung cancer, gastrointestinal cancer, and laryngeal cancer (Dupré 1984). Several of the recommendations made in three reports by Paul Weiler in the 1980s related to the compensation of occupational disease claims (Weiler 1980, 1983, 1986).

Many of Weiler's recommendations were enacted in legislation in 1985. In particular, the definition of industrial disease was expanded to include four distinct types of disease, provision was made for a new schedule of diseases, called Schedule 4, and an external scientific and political body, the Industrial Disease Standards Panel (IDSP), was created to make recommendations to the Board on new industrial diseases, eligibility rules, and criteria for entitlement.[1]

The Ontario Workers' Compensation Act

According to the Act, an industrial disease is a condition meeting one of four criteria:

(a) a disease resulting from exposure to a substance relating to a particular process, a trade or occupation in an industry,

(b) a disease peculiar to or characteristic of a particular industrial process, trade or occupation,

(c) a medical condition that in the opinion of the Board requires a worker to be removed either temporarily or permanently from exposure to a substance because the condition may be a precursor to an industrial disease, or

(d) any of the diseases mentioned in Schedule 3 or 4; . . .

1 On Decmber 9, 1994, *An Act to Amend the Workers' Compensation Act* received Royal assent. This amendment chan05ged the words 'industrial disease' to 'occupational disease' and the Industrial Disease Standards Panel to the Occupational Disease Panel. There were no substansive changes in these sections of the amendment. In the context of this chapter, the terms 'industrial disease' and 'Industrial Disease Standards Panel' will continue to be used.

Section 134(1) of the Act indicates that a worker who suffers from an industrial disease, where the disease leads to the worker's impairment or death and where the disease is 'due to the nature of any employment in which the worker was engaged,' is eligible (or in the case of death of the worker, his/her dependent is eligible) for compensation 'as if the disease was a personal injury by accident and the impairment was the happening of the accident.'

Schedules 3 and 4, which are presented in appendices to this chapter, enumerate diseases and corresponding occupational processes.[2] As indicated by Sections 134(9) and 134(10) of the Act, the diseases listed in Schedule 3 'shall be deemed to have been due to the nature of that employment unless the contrary is proved,' while those in Schedule 4 'shall be conclusively deemed to have been due to the nature of the employment.'

In other words, to establish an industrial disease claim, an afflicted worker must simply demonstrate that he or she suffers from a disease listed in either schedule and that he or she was engaged in the corresponding process. However, the presumption of occupational causation for Schedule 3 diseases may be contested; this presumption cannot be rebutted for Schedule 4 diseases.

Many of the diseases listed in Schedule 3 are acute-onset conditions, such as poisoning or ulceration of the corneal surface of the eye, or do not have a process listed opposite the disease in column 2 (for example, dermatitis venenata, tuberculosis, and the pneumoconioses other than silicosis).

Although Schedule 4 was created in 1985, it did not list any diseases until May 28, 1992. The schedule now includes asbestosis, mesothelioma and cancer of the nasal cavities and paranasal sinuses.[3]

In addition to diseases listed in Schedules 3 and 4, the Board has issued more than forty guidelines recognizing as industrial diseases certain conditions that are peculiar to or characteristic of a particular occupation or process. For example, policies and guidelines exist for lung cancer and gold mining, lung cancer and radiation, lung and sinus cancer and nickel smelter work, occupational noise-induced hearing loss, vibration-induced white finger disease (now known as hand-arm vibration syndrome), and chronic obstructive lung disease and sulpher particulates exposure.

2 The Schedules are not contained in the Act but in Regulation 1102.
3 The International Labour Organisation is updating a list of occupational diseases. Mullan and Murphy (1991) published their own list and suggest that it be used by physicians in the community and for public health surveillance.

Definition of Occupational Disease

One of the more problematic aspects of occupational disease compensation is the accurate identification of a particular disease process or condition as occupational.

According to *Dorland's Illustrated Medical Dictionary* (1989) 'disease' may be defined as

Any deviation from or interruption of the normal structure or function of any part, organ, or system (or combination thereof) of the body that is manifested by a characteristic set of symptoms and signs and whose etiology, pathology, and prognosis may be known or unknown.

The definition used by the International Labour Organisation (ILO), is primarily based on etiological or causal considerations; the ILO defines occupational disease to include all pathological conditions induced by prolonged work (ILO 1989). This broad definition encompasses a wide variety of conditions.

Diseases may have either a sudden or immediate onset or a delayed onset. Sudden-onset diseases (that is, those related to acute exposures, such as traumatic hearing loss, acute poisoning, or needle-stick injuries) normally fall under the definition of 'accident' in section 1(1) of the Act[4] and are adjudicated under s.4(1) of the Act, which states that

where . . . personal injury by accident arising out of and in the course of employment is caused to a worker, the worker and the worker's dependants are entitled to benefits in the manner and to the extent provided under the Act.

Diseases with a delayed onset, which include both long-latency diseases and diseases that result from cumulative exposure, could be described as 'occupational diseases.'[5] They are adjudicated either under s.134(1) of the Act or under s.4(1) and the disablement definition of 'accident' in s.1(1).

Mullan and Murphy (1991) have identified two categories of occupational diseases. The first consists of 'true' occupational diseases—

4 Section 1(1) of the Act defines an accident to include: '(i) a wilful and intentional act, not being the act of the worker, (ii) a chance event occasioned by a physical or natural cause, and (iii) disablement arising out of and in the course of employment.' Clause iii the disablement provision referred to previously.

5 Diseases, such as some forms of cancer, that are only manifested long after exposure to the causal agent are called long-latency diseases. Sensorineural hearing loss is an example of a disease caused by cumulative exposure; manifestation of the disease occurs after gradual and accumulated exposure to the causal agent.

those diseases that are inherently occupational. It is unlikely that these diseases would occur in the absence of the occupational exposure agent. Asbestosis and silicosis are examples of 'true' occupational diseases.

The second category is composed of diseases that may or may not be occupationally related. Further information on the industry and occupation is required before a causal link between the disease and the occupation or occupational exposure can be established. Examples are lung cancer among uranium miners or tuberculosis among health-care workers. To determine if a link exists between these diseases and an occupation, scientists often use criteria developed by Bradford Hill (1965): strength of association between disease and the occupation (from epidemiological studies), consistency of results across studies conducted in different settings, specificity, temporality, biological gradient (a dose-response pattern), biologic plausibility, coherence, experimental evidence, and analogy. All of these criteria need not be satisfied to establish occupational causation. However, the likelihood of a causal relationship between the occupation and the disease increases as the number of criteria satisfied increases. Although the Bradford Hill criteria are widely accepted as useful guidelines for assessing causation with respect to occupational disease, it it not generally agreed when causation has been established for any particular disease and occupation combination.

The Development of Disease Policy and Guidelines

Until 1987, policymaking with respect to occupational disease at the Ontario Board depended primarily on the recommendations of medical experts employed by the Board. Rather than using Schedule 3 to identify industrial disease and assist in decisionmaking, the Board developed policy guidelines. These guidelines have been criticized by labour groups, who claim they are overly restrictive, provide little or no guidance to decisionmakers, and lack fundamental fairness.

Today, in addition to an internal policy team of the Ontario Board, called the Medical and Occupational Disease Policy (MODP) Branch, the Industrial Disease Standards Panel plays an important role in disease-policy development. The IDSP was created in 1985 in response to Weiler's recommendation that an independent body should be responsible for advising the Board on industrial disease. Prior to the Weiler report, the Board had been criticized for being secretive, for not considering the viewpoints of stakeholders, and for being biased toward employers. Consequently, the IDSP was designed to combine technical expertise with social and political viewpoints on industrial disease issues.

The function of the IDSP is to investigate possible industrial diseases; determine whether or not a probable connection exists between a disease and an industrial process, trade or occupation in Ontario; create, develop, and revise criteria for the evaluation of claims respecting industrial diseases; and recommend eligibility rules for compensating industrial-disease claims. The Panel's findings and recommendations are submitted to the Board in the form of IDSP reports and, as required by s.95(12), are published in *The Ontario Gazette*, to allow interested parties to comment. The Board is then required to accept, reject, or revise the Panel's findings and recommendations, and to provide reasons for whatever approach is chosen. The Board's response must then be published in *The Ontario Gazette*.

Since its creation in 1985, the IDSP has submitted 17 reports to the Board. Most have been initiated by questions from the Board (for example, about gold mining, PCBs, asbestos, aluminum), although more recently, the IDSP has initiated its own reports (for example, on scleroderma, a progressive connective tissue disease, and non-malignant respiratory disease). Over the years, the Board has accepted, rejected, and amended the Panel's findings; when the Panel was unable to arrive at a consensus, the Board chose from among several options contained in Panel reports.

Scleroderma/Silica Dust Policy

The development of the Board's new policy on scleroderma and silica-dust exposure illustrates how the Board and the IDSP function together. In the fall of 1991, the Board's disease adjudication unit, the Complex Case Unit - Diseases (CCU-D), asked the Medical and Occupational Disease Policy Branch for advice on a claim file from a miner who was diagnosed with scleroderma. The Branch's epidemiologist reviewed the literature and concluded, in a report to the CCU-D dated December 1991, that there was evidence to support a causal association between scleroderma and working as a miner. When the Board was reviewing the issue, the IDSP began its own review, prompted by a question from a provincial member of parliament. The IDSP submitted an interim report on scleroderma to the Workers' Compensation Board, and the Board published the report in *The Ontario Gazette*, with a deadline for comments.

The IDSP concluded that there was a probable connection between scleroderma and silica-dust exposure and developed recommendations for adjudication. The MODP Branch reviewed the IDSP findings and recommendations and the two submissions received by the Board, met with the IDSP to clarify certain issues, and developed a draft policy on scleroderma. The Board of Directors approved a policy on April 1, 1993.

The Board is reconsidering scleroderma claims which were previously denied and informing physicians and the mining community about the new policy.

Current Adjudication Practice

The Board handles five different types of 'disease' claims: (1) diseases that occur as a result of an accident (e.g., fume toxicity as a result of a chemical spill; exposure to HIV as a result of a traumatic event in a hospital emergency room); (2) long-latency 'occupational diseases' (e.g., asbestosis; nasal cancer among nickel smelter workers; lung cancer among nickel smelter workers); (3) occupational diseases caused by cumulative exposure (e.g., hearing loss, degenerative disc disease, hand-arm vibration syndrome, carpal tunnel syndrome); (4) pre-existing diseases that are accelerated or aggravated by the workplace; and (5) diseases for which there is no known cause, but growing evidence of a possible occupational relationship. All these claims, are adjudicated by reference to Schedule 3 or 4, to existing policy guidelines, or on a case-by-case basis.

The vast majority of disease claims are considered on a case-by-case basis. Case-by-case adjudication of benefit entitlement for disease claims entails the same process used to determine entitlement for accident claims. However, these two types of claims differ in the way evidence is assembled and the technical nature of the condition and workplace factors. In an accident claim, it is necessary to ascertain whether or not the accident arose out of and in the course of employment. In a disease claim, it is necessary to determine the nature of the disease, the nature and extent of the exposure, and the likelihood that the disease was due to the nature of the employment. Medical advice is sought from the Board physicians, and an occupational hygienist assists the adjudicator in determining whether or not the nature and extent of the exposure in the workplace could have been responsible for the development of the disease. Toxicological and epidemiological advice may also be sought from experts in the MODP Branch.

Incidence of Occupational Disease Claims 1987-1992

According to the WCB's Occupational Disease Information and Surveillance System database (ODISS), which records claims handled by the Complex Case Unit—Diseases, almost fifty-seven hundred 'disease' claims were handled in 1992. This excludes noise-induced hearing loss and repetitive strain injury, which are not recorded on ODISS because they are not handled by the CCU-D. Most claims are for vague symptoms, such as dizziness, fatigue, or chest pains; contact dermatitis; or 'exposure' claims where no condition or symptoms exist. The other major categories are for hand-arm vibration, asthma, and ischaemic heart disease (heart attack). Cancers make up about 5 percent of the caseload in this unit, and the number of asbestosis and silicosis claims allowed each year is relatively small (25 and 23, respectively in 1992).

Disease claims account for approximately 5 percent of the total allowed lost-time claims (see Table 1). However, they make up a much larger proportion of allowed fatal claims (see Table 2). In 1992, 53 percent of allowed fatal claims were disease claims. Some of the deaths among 100 percent pensioners were also caused by work-related disease so that these data actually understate the incidence of fatalities due to occupational disease. Moreover, it can be noted in Table 3 that the percentage of fatalities caused by disease has increased in recent years, although the actual number has not changed substantially.

Table 1

Allowed Lost-Time Claims in Ontario, 1992

Type	Number	Percent
Injuries	130,431	95.3
Diseases	6,364	4.7
Total	136,795	100.0

Source: Workers' Compensation Board of Ontario (1992).

Table 2

Occupational Fatalities Allowed in 1992

	Number	Percent
Diseases	238	53
Immediate deaths	114	25
Not immediate deaths	30	7
100% pensions	70	15
Total	452	100

Source: Workers' Compensation Board of Ontario (1992).

Table 3

Fatality Type by Year of Registration

	1988		1989		1990		1991		1992	
Fatality type*	No.	%	No.	%	No.	%	No.	%	No.	%
Diseases	228	49	226	50	256	58	207	54	238	62
Accidents**	235	51	226	50	185	42	178	46	144	38
Total	463	100	452	100	441	100	385	100	382	100

Source: Workers' Compensation Board of Ontario (1992).

* Excludes deaths from 100% pensions.
**Total of immediate and non-immediate deaths from accidents.

Table 4 examines the number of claims submitted to the Board from 1987 to 1992 by selected type. Because these data were extracted from ODISS, claims for some delayed-onset conditions are not included. In addition, the completeness of ODISS, particularly in its early years, has been questioned. Therefore, these data should only be considered as illustrative of the type of data that exist or as a means of identifying issues for further research. With those caveats in mind, this table shows that (1) the number of asbestosis and silicosis claims submitted to the Board is low, (2) the number of dermatitis claims has declined substantially since 1987, (3) claims for hand-arm vibration (a condition often seen in miners) have declined, (4) claims for 'symptoms, signs, and ill conditions' have increased.

The incidence of occupational disease claims submitted to the Board depends on a number of factors including the size of the workforce, stakeholder knowledge, the presence of disease-causing exposures in the workplace, and the incidence and prevalence of disease. Therefore, interpretations of these data must be made cautiously.

Tables 5 and 6 provide information on the Board's decision-making on disease claims. Again, these data are obtained from ODISS, and only those diseases handled by CCU-D are included. These tables indicate that: (1) 53 percent of lung-cancer claims were allowed; (2) 86 percent and 81 percent of asbestosis and mesothelioma claims, respectively, were allowed; (3) 54 percent of hand-arm vibration claims were allowed; (4) 22 percent of ischaemic-heart-disease claims were allowed

Table 4

Number of Claims Submitted, Selected Types by Year of Registration

Disease category	1987	1988	1989	1990	1991	1992
Lung cancer	76	552*	109	145	120	109
Mesothelioma	24	32	38	42	51	40
Skin cancer	4	4	7	8	11	7
Hand-arm vibration syndrome	488	414	406	400	289	280
Ischaemic heart disease	203	171	161	192	206	215
Asbestosis	27	17	23	34	21	25
Silicosis	30	26	25	32	23	28
Asthma	115	121	148	177	153	183
Dermatitis	877	646	579	370	466	428
Symptoms, signs, ill-defined conditions	921	1164	1088	1403	2355	2230
Exposures	240	138	209	592	750	851
All diseases on ODISS	4217	4696**	3772	4439	5418	5397

* Includes 463 lung cancer claims set up as part of special gold miner project.
**Includes 775 claims set up as part of special gold miner project.

Table 5

Disease Claim Adjudication in Ontario, Decision Year = 1992

Disease category	Allowed Number	Allowed Row%	Denied Number	Denied Row%	Total Number	Total Col.%
Infectious and parasitic	49	65	26	35	75	1.3
Neoplasms						
Lung cancer*	93	53	84	47	177	3.7
Mesothelioma	34	81	8	19	42	0.7
Skin cancer	7	58	5	42	12	0.2
All others	17	22	59	78	76	1.3
Blood and blood						
forming organs	1	50	1	50	2	0.04
Mental disorders	1	17	5	83	6	0.1
Nervous system and						
sense organs	25	66	13	34	38	0.7
Circulatory system						
Hand-arm vibration						
syndrome	177	54	153	46	330	5.8
Ischaemic heart disease	53	22	187	78	240	4.2
All others	14	27	37	73	51	0.9
Respiratory system						
Asbestosis	25	86	4	14	29	0.5
Silicosis	23	82	5	18	28	0.5
Asthma	140	92	13	8	153	2.7
All others	521	92	48	8	569	10.1
Digestive system	3	20	12	80	15	0.3
Genitourinary	2	67	1	33	3	0.1
Skin						
Contact dermatitis	394	95	19	5	413	7.3
All others	2	33	4	67	6	0.1
Musculoskeletal system	7	88	1	12	8	0.1
Symptoms, signs,						
ill-defined conditions	1241	54	1051	46	2292	40.6
Injury, poisoning	147	78	41	22	188	3.3
'Exposures'	508	59	354	41	862	15.3
Missing	21	64	12	36	33	0.6
Total	3505	62	2143	38	5648	99.8

* Includes 47 decisions made as part of a special gold miner claim re-adjudication project.

Table 6

Disease Claim Adjudication in Ontario, Claim Status by Decision Year

Decision year	% Allowed	% Denied	Decision year	% Allowed	% Denied
1987	85	15	1991	66	34
1988	73	27	1992	62	38
1989	65	35	1993 to date*	61	39
1990	64	36			

* November 1993.

(as an aggravation of a pre-existing condition); (5) 92 percent of asthma claims were allowed (this includes both 'occupational asthma' and asthma as an aggravation of a pre-existing condition); and (6) the percentage of allowed claims has declined from 85 percent in 1987 to 61 percent as of November, 1993 (see table 6).

There are two possible explanations for the drop in the proportion of allowed claims. Either the Board is scrutinizing occupational disease claims more carefully, or the number of marginal claims (i.e., claims where it is difficult to establish a causal link between occupational exposure and the disease process) has increased. While the data do not allow a conclusive test of these alternative hypotheses, data presented in Table 4 support the latter explanation. In particular, it can be noted that the number of disease claims has risen dramatically between 1987 and 1992 (by over 25 percent) and that the largest share of this increase was due to the rising number of diseases classified as 'symptoms, signs, ill conditions,' which increased by over 142 percent and 'exposures,' which increased by nearly 255 percent. Both classifications include, by definition, a large number of marginal claims. And, as can be seen from Table 5, the Board denied a large number and percentage of both types of claim: 46 percent or 1,051 of all 'symptoms, signs, ill-defined condition' claims and 41 percent or 354 of all 'exposure' claims.

Complexity of Disease Claim Adjudication

Weiler (1983) referred to industrial disease as the 'soft underbelly' of workers' compensation. There are those who maintain that such a description applies today.

Compared to accidents, disease claims are complex and require scientific and technical expertise to adjudicate. Some diseases are multicausal so that the development of the disease may be attributed to both work and nonwork factors. In addition, although it is possible to identify occupational groups in which workers are at high risk to develop a particular disease, once the disease has been diagnosed in a worker, there is no reliable method of determining whether or not and to what extent the workplace contributed to his or her disease. Work-related lung cancer and lung cancer caused by cigarette smoking look exactly the same to a physician or a pathologist.

Another problem in disease claim adjudication involves the limitations of epidemiology, the field most often relied upon to identify work-disease relationships. Epidemiological studies use a statistical analysis of the incidence of disease by occupation or industry to determine etiology. A disease that has a statistically significant relationship with a particular occupation, industry, or process is considered to have an occupational origin when other criteria are also met.

Critics of the Ontario Board have maintained in the past that the Board relies too heavily on epidemiology and does not consider its limitations. It is noted that epidemiological studies often cannot identify hazardous work exposures when the size of the workforce is small. Therefore, a negative finding in an epidemiological study does not necessarily mean that the workplace is safe. In addition, because of technological advances, exposures in the workplace are changing every day, and reliance on epidemiology alone may not identify hazards. Finally, many diseases have a long latency. Therefore, conducting reliable epidemiological studies and assembling evidence of workplace exposure once the disease is diagnosed are particularly problematic.

Recognizing these problems, the Ontario Board develops policies on disease-claim adjudication, which provide adjudicators with advice on whether it is more probable than not that a worker's disease is attributable to the workplace. The Board's gold miner policy, originally approved on 8 January 1988, is an example.

The Gold Miner Policy

The gold miner policy stated that compensation was available to workers who met a number of conditions: the worker must have worked in an Ontario gold mine, been diagnosed with primary lung cancer, had a biologically plausible latency period, worked during the dustiest years of gold mining, and had sufficient and consistent evidence of occupational exposure. The policy also addressed the issue of what and how much evidence was necessary to establish a causal relationship between the disease and employment (e.g., a 15-year latency was considered to be a biologically plausible latency after first employment in a 'dusty occupation'; a chest x-ray of code 4 or more *and* a weighted dust-exposure index of 60 or more would be one way of demonstrating sufficient and consistent evidence of occupational exposure).

The policy was based primarily on an IDSP report which reviewed findings in epidemiological studies of a cohort of Ontario gold miners, further analysis of this cohort, and input from workers' and employers' representatives. When legal questions arose and new scientific information became available, the policy was revised, on August 29, 1991, to modify the evidence requirements. For example, work in mines with significant levels of arsenic or radon progeny was also considered to be persuasive evidence of a causal relationship of disease with employment. If no evidence of arsenic or radon exposure was present, then the equivalent of 10 years of 'dusty gold mining' would also be persuasive.

Occupational Disease and Workers' Compensation Costs

It would be premature to conclude that the rising costs of workers' compensation in Ontario are due to occupational disease. While the proportion of allowed occupational disease claims has grown, it is still a very small proportion of total claims. In addition, aside from the effects of a reduction in the workforce, there does not seem to be a major change in the number and type of disease claims submitted to the Board with the exception of claims submitted for 'symptoms, signs, ill-defined conditions'. Finally, decisionmaking on disease claims continues to be done primarily on a case-by-case basis, and few conclusions can be drawn about trends.

Progress and Future Directions

The Ontario Board has made considerable headway in raising the profile of occupational disease and in initiating discussions between workers and employers on complex issues. Board staff are (1) informing workers and employers of known occupational diseases, (2) identifying more occupational diseases, (3) working with workers and employers to ensure that the effectiveness of Board disease policies are satisfactory, and (4) seeking information on alternative compensation mechanisms.

Work is proceeding, for example, on identifying known 'occupational diseases' for entry in Schedule 4 and Schedule 3 and on informing workers and employers about well-established occupational diseases. The IDSP continues to identify 'industrial diseases' for Board approval. The Board also has an important role (through review of the world scientific literature and the development and improvement of a disease database) in recognizing potential industrial diseases.

The Board is also working with workers and employers to ensure that Board policies are not only legally and scientifically supportable but are also satisfactory to both groups. Ideally, policies will result that can identify a high proportion of allowed claims that are truly work-related and a high proportion of denied claims that are truly *not* work-related. What is known epidemiologically about occupational disease, and where the Board draws the lines beyond epidemiological findings, will affect the Board's effectiveness in disease-claim adjudication.

Another goal of the Ontario Board is to explore alternative forms of compensation, such as universal disability. With universal disability, it would be unnecessary to attribute causation to the workplace, and the complexity of disease-claim adjudication would be eliminated. If such a system were implemented, the only reason to assess the determinants of occupational diseases would be to prevent them.

References

Bradford Hill, Austin. 1965. The environment and disease: Association or causation? In *Proceedings of the Royal Society of Medicine*, vol. 295, p.385. London: Longmans, Green.

Dorland's Illustrated Medical Dictionary. 1989. Philadelphia: Saunders.

Dupré, J. Stefan. 1984. *Report of the Royal Commission on Matters of Health and Safety Arising from the Use of Asbestos in Ontario*. Toronto: Queen's Printer.

Ham, James M. 1976. *Report of the Royal Commission on the Health and Safety of Workers in Mines*. Toronto: Ministry of the Attorney General.

International Labour Organisation. 1989. *Encyclopaedia of occupational safety and health*. 3rd ed. Geneva: International Labour Office.

Meredith, W.R., Sir. 1913. *Final Report on laws relating to the liability of employers to make compensation to their employees for injuries received in the course of their employment which are in force in other countries*. Toronto: L.K. Cameron, Printer to the King's Most Excellent Majesty.

Mullan, R.J. and L.I. Murphy. 1991. Occupational sentinel health events: An updated list for physician recognition and public health surveillance. *American Journal of Industrial Medicine* 19: 775-99.

Weiler, Paul C. 1980. *Reshaping workers' compensation for Ontario*. Toronto: Ontario Ministry of Labour.

———. 1983. *Protecting the worker from disability: Challenges for the eighties*. Toronto: Ontario Ministry of Labour.

———. 1986. *Permanent partial disability: Alternative models for compensation*. Toronto: Ontario Ministry of Labour.

Workers' Compensation Board of Ontario. 1992. *Statistical Supplement to the Annual Report 1992*. Toronto.

Appendix A

Schedule 3 Entries

1   Anthrax
    Process: Handling of wool, hair, bristles, hides

2   Infected blisters
    Process: Any process involving continuous friction

3   Bursitis

4   Epitheliomatous cancer or ulceration of the skin due to tar, pitch, bitumen, mineral oil or paraffin or any compound, product or residue of any of these substances
    Process: Handling or use of tar, pitch, bitumen, mineral oil or paraffin or any compound, product or residue of any of these substances

5   Compressed-air illness or caisson disease
    Process: Any process carried on in compressed air

6   Dermatitis venenata

7   Poisoning and its sequelae by
    i.   arsenic
          Process: Any process involving the use of arsenic or its preparations or compounds
    ii.   benzol
          Process: Any process involving the use of arsenic or its preparations or compounds
    iii. beryllium
          Process: Any process involving the use of beryllium or its preparations or compounds
    iv.   brass, nickel or zinc
          Process: Any process involving the use of brass or nickel or melting or smelting zinc
    v.   cadmium
          Process: Any process involving the use of cadmium or its preparations or compounds
    vi.   carbon bisulphide
          Process: Any process involving the use of cadmium or its preparations or compounds
    vii. carbon dioxide
          Process: Any process involving the evolution of carbon dioxide
    viii. carbon monoxide
          Process: Any process involving the evolution of carbon monoxide
    ix.   chlorinated hydro-carbons (carbon tetrachloride, trichloroethylene, tetrachlorethane, trichlornaphthalene and others)
          Process: Any process in the manufacture or involving the use of these substances
    x.   chrome
          Process: Any process involving the use of chromium or its compounds
    xi.   lead
          Process: Any process involving the use of lead or its preparations or compounds
    xii. mercury
          Process: Any process involving the use of mercury or its preparations or compounds
    xiii. nitro, derivatives and amino derivatives of benzene, phenol and their homologues (trinitrotoluene, dinitrophenol, anilin and others)
          Process: Handling any nitro derivatives or amino derivatives of benzene or phenol or any of their homologues or any process in the manufacture or involving the use thereof

xiv. nitrous fumes
Process: Any process in which nitrous fumes are evolved

xv. phosphorous
Process: Any process involving the use of phosphorus or its preparations or compounds

8 The pneumoconioses other than silicosis

9 Any disease due to exposure to X-rays, radium, or other radioactive substances

10 Respiratory disease due to the inhalation of materials used in non-offset sprays
Process: Any process or occupation involving the use of non-offset sprays in the printing industry.

11 Retinitis due to electro-welding or acetylene-welding

12 Silicosis
Process: Mining or quarrying, cutting, crushing, grinding or polishing stone, or grinding or polishing metal

13 Teno-synovitis

14 Tuberculosis contracted by an employee employed by and in,
i. a hospital, jail, sanatorium, convalescent home, nursing home, home for the aged, health unit or visiting nursing association to which Part I of treatment centre operated by the Province of Ontario the Act applies; or
ii. a laboratory, reform institution, health unit, or treatment centre operated by the Province of Ontario

15 Ulceration of the corneal surface of the eye, due to tar, pitch, bitumen, mineral oil or paraffin, or any compound, product or residue of any of these substances
Process: Handling or use of tar, pitch, bitumen, mineral oil or paraffin, or any compound, product or residue of any of these substances

16 Primary cancer of the nasal cavities or of paranasal sinuses
Process: Concentrating, smelting or refining in the nickel producing industry

Appendix B

Schedule 4 Entries

1 Asbestosis
Process: Any mining, milling, manufacturing, assembling, construction, repair, alteration, maintenance or demolition process involving the generation of airborne asbestos fibres.

2 Primary malignant neoplasm of the mesothelium of the pleura of peritoneum
Process: Any mining, milling, manufacturing, assembling, construction, repair, alteration, maintenance or demolition process involving the generation of airborne asbestos fibres.

3 Primary cancer of the nasal cavities or of paranasal sinuses
Process: Any process at the Copper Cliff sinter plant of Inco Limited.

4 Primary cancer of the nasal cavities or of paranasal sinuses
Process: Any process in the Port Colborne leaching calcining and sintering department of Inco Limited that was practised before January 1, 1966.

Workers' Compensation Costs in Québec, Ontario and British Columbia, 1982-1991

François Vaillancourt

This chapter presents information on the costs of Workers' Compensation Boards (WCBs) in Canada in recent years, and analyzes the principal determinants of these costs. Although these costs have been increasing rapidly, often leading to growing unfunded liabilities for WCBs, they have been the object of little research in Canada. The first part of the chapter describes the evolution of the costs and revenues of workers' compensation programs in the recent past. The second indicates the separate components of these costs and attempts to identify key factors accounting for their growth. The analysis helps to explain why the financing of workers' compensation has been described as 'resulting in a financial crisis in some provinces' (Canadian Manufacturers' Association 1989, i).

Financial and accident data from 1982 to 1991 for three Canadian provinces, Québec, Ontario, and British Columbia, are examined. Financial data are taken from ten-year summaries available from the annual reports of these three provinces. Accident data are provided by Statistics Canada, which first compiled them in 1982. While financial and accident data are available from other provinces and for earlier years, these data are not necessarily comparable to the data reported in this chapter, due to differences in data collection and data reporting across time and jurisdictions. The three provinces chosen for study account for a substantial proportion of Canadian workers' compensation costs—about 80 percent of total compensation costs in 1986–1987, the mid-point of the interval used in this analysis (Vaillancourt 1994, Table 2-1).

Note: Part of this work was funded by the Canadian Tax Foundation and by the Public Sector and Competitiveness Project, Government of Canada. The author thanks participants at the Challenges to Workers' Compensation Conference for useful comments, as well as Michel Briskin and Stéphane Fortin for able research assistance.

The Growth of Compensation Costs in Canada

Before examining data on workers' compensation costs, it is important to note that in Canada, WCBs are provincially or territorially owned public monopolies. The finances of the WCBs are not consolidated with the general budgets of the provincial or territorial governments, and the WCBs have a large degree of autonomy in policymaking and day-to-day operations. Nonetheless, WCBs are subject to both legislative and governmental directives on policy matters, such as the level of benefits paid to injured workers and assessment rates charged to covered employers.

Indeed, the real value of compensation benefits is established through legislative enactment. In Ontario, for example, when Bill 162 was passed in 1989, indemnity benefits were retroactively increased for about 22 thousand WCB recipients. New real benefits were created for claimants who had been injured prior to the enactment of this legislation. In addition, prior to Bill 162, indemnity benefits in Ontario were adjusted for inflation through annual legislative acts. Bill 162 amended the *Workers' Compensation Act* to provide for automatic indexing of benefits. Assessment rates are also affected by legislative acts. During part of the 1980s, legislative mandate held assessment rates below levels necessary to completely fund accident costs in Québec; this was done in order to increase provincial employment by restraining the growth of nonwage labour costs.

WCB budgeting involves forecasting the cost of covered accidents in a given year. This means predicting the frequency and severity of accidents as well as their distribution by wage level, since benefits are based on claimants' wages. Based on this forecast, the WCB sets appropriate assessment rates.[1] The cost of covered accidents includes expenditures that are paid during the year in which the accident occurred, as well as expenditures that the WCB estimates will be paid out for current-year accidents in future years. Future expenditures are financed through the funding of a reserve and the investment income earned on that reserve.

This description of the WCB budgeting cycle implies that accident costs for a given year are known with a fair degree of certainty before that year begins. In practice, this has not always been the case, since provincial governments have often increased benefits retroactively and the funding of accident reserves did not provide for these unexpected legislative acts.

---

1 This may or may not lead to full funding of expected costs, depending on governmental policies.

Total expenditures, in nominal terms, of each of the WCBs studied are shown in Table 1. Costs have been increasing in nominal terms from 1982 to 1991 in all three provinces.[2]

Are WCB revenues keeping pace with costs? Revenues are also reported in Table 1. When annual revenue growth rates are compared with the growth rates of expenditures, it is apparent that revenues have increased more slowly than expenses in British Columbia, as fast as expenses in Québec, and faster than expenses in Ontario. However, this comparison hides the impact of one-time increases in expenditures, which occurred in Ontario in 1985 and 1989 and in Québec in 1985, that are smoothed by rate-of-growth calculations. As a result, the annual coverage ratio (revenues/expenses) reported in Table 1 is usually less than 1 for most of the period in Québec and Ontario. Continuing undercoverage of costs by revenues leads to diminishing surpluses or increasing accumulated deficits, which are referred to as unfunded liabilities by WCBs.

Table 2 shows the development of these unfunded liabilities in Québec and Ontario as well as the surpluses reported by British Columbia. Since 1982, unfunded liabilities have quadrupled in Québec, increased seven-fold in Ontario, and have disappeared in British

Table 1

Revenues and Expenditures of Workers' Compensation Boards in Québec, Ontario, and British Columbia, 1982–1991 ($000,000)

Year	Revenues			Expenditures			Ratio of revenues to expenditures		
	Québec	Ontario	BC	Québec	Ontario	BC	Québec	Ontario	BC
1982	887.9	951	619.2	945.7	1,563	608.5	0.939	0.608	1.018
1983	921.2	1,049	596.2	968.2	1,646	526.8	0.951	0.637	1.132
1984	919.6	1,336	642.5	1,147.8	2,021	460.7	0.801	0.661	1.395
1985	990.8	1,610	679.1	1,538.7	4,281	387.1	0.644	0.376	1.754
1986	1,184.9	1,954	648.8	1,542.3	2,780	407.9	0.768	0.703	1.591
1987	1,435.9	2,364	567.4	1,526.6	2,848	609.8	0.941	0.830	0.930
1988	1,754.0	2,693	711.9	1,650.9	3,352	732.8	1.062	0.803	0.971
1989	1,966.3	3,087	831.2	1,753.2	4,206	816.6	1.122	0.734	1.018
1990	1,848.4	3,036	875.9	2,037.1	3,655	987.6	0.907	0.831	0.887
1991	1,641.4	2,955	905.2	2,408.3	4,214	970.1	0.682	0.701	0.933
Growth rate	9.76%	14.28%	4.49%	9.65%	10.59%	8.35%			

Sources: CSST (1992, 79-80); Workers' Compensation Board of Ontario (1992, 44); Workers' Compensation Board of British Columbia (1991, 64).

2 Growth rates are calculated as follows:

ln $Y = B_0 + B_1 t$,

with B_1 equal to the growth rate and B_0 and B_1 obtained through OLS.

Table 2

Surplus (Deficit) of the Accident Fund, Québec, Ontario and British Columbia, 1982–1991 ($000,000)

Year	Québec	Ontario	British Columbia	Year	Québec	Ontario	British Columbia
1982	-679.6	-1,428	-492.4	1987	-2,360.4	-6,691	249.5
1983	-866.7	-2,025	-423.0	1988	-2,257.2	-7,350	228.6
1984	-1,322.9	-2,710	-241.1	1989	-2,015.1	-8,469	243.2
1985	-1,870.8	-5,381	50.9	1990	-2,203.8	-9,088	131.5
1986	-2,228.1	-6,207	291.9	1991	-2,970.7	-10,347	66.6

Sources: CSST (1992, 79–80); Workers' Compensation Board of Ontario (1992, 44); Workers' Compensation Board of British Columbia (1991, 64).

Columbia, where they are being funded as part of a long-term (15- to 20-year) plan to re-establish a fully funded reserve. As can be seen from the data presented in Tables 1 and 2, it seems reasonable to conclude that the financial position of Canadian workers' compensation boards has been deteriorating and that this deteriorating financial position is at least partially explained by higher levels of expenditures.

An Analysis

As indicated above, WCB expenditures for a given year, including transfers to reserves, depend not only on the costs of current claims, but also on legislative decisions with respect to issues such as retroactive increases in benefits. The following analysis isolates the costs of current claims from 1982 to 1991 (or from 1986 to 1991 for Ontario), excluding increased expenditures due to changes in the valuation of claims initiated in previous years.

Current claims costs in nominal dollars are shown in Table 3. These costs represent the costs of accidents occurring in a given year, including both current expenses and future expenses (reserves). Table 4 reports the ratio of the cost of current claims to total expenses. As can be seen, this ratio varies significantly from year to year.

Note that current claims costs are smaller than total costs. This reflects the expensing of retroactive improvements in compensation benefits. For example, in Ontario from 1980 to 1990, more than six billion dollars (in nominal terms) can be attributed to costs associated with retroactive benefit improvements. In particular, benefit indexing resulted in a $1,860 million cost increase in 1985 following the passage of Bill 101, while, as mentioned above, retroactive benefits associated with the introduction of a dual award for permanent partial dis-

Table 3

Expenses for Current Claims, Québec, Ontario and British Columbia, 1982–1991 ($000,000)

Year	Québec	Ontario	British Columbia	Year	Québec	Ontario	British Columbia
1982	584.1	n.a.	310.4	1988	837.2	1,732	400.2
1983	590.2	n.a.	293.0	1989	898.0	1,843	545.3
1984	591.6	n.a.	288.4	1990	1,018.6	1,727	534.7
1985	759.8	n.a.	285.7	1991	1,133.9	1,465	557.6
1986	819.0	1,237	297.3	Growth			
1987	837.1	1,516	335.8	rate	7.39%	3.71%	7.81%

Sources: CSST (1983, 18; 1985, 19, note 12; 1987, 24, note 10; 1989, 35, note 4; 1991, 30, note 3); Ontario: Private Communication with P. Banel, Manager, Actuarial Services Branch, WCB, July 27, 1993. British Columbia: Workers' Compensation Board of British Columbia (1991, 64). n.a. - not available.

Table 4

Ratio of Expenses for Current Claims to Total Expenses, Québec, Ontario, and British Columbia, 1982–1991

Year	Québec	Ontario	British Columbia	Year	Québec	Ontario	British Columbia
1982	0.618	n.a.	0.510	1987	0.548	0.532	0.551
1983	0.610	n.a.	0.556	1988	0.507	0.517	0.546
1984	0.515	n.a.	0.626	1989	0.512	0.438	0.556
1985	0.494	n.a.	0.738	1990	0.500	0.473	0.541
1986	0.531	0.445	0.729	1991	0.471	0.348	0.575

Sources: Tables 1 and 3. n.a. not available.

ability (Bill 162) and affecting 22 thousand recipients, led to a 630 million dollar increase in 1989.

Total expenses and current claims costs in real terms are shown in Table 5. Alternatively, these costs are shown on a per-accident basis in Table 6. Examination of Table 6 shows that real, per-accident current claim costs grew in all three provinces, but most rapidly in Ontario. However, comparison of the total and per-accident cost data for Ontario reveals that while per-accident costs grew, total costs declined, albeit slightly. Examination of particular years shows that total per-accident expenses increased dramatically from 1990 to 1991 in both Québec and Ontario. Approximately one-half of this growth is explained by declines in the accident rates of the two provinces (see Table A.1). The remainder is due to an increase in the duration of dis-

Table 5

Total Expenses and Expenses for Current Claims, Québec, Ontario and British Columbia, Constant (1981) Dollars, 1982–1991 ($000,000)

	Total expenses			Current claims expenses		
Year	Québec	Ontario	British Columbia	Québec	Ontario	British Columbia
1982	853.5	1,410.6	549.2	527.2	n.a.	280.1
1983	826.1	1,404.4	449.5	503.6	n.a.	250.0
1984	938.5	1,652.5	376.7	483.7	n.a.	235.8
1985	1,209.7	3,365.6	304.3	597.3	n.a.	224.6
1986	1,164.9	2,099.7	308.1	618.6	934.3	224.5
1987	1,104.6	2,060.8	441.2	605.7	1,097.0	243.0
1988	1,148.1	2,331.0	509.6	582.2	1,204.5	278.3
1989	1,161.1	2,785.4	540.8	594.7	1,220.5	300.9
1990	1,301.7	2,335.5	631.1	650.9	1,103.5	341.7
1991	1,475.7	2,582.1	594.4	694.8	897.7	341.7
Growth rate	5.43 %	6.36 %	4.12 %	3.16 %	-0.48 %	3.58 %

Sources: Tables 1, 3, and A.1.
n.a. not available.

Table 6

Total Expenses and Current Claims Expenses Per Accident, Québec, Ontario and British Columbia, Constant (1981) Dollars, 1982–1991

	Total expenses			Current claims expenses		
Year	Québec	Ontario	British Columbia	Québec	Ontario	British Columbia
1982	5,358	9,940	8,211	3,310	n.a.	4,189
1983	5,138	9,658	7,141	3,132	n.a.	3,971
1984	5,332	9,851	6,350	2,748	n.a.	3,975
1985	6,223	18,032	4,977	3,073	n.a.	3,673
1986	5,460	10,716	4,992	2,899	4,768	3,639
1987	5,097	10,040	6,665	2,795	5,344	3,670
1988	5,265	11,180	6,941	2,670	5,777	3,791
1989	5,309	13,860	6,793	2,719	6,073	3,779
1990	6,358	12,662	7,471	3,179	5,983	4,045
1991	8,258	16,608	7,479	3,888	5,774	4,299
Growth rate	2.90 %	4.07 %	0.67 %	0.63 %	3.84 %	0.13 %

Sources: Tables 1, 3, and A.1.
n.a. not available.

ability benefits, which may depend partly on the increase in unemployment over that period, since there is some substitution between unemployment insurance and worker's compensation (Fortin and Lanoie 1992). This relationship may also explain why Butcher (1990) and Vaillancourt et al. (1993) were unable to successfully account for WCB costs with a multiple regression model that did not include this variable. Increases in the duration of disability benefits affect the cost of both past and current claims and may explain the higher growth rates for total expenses than for current claim costs.

Conclusion

WCB costs increased in Canada over the 1982-1991 period in real terms, both in the aggregate and on a per-accident basis. Important factors explaining recent changes (from 1989 to 1991) include the decline in the accident rate and an increase in the duration of disability benefits. While the decline in the accident rate may be due to reduced economic activity, reduced economic activity also lengthens the period of receipt of benefits. In future work, it would be useful to examine the differences between the experiences of Québec, Ontario, and British Columbia.

Table A.1

Number of Accidents With Time Loss,Québec, Ontario and British Columbia, Consumer Price Index and Real GDP per Capita, 1982–1991

| | Number of Accidents Reported | | | | |
Year	Québec	Ontario	British Columbia	Consumer price index	GDP at factor cost, 1981$/per capita
1982	159,288	141,917	66,882	1,108	12,785
1983	160,796	145,412	62,949	1,172	13,203
1984	176,001	167,748	59,319	1,223	13,962
1985	194,377	186,648	61,146	1,272	14,574
1986	213,366	195,937	61,711	1,324	14,964
1987	216,724	205,259	66,200	1,382	15,567
1988	218,057	208,499	73,418	1,438	16,213
1989	218,708	200,967	79,613	1,510	16,533
1990	204,734	184,444	84,464	1,565	16,427
1991	178,689	155,473	79,484	1,632	16,069
Growth rate	2.53%	2.28%	3.46%	5.00%	2.74%

Sources: Statistics Canada (annual; monthly, 22; and 1992, 51, 27, 28, and 98).

References

Butcher, Paul. 1990. Evolution des dépenses des CSST et du taux d'accident au Canada 1975–1987. Master's essay, Département de sciences économiques, Université de Montréal.

CSST (Commission de la Santé et de la Sécurité du Travail). Various years. *Rapport d'activité.* Québec.

Canadian Manufacturers' Association. 1989. *Workers' compensation in Canada: Facing new realities.* Toronto: The Association.

Fortin, Bernard and Paul Lanoie. 1992. Substitution between unemployment insurance and workers' compensation. *Journal of Public Economics* 49:287–312.

Statistics Canada. Annual. Work injuries in Canada. Cat. no. 72-208 Ottawa.

———. Quarterly. *Consumer Prices and Price Indexes.* Cat. no. 62-010. Ottawa.

———. 1992. *Canadian Economic Observer: Historical Statistical Supplement 1991/92.* Cat. no. 11-210. Ottawa.

Workers' Compensation Board of Ontario. 1992. *Annual report 1991.* Toronto.

Workers' Compensation Board of British Columbia. 1991. *Annual Report.* Victoria.

Vaillancourt, François, Michel Briskin and Paul Butcher. 1993. The cost of WCBs in Canada (1980–1990): A note. Public Sector and Competitiveness Project, Ottawa. Mimeographed.

Vaillancourt, François. 1994. *The financing of workers' compensation boards in Canada 1960–1990.* Toronto: Canadian Tax Foundation.

Name and Author Index